NATIONAL
GEOGRAPHIC

BUCKET LIST
FAMILY TRAVEL

BUCKET LIST
FAMILY TRAVEL

Share the World With Your Kids on
50 Adventures of a Lifetime

JESSICA GEE
of The Bucket List Family

NATIONAL GEOGRAPHIC
WASHINGTON, D.C.

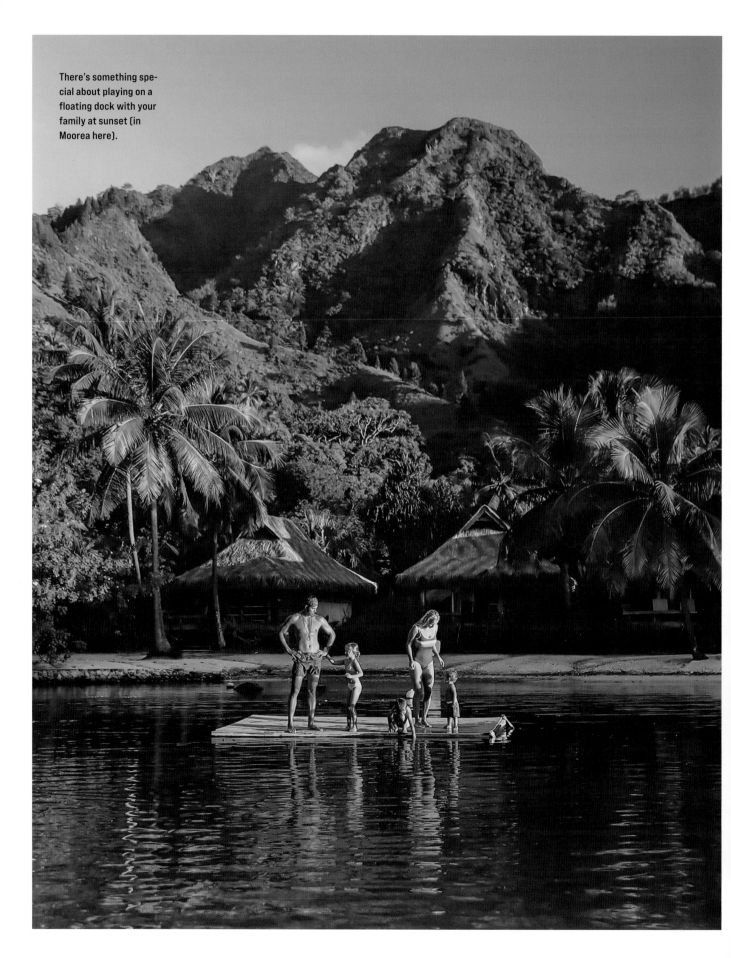

There's something special about playing on a floating dock with your family at sunset (in Moorea here).

CONTENTS

....

This picture was taken just moments after Garrett and I were officially married in April 2009. I could never have imagined the adventure that life had in store for us.

JUST A NORMAL MOM

....

If you ask Jess, she was never supposed to write this book. She was never meant to live out of a suitcase and explore the world. She doesn't like to step outside her comfort zone. And yet, Jess was the one who made the life-changing choice to hit the reset button for our family and "do a little bit of traveling." That courageous out-of-character decision changed everything.

Jess might be known now as "The Bucket List mom," but she'll be the first to tell you she's just a normal mom who really likes to sleep in her own bed. That's exactly why she's the perfect person to write the book you hold in your hands. She is proof of what happens when you sacrifice some of the comforts of your life for something grander.

Traveling the world with three young children is no easy task. I am the one with the crazy, out-there ideas, but Jess is the one who makes it all happen. While we traveled full-time, she was a full-time mommy, homeschool teacher, travel planner, and business manager. Jess spent her entire third pregnancy (save the last four weeks) living out of a suitcase and traveling to 10 different countries. She knows the code for every major airport in the world, how to convert Fahrenheit to Celsius and pounds to kilograms, and she can switch between driving on the left- and right-hand side of the road like it's nothing.

As the mastermind behind The Bucket List Family, Jess put everything she knows into this book. She'll help you learn how to plan, budget, pack (or not pack), and survive a 36-hour travel day with a baby and a toddler. She also gives you an insider's tour of 50 of our favorite destinations around the world and offers her most valuable tips—the ones we learned the hard way.

Dear Jess, *you did it!* (Oh, my! I just realized that I'm married to a published National Geographic author!) This book represents the world and its cultures so beautifully. It will be a timeless keepsake for our family—our great-grandkids will be able to read stories of their adventurous great-grandma, who was, and will forever be, Captain Jessica Gee. And for you, reader, I'm sure this book will become motivation to follow in our footsteps, in your own way.

—GARRETT GEE

Our time in Uganda was spent with our three favorite things: family, friends, and wildlife. We stayed at the beautiful Kyambura Gorge Lodge.

ONE ORDINARY FAMILY, ONE EXTRAORDINARY ADVENTURE

....

In 2015, my husband, Garrett, and I sold everything we owned to travel the world full-time with our one- and three-year-old children. Since then, our now family of five (myself, Garrett, Dorothy, Manilla, and Calihan) has traveled to more than 90 countries. We've slept in castles, swum with humpback whales, lived on safari, and jumped out of helicopters. This book is about our journey—and how you can create and live a family bucket list of your own.

Never in a million, billion years would I have believed you if you'd told me I'd be a world traveler when I grew up.

I was raised in Denver, where I led a quintessential all-American-girl existence: I was a cheerleader, the student body president, and the prom queen. The plan after high school? Attend a Division 1 college, go on a church service mission, find a husband, have kids, and be a stay-at-home mom. That was what was expected. That was the plan, and I rarely strayed from the plan. A comfortable and conventional life was everything I thought I wanted.

My dad was a computer software salesman, and my mom was a stay-at-home mom. I liked to travel, but for my family growing up that meant a road trip to Phoenix to see relatives or an annual trip to Walt Disney World. We took one international trip to England and northern France when I was 11.

Garrett, on the other hand, had parents who split up when he was nine. You couldn't pay his dad enough money to get on a plane. But his mom moved to the United States from Manila, Philippines, when she was eight. She studied journalism and turned her love of travel into a career as a travel writer. Garrett grew up spending many of his summers traveling around Europe with his mom.

Garrett thrives on questioning the norm and proving to people that he can do things differently—

9

and better. He prides himself on being a three-time college dropout who found success on his own terms. Garrett is successful at whatever he puts his mind to, whether that's health, family, business, or sports. Whatever he puts his efforts into, he goes for it 1,000 percent. He was actually the *best* boy-friend because of this! When he commits, he commits. Garrett has not had a drop of soda in 25 years. He takes cold showers. He is a millionaire who doesn't own a wallet.

I admire his unwavering confidence and optimism. While I would never call myself a pessimist, I am definitely the realist in the relationship. He is the King of Extreme and I'm the Queen of Moderation.

I've been blessed beyond measure to be married to Garrett. He's gone way above and beyond to provide our family with a wonderful, fulfilling life. But without me, he would absolutely be dead in a gutter. He shoots for the stars, and I make sure he lands softly back in this atmosphere.

To understand how we made the decision to travel full-time, you need to know a bit of our family history.

Rewind to 2011: We were newlyweds at Brigham Young University in Provo, Utah. Garrett was playing collegiate soccer. I had already graduated and was working full-time at a marketing company. That year, while playing soccer and taking college courses, Garrett developed an app called Scan with two of his buddies. The app scanned QR codes and barcodes—nothing that exciting (we thought)! Scan started as a small college project meant to get their feet wet in the app world. Well, the app quickly picked up traction and captured the attention of Silicon Valley investors. Garrett ended up dropping out of college and leaving soccer behind to go join the hustle of the tech world and build Scan into a successful startup.

Before we left home to travel, Dorothy, Manilla, and I cheered Garrett
on for his final year on the Brigham Young University soccer team.

India is one of the hottest and most humid places we have traveled to.
We gave the kids a break from the sun at the Red Fort in New Delhi (page 334).

We had an amazing two-bedroom apartment in San Francisco and loved living in the city. It was so different from Provo. Garrett was working tirelessly on the Scan app. I owned and managed two e-commerce websites, which I ran from a home office.

In San Francisco, being around some of the world's wealthiest and most successful people, we learned many lessons. Most important: *Wealth and status don't matter without health, family, and friendships.* Long story short, we picked up and moved back to Provo, Utah, for a life that fit us better. Garrett re-enrolled at BYU and rejoined the soccer team. For the next two years, Garrett took classes, played soccer, and continued to grow Scan. We also had our daughter, Dorothy. Those busy and scrappy years are some of the most cherished times of our lives.

In 2014, Garrett got an email from the CEO of Snapchat inviting him to come out to Los Angeles to talk about Scan. After an hour-long walk on the beach, Garrett had an offer for Snapchat to acquire Scan for $54 million dollars. That number is still crazy to me. The result: In September 2014, now a family of four (Manilla was born that same year), we moved to Venice Beach, California, so Garrett could work for Snapchat. I was thrilled to be in Los Angeles with a husband who, for the first time, worked a 9 to 5 job. When Garrett came home at 5 p.m., he didn't even have his computer with him! I had been so used to him working around the clock to build Scan and loved having him turn off at the end of the day.

Seeing wild elephant seals on Sea Lion Island in the Falkland Islands (page 306) was one of our most remote adventures!

Unfortunately, Garrett's happiness and confidence quickly began to decline while working a typical nine-to-five. We had a great home in L.A., with the prospect of making quite a bit of money over the next few years, but I could see that Garrett was unhappy.

Garrett had dropped out of school when he sold his business to Snapchat and was forgoing his senior season of soccer. It was a huge sacrifice for him after working so hard to get on the soccer team. But with so many business partners and investors benefiting from the acquisition, he knew he couldn't be selfish.

One day, we serendipitously ran into Garrett's college soccer coach in L.A. He told Garrett that if he wanted to come back and play, his spot was still open. I thought that ship had sailed, and we were moving on with our lives in Southern California. But I could see the glimmer of hope in Garrett's eyes. I don't recall how this conversation started, but the idea of quitting Snapchat—after just a few months working there—to go back and play soccer was suddenly on the table. I could see how unhappy Garrett was, but I did not want to go back to Provo. I loved my time in college, but it felt like moving back there would be taking a step backward in life.

I'll forever admire Garrett for not being motivated by money. He knew that no amount of money could bring back his youth, or in this case, his senior year of soccer.

So we made a deal. I would follow him one last time back to Provo to enjoy his senior season of soccer, then I would get to choose what we would do next. What did I want?

My words exactly: *"I want to do a little bit of traveling."*

Those turned out to be famous last words. Somehow, I forgot who I was married to. After Garrett finished his final soccer season, it was time to start thinking about our travels. Garrett, of course, went in 1,000 percent. Instead of just booking a fantastic getaway, he came up with the idea to *sell everything we owned to travel the world.*

Quite honestly, I was only ready for a four-month family vacation. Garrett, on the other hand, quickly came up with a name, logo, and brand behind what we were doing. He started The Bucket List Family account on Instagram and created a YouTube channel—and he had big plans for both. This was back in 2015, before social media and "influencing" were really a thing. From the get-go, Garrett had this big, long-term vision. Garrett went to the Outdoor Retailer trade show in Salt Lake City, Utah, and worked every booth he could. He told them what we were doing and how we'd take pictures in exchange for free gear.

We both saw this point in our lives as a huge reset. Although we had come into a huge chunk of money from the sale of Scan, it didn't feel right to touch it. We were afraid it could disappear as quickly as it had come. It felt wrong to buy a new house or a fancy car. And we also didn't know where we wanted to end up raising our children. We were both under 30 years old and felt we had some more growing up to do. We hoped some international travels could teach us a little more about what was out there in the world and how we wanted to raise our little family. So we sat down and wrote a list of goals for our travels:

1. Become closer, in our marriage and as a family.
2. Remain good friends to the people in our lives.
3. Live a life of service and compassion.
4. Learn to find happiness with less.

5. Become more open-minded and open-hearted.
6. Love and respect nature and the planet.
7. Create lifelong memories.

The plan was to take off for three to four months of travel, for starters. We didn't own a home, but we sold our car, furniture, and most of our clothing and other belongings. In the end, we made $45,000 for our travels. Once that money was gone, we would stop traveling and decide what was next. Most likely, we would use our Scan acquisition money to buy a home and Garrett could start his next venture, we thought.

On August 15, 2015, we set off for the South Pacific. We had plans to go to Hawaii, Fiji, Tonga, New Zealand, Australia, Thailand, and Indonesia. In December of that year, our funds were starting to dwindle, so we returned to Utah to celebrate Christmas and make a big decision: Do we buy a house and start our next life chapter, or do we keep traveling and leveraging social media? I wasn't surprised when Garrett's vote was to keep traveling. But I was surprised that I also wanted to keep going.

So our initial trip got extended once, twice, three times. It ended up lasting a full year. Then another. And another. In 2018, when Dorothy was of kindergarten age, we bought a home in Hawaii. I smile realizing that our first stop on our life of travel became our home base. It is a place we return to as we continue to journey near and far, with no end in sight.

Maybe you are like Garrett. Maybe you have that rare go-big-or-go-home, glass-is-always-half-full, and no-pain-no-gain mentality.

But if you're like me, you grew up taking the path *most* traveled because it is just the way things are done. I'm a privileged, blessed American girl who has spent the majority of my life in a really comfortable zone.

Then I opened myself up to "a little bit of traveling." I took a baby step outside of my suburban comfort zone and found that I not only enjoyed a life outside the box but thrived there! I felt myself grow mentally and spiritually as I learned from different cultures. I loved teaching my son what an elephant says while seeing them in Thailand. I loved watching my daughter make friends with complete strangers who don't look or talk like her. And I loved how our journey brought Garrett and I closer together.

I suspect that most of you reading this book are not looking to trade all your belongings for full-time travel. You might just be looking for some ideas for your next family vacation.

Whatever your personal travel goals are, my hope is that as you read this book and see the adventures that one young family has had, you remember that behind these beautiful pictures and exciting stories is an average mom from Denver, Colorado, who is generally very traditional in her life. She has all the doubts, fears, and anxieties that come along with being a mother. But she has learned that the blessings of getting outside your comfort zone are endless. That doesn't apply just to travel but to all of life.

I hope this book inspires you to try something new. To get out there and explore. To meet people and discover new places—whether that's for one week of the year or for a lifetime.

Happy travels! I'm so glad you're joining us on our ongoing journey and, most important, starting your own. ≡

This photo taken in Belize served as our profile picture on Instagram for years.

Just like her daddy, Dorothy found her own ways of capturing memories along the way in her sketchbook.

PART ONE

PLANNING

We've found plenty of bucket list adventures near and far. This one looks far, but it's at Disney's Animal Kingdom Theme Park (page 388).

CHAPTER ONE

WHAT TYPE OF TRAVELER ARE YOU?

Plan Your Family's Next Adventure

· ·

First things first: You have to decide where to go. And you only have the whole world to choose from! I know it can feel overwhelming. But if you are reading this, my guess is that you are ready to take a break from your family's usual trips and try something new. So where to start?

Every person and every family has a different travel style. Are you a sit-by-the-pool-and-read-a-book type of traveler? Or an every-minute-of-the-day-planned-out type of traveler? Do you want to relax? Or go on an adventure? Are you a foodie? A camper? A backpacker? A luxury or budget traveler? A museumgoer? Do you like guided tours? Do you like meeting locals? Do you shop on vacation?

Whatever your style, here are some planning tips catered to you:

• The Last-Minute Traveler: For those of you who can pick up and leave town when you see a last-minute deal, good for you! I'm impressed! Some really awesome platforms like Priceline, Travelzoo, Groupon Getaways, or Going (formerly Scott's Cheap Flights) offer last-minute trip deals to destinations all over the world. Find the right deal, pack your bags, and go! Back in 2013, our friend found a Groupon for an all-inclusive in Mexico. It was for five nights at $294 per person. Eight of us enjoyed a few days at the Riviera Maya, just south of Cancun. It was right before any of us had kids, so it was way easier to pick up and go.

• The Bucket Lister: For those of you who want to go on those once-in-a-lifetime bucket list trips, they'll take planning! Most people don't just pick up and go to Zimbabwe or Antarctica; these trips take years of planning and saving.

One of the best ways to find your bucket list destinations is by following photographers, travel journalists, and influencers who can give you the inside scoop. We learned that you can

The ultimate playdate: Parents introduce their young to each other—in this case, Dorothy and her daddy with wild humpback whales in Tonga (page 342).

swim with humpback whales in Tonga from a nature photographer named Scott Portelli. Less than a year after my husband first saw a photo Scott posted on Instagram, we were on a boat with him in Tonga swimming with whales ourselves!

The beautiful thing about the internet is that you can connect with like-minded people. You'd be surprised by the communities within communities that you can find. If you're trying to connect with an influencer or professional photographer, become an active member of their community and on their page. They're much more likely to respond to questions if they've seen you around. Chances are, these experts have answered your same questions somewhere on their blog, website, or social media pages, so check there first.

But you don't have to make contact with anyone to be inspired by their travels. Once something sparks your interest, do a deep dive into how to make it happen. Read travel blogs, consult with travel agents if you need help planning, and talk to tour companies that might be able to assist with making travel arrangements to go on an expedition.

Sometimes the bucket list trip is about an experience more than a destination. The Great Migration (when more than two million zebras, wildebeests, and gazelles travel from the Serengeti in Tanzania to the Masai Mara National Reserve in Kenya) is late June through September; the Holi festival throughout India is usually in March; whale season in Hawaii is December to March; the crowds are low and the weather is nice in Paris in the fall. If someone flew all the way to Tonga in January to see whales, they'd be pretty disappointed that there are no whales that time of year! Do your research and plan your trip accordingly.

• The Holiday Traveler: Traveling during holidays is tricky. Prices and crowds will be high. If you can, avoid holiday travel. But if it's the only time you can make it work, be sure to book flights and reservations far in advance. You'll need to be extra prepared. If you're traveling during the December holidays, expect inclement weather. Be ready for delayed and canceled flights and have a good backup plan. It can be extra stressful, so show yourself and others grace and patience.

Here are a couple of extra tips: Consider driving. It may take a little longer, but at least your flight won't get canceled. If you do fly, don't check bags. (Checked bags make last-minute flight changes even trickier.) Avoid peak travel days if you can (such as the days right before and after Thanksgiving and Christmas).

It's fun to meet up with friends and extended family in far-off places around the globe, like Uganda.

• The Spring and Fall Break Traveler: Honestly, both seasons are a great time of year to travel. Weather is more temperate around the world and prices are lower. Sure, you could go on a cruise or find an all-inclusive in Mexico or the Bahamas for spring break. But if you're looking for some unique bucket list trip ideas for your school holidays, here are some thoughts. In April and May, you can see (and touch!) the gray whales in Mexico or take in the tulips in the Netherlands. For fall break, take advantage of the changing leaves in places like New England. In October, enjoy Mickey's Not-So-Scary Halloween Party at Walt Disney World in Florida or the Albuquerque International Balloon Fiesta in New Mexico.

• The Group Traveler: We love to travel with friends and family, but it's easier said than done. Mainly because, as I mentioned already, *everyone has a different travel style!* The goal is to find common ground so everyone can have an enjoyable time.

When we travel, we get up early, exercise, and have a healthy breakfast, all before 8 a.m. We don't do a lot of hiking or guided tours. We prefer a lot of water and wildlife adventures. We play all day, have dinner early, and are usually in bed by 9 p.m. I imagine that sort of travel sounds like a nightmare to some people. That's why it's key to find friends and family with similar travel styles—and it's okay if not everyone in your friend group is someone you want to vacation with. When you find a good travel buddy, keep them close!

If you are traveling with friends or family members for the first time, it's worth a conversation before the trip to set expectations. Let everyone share their goals. Agree to split up for certain activities. And establish a few basic rules. For us, "No whining, no crying, have fun" applies to every group we travel with—and not just the kids! We want to make sure everyone is upbeat, positive, and having a good time.

• The Hobby Traveler: I encourage more people to choose destinations based on family hobbies. As our kids have gotten older, our trips are less about where we want to *go* and more about what we want to *do*—what fits our family's style.

When our middle child, Manilla, was two years old, he was obsessed with cars. The kid always had a Hot Wheel or two in his hands. In Germany we heard of a place called Autostadt in Wolfsburg, a small town a few hours west of Berlin that's home to the headquarters of Volkswagen. At the factory they have a car museum, a theme park, and a super family-friendly town center. I can't think of a more random place we could have wound up, but my little two-year-old boy was in car heaven.

When Dorothy was five years old, she had just started gymnastics and was really beginning to find a passion for it. After a little research, we learned that Club Med has a few properties that partner with Cirque du Soleil to let guests try their hand at air gymnastics, bungees, and the flying trapeze. So off we went to Club Med Punta Cana.

Wherever you end up, remember: More important than where you are going is who you are going with (and who you meet when you're there!). ≣

Our kids, in Bucket List backpacks, follow the leader on safari in Zimbabwe (page 372).

Some things can only be fully experienced in person. Waterfalls are at the top of that list, including Iguazú Falls in Brazil (page 290).

CHAPTER TWO

MY TOP MONEY-SAVING TIPS

How to Budget for Your Trip

. . . .

"How do I save for a family vacation?" This is the question we get the most. As I've mentioned, our financial situation is unique and unrelatable to most. We sold all our belongings and made $45,000 to fund our first four months of full-time travel. On top of that, we were lucky enough to have a financial safety net from the sale of Garrett's business to fall back on when we were ready to settle back down.

From my perspective, our travels were meant to be a family vacation. My husband, however, had other plans. He created our Instagram account and YouTube channel first and foremost as a family journal. But he also knew the potential our story held. Back in 2015, the term "influencer" didn't really exist. We'd reach out to a resort property or travel brand and ask if they'd like to host us in exchange for photography and social media coverage—but it was a new concept for most companies. Just as our initial budget of $45,000 began to run out, airlines, hotels, tourism boards, and other brands began to work with us. At first, we were just breaking even, not making very much money but having enough to continue to travel. As we continued to work hard and our following on social media continued to grow, we began to pave the path for what would eventually become travel-influencer marketing. We partnered with companies to help support some of our travels and began earning an income from our content.

But even without these circumstances, I truly believe that if travel is a priority, you can make it work. Travel can come from all sorts of budgets: You can camp in your backyard, road-trip just a few hours away, or fly across the world. In my opinion, money spent on travel is money well spent. With that said, you should have enough saved in the bank for an emergency or random travel incidentals such as a visa, luggage fees, park fees, and taxes. Even the best-laid budget needs that safety net!

I've traveled enough to really know how to be a budget-savvy traveler. I know the ways airlines sneakily add fees, how and where and when to book travel, and that you should always grab an extra yogurt and apple from the breakfast buffet for a midday snack. Even when some of our travel is compensated for work, I'm naturally frugal and will always try to save money wherever I can.

Here are my top budgeting and money-saving tips:

• Use a travel agent. When my husband and I were newlyweds, we saved and saved to go to Tahiti. After our first trip, we fell in love with the country and visited multiple times long before The Bucket List Family began. Our trips to Tahiti taught us that there are a handful of destinations that most definitely should be booked with a travel agent. If you book Tahiti on your own, for example, you can spend upwards of $1,200 on flights, $1,000 a night on bungalows, and around $100 per meal. A five-night trip can end up costing more than $10,000. But many travel agencies have deals to places like Tahiti or Fiji for $2,000 to $3,000 that include round-trip flights, great accommodations, and daily breakfast. Usually, the agency also has perks like airport pickups, transfers, welcome treats, and drinks in your room. You also have someone on standby in case of emergencies. Plus, most travel agencies don't charge you anything! They take a commission from the hotels and airlines.

Still, a lot of people find joy in booking a trip on their own. I've been there. Definitely no judgment if that's the way you want to go!

Early in our travels, we were able to budget by using points and rewards systems.
(Here we are at Belle Mont Farm on the island of St. Kitts.)

Homestays and other unique accommodations, like a small stone village in Switzerland, can help save money—and provide cultural experiences!

• Check online flight platforms. There are so many great flight platforms that offer alerts for routes you want to take and notifications when prices drop. Google Flights, Hopper, and Kayak are just a few.

You can also search on websites like Going (formerly Scott's Cheap Flights) or Travelzoo, which offer paid subscriptions for tips on mistake fares (also known as error fares or airline price glitches) or just insanely great deals. Keep in mind: These are generally for people who are willing to book quickly and have some flexibility in their schedule.

• Watch for airline sales. Almost every airline has its designated time of year for sales. British Airways has a worldwide sale starting on Boxing Day (December 26) that lasts through the end of January. Many airlines (resorts too) have Black Friday sales on the day after U.S. Thanksgiving. Instead of looking for deals on vacuums and TVs in November, check for discounts on your next adventure! Some airlines, like Southwest, have deals throughout the year. I've bought tickets from Denver to Salt Lake City for $49 on Southwest.

• Search smart. There are some destinations that are served by more than one airport, such as New York City (LaGuardia, JFK, and Newark) and London (including City, Heathrow, Stansted, and Gatwick). Prices can vary so much depending on the airport, so check them all.

Sometimes breaking up your flight can save you money. If you know you have a layover at LAX in Los Angeles, look at ticket prices just to LAX and add on a separate ticket to your final destination. This doesn't always work, but I've had some luck doing this in the past.

Look at pricing for one-way fares as well as round-trip. Sometimes booking separately costs more, sometimes less.

• Research transportation options. The more budget-friendly car rental options are usually located some distance from the airport, or with smaller or locally owned companies. In some destinations, you can skip the rental car when a bus or a ride-share app will suffice. In others, it's best (and safest) to hire a driver for your stay: You'll have someone familiar with the roads and language, and they might even become a friend.

• Consider alternate accommodations. Hotels are often the biggest line item in your travel budget, and sometimes house rentals are just as pricey. Look into options like house swapping, couch surfing, or renting campers. Browse sites like Outdoorsy.com, HomeExchange.com, or CouchSurfing.com to see if these accommodations are right for your family.

Homestays are a great way to be immersed in the local community and are typically a fraction of the cost of a hotel. You can also find cultural experiences. Websites like Airbnb are definitely worth checking out (look for the Experiences section). Instead of paying a big tour company, you put your money directly into the pockets of locals. We once hooked up with a local in Hawaii who showed us a secret spot to find dolphins!

• Utilize frequent-flier and credit card rewards. This is a whole world of its own. Really! We have friends (popular YouTubers Kara and Nate) who have traveled the world for years doing what is called "travel hacking." I'll hardly scratch the surface on how complex this can get. Start by finding the best credit card to maximize points toward flights and hotel stays. Consider sticking to one or two main airlines to quickly rack up miles. Do the same for hotel chains to earn points toward free nights or upgrades.

• Use budgeting tools. If you need some extra help budgeting in your daily life to afford your next vacation, use a website like Mint or You Need a Budget. They can help you understand where you're spending your money and where you can cut back to afford a trip. You can even set savings goals, and these apps or sites will help you get there!

• Ask yourself: What's the opportunity cost? If your goal is to save money, then book the cheaper flight route, even if it's the longer option. But if you're bringing kids, consider what added travel hours look like for your family versus paying a little extra per ticket for a day that might run more smoothly. But always remember: Sometimes the journey is half the fun! ≡

We believe money spent to create memories is money well spent (Mnemba Island, Zanzibar, Tanzania).

A small hopper plane dropped us off
on this tiny island in the Falkland
Islands with only five residents. We
doubled the population (page 306).

CHAPTER THREE

WHERE SHOULD I STAY?

How to Research and Book Accommodations

· ·

Once you know where you're going and how you're getting there, it's time to decide where to sleep. There are so many options to choose from—big hotels, small inns, house rentals—and each has its pros and cons. And where you stay very much depends on the place: Some destinations are best experienced as a local, and some are more easily navigated with the help of a hotel concierge.

My family likes to switch things up. Sometimes I just want to be in a nice hotel with a breakfast buffet and not make my bed for a week. Other times I want to really feel what it's like to live in a city. Let me help you make the right decision for your vacation.

HOTELS AND RESORTS

We love staying in a family-friendly resort or hotel. I am a sucker for a really good breakfast buffet. It can be nice to enjoy a hotel pool and room service and not have to make your own bed. Ideally, we like to find a hotel with suites, where we have enough beds for all of us but the kids aren't in an entirely separate room. We also like to have a kitchenette so we can keep snacks on hand. Sometimes we even have lunch or dinner in our room. It's nice to have a place feel more like a home, and it definitely keeps us healthier when we can have a little more control over our meals.

Hotels can do a great job offering unique activities that highlight their location. We've enjoyed mermaid swim lessons at the Fairmont in Maui, pizza-making class at the Sheraton in Rome, and a visit from Saint Nicholas during Christmastime at the Ritz-Carlton in Berlin.

We especially love finding properties that have a kids' club. Our kids love to have their own spot where they can do crafts and kid-focused activities, plus they get to play with other children from around the world. Kids' clubs also give Mom and Dad the chance to go to the gym or have a date night. The cost is usually included, but sometimes they charge for off-hours or late nights.

Of course, some hotels aren't so kid friendly. Look for hints: Are there any pictures of kids on the website? Does it have a section with suggestions for family activities? If they're not marketing to families, they might not be very welcoming to yours. You might want to consider staying elsewhere.

HOME RENTALS

In general, I prefer home rentals to hotels. Our trips have become more of a lifestyle than a vacation, so having a "home away from home" can feel nice. But I also believe a home rental allows me to get a better feel for a country or a culture. We enjoy shopping in the neighborhood grocery stores, finding nearby gyms, playing at local parks, and having our own space to retreat to.

Staying in a home makes for really unique experiences and memories. In 2016, we stayed in a gray stone village in Switzerland. Every morning a bread truck came up the winding road and the driver rang the church bells in our little village. The few people who lived there came out to purchase eggs and fresh, warm bread. It was absolutely charming to watch—and be a part of.

In Scotland, we went to Loch Ness and stayed in an old abbey that looks like Hogwarts. And in Norway, we rented a tiny red house on a tiny island with a tiny boat to cruise around the water. There are so many unique homes all over the world! Airbnb and Vrbo have different listings, search functions, and pricing, so I always check both.

ALL-INCLUSIVE RESORTS

If you're looking to travel and really relax, an all-inclusive is a great way to go. You have activities and all of your meals at your fingertips. It can also be a great budget travel option. We've stayed at some

Our family stayed in this very tiny home on a small private island in Norway (page 396). Hide-and-seek was especially fun here.

This small village in the Verzasca Valley on the Switzerland-Italy border is famous for its crystal clear river; it is one of our favorite places on Earth!

The family-friendly Zion Red Rock Oasis is just outside Zion National Park in Utah (page 264).

really amazing all-inclusive resorts, and we've stayed at some really not-so-great all-inclusive resorts. When planning a visit, make sure to understand that it can come at a price. Sometimes an all-inclusive can lack quality and feel overcrowded.

Beaches Resorts are all-inclusives throughout the Caribbean that are specifically geared toward families. Their sister company, Sandals, is for adults only. Our kids really enjoyed the Beaches Resort in Negril, Jamaica. They spent their days playing at the kids' club and swimming in pools and water parks. Their days ended with Sesame Street characters Elmo and Big Bird reading them bedtime stories.

Frankly, our kids love this sort of stuff. The endless food and entertainment are everything they could want. To me, these resorts are often a bit much, and they can be quite manufactured and lack culture. But hey, maybe that's exactly what you're looking for?

CRUISES

We went on a cruise for our honeymoon, and it was perfect for that time in our lives. We spent five days cruising around the Hawaiian Islands and then another five sailing up to Vancouver, Canada. We couldn't afford many off-the-boat excursions, but there was plenty to do on board that was included in the price of our passage. We loved taking dance lessons and going to the shows every night.

Cruises can also be a great way to visit a lot of different destinations in a short amount of time. In 2017, we went on a European cruise that stopped in Mallorca, Barcelona, Milan, and Rome.

My kids love cruises! My eldest daughter says she'd rather go on a Disney cruise than to Walt Disney World. (That's blasphemy in my book, since I grew up visiting the Disney parks every year.) And although cruises are not my first or second choice, I can't deny how much fun my kids have on them.

I think cruises feel a bit too manufactured, too manicured, and too crowded. However, I do enjoy smaller cruises. Garrett and I have returned time and time again to Tahiti to go on the *Paul Gauguin*. The boat holds about 300 guests and cruises around the islands of Tahiti and other places in the South Pacific. The service is incredible, and it feels much more intimate.

By the time you're reading this, we will have been on two other small cruises: one on Lindblad Expeditions to see the polar bears in the Arctic, and another in Europe to see the Christmas markets. If you're looking for something more authentic or intimate, these are the types of ship options to explore.

BOAT CHARTERS AND LIVEABOARDS

Chartering a boat is one of my all-time favorite ways to travel. One big caveat: I don't love traveling with young kids on a boat until they are a bit older. As a mom, I stress nonstop over their safety. So our boat trips are often adults only. Garrett and I try to take one or two trips a year with some friends for some special time alone. We love to charter a boat for these trips.

Chartering a boat can be more reasonably priced than you might think. In 2015, we chartered a catamaran with two other couples in Tahiti for a week for $15,000. That came out to $2,500 per person, which might seem expensive, but for a full week that price included a skipper, tour host, on-board chef (and by default, all of our meals and food), accommodations, and all of our activities. In the end, we spent the same as we might have on a hotel, meals out, and excursions in another destination—all those costs add up! We had endless time to explore and relax, and the crew took us wherever we

One of our favorite ways to travel is by small boat, like we did in the Greek islands (page 250).

wanted to go around the islands. I highly recommend considering this all-inclusive option for group travel if your budget allows.

GROUP EXPEDITIONS

Are you a social traveler? Nowadays with social media it's easy to connect with like-minded people and travel with them, whether it's a trip focused around yoga or surfing or cooking. It's also easy to find tour groups that cater to your hobbies and interests. I've seen really cool trips and expeditions for aspiring photographers, community service, female getaways, fitness retreats, and so much more. My best friend went to Sweden for four weeks one summer for a swing-dancing camp. You can find a trip for any type of hobby; all you have to do is look!

You can find expeditions in various price ranges, from budget friendly to luxury. Typically, the fee includes lodging, meals, and activities. We went on a group expedition to see the sperm whales in Dominica with other aspiring underwater photographers. We have also led a handful of group expeditions ourselves, visiting Guatemala, Mexico, the Galápagos, Fiji, and Tanzania. Joining a tour group offers you a guided experience, often from a local perspective, and introduces you to people around the world who likely have interests similar to yours. The people we've met along the way have changed our lives, and we are still good friends with many of them. ≋

We came across a pod of curious and playful spotted dolphins in the Bahamas (page 294).

CHAPTER FOUR

PLAN IT OUT

How to Create Your Itinerary

. . . .

In my family, I'm the planner. I research the destination, book the flights, rent the car, and schedule all of our activities. Garrett usually gives me a list of his must-dos, and then I do my best to fit those into the trip. As my kids grow older, I try to include them in the planning too.

My planning style has evolved over the years. Back when we only did one family vacation a year, I organized like crazy. And I loved it! I had Google spreadsheets to help plan and budget for every minute and every cent. I'm a little looser about our plans now. I no longer schedule everything minute by minute. Instead, I book a few activities but leave some time open for spontaneity and local suggestions. Here's how I go about thinking through our trips.

IDENTIFY AND PRIORITIZE YOUR GOALS

Even if you are returning to your favorite family vacation spot for the 100th time, set goals for your trip. The goal can be to try something new—a cool restaurant, a more difficult hike—or just aim to talk to more strangers and go a little deeper into the local culture. Maybe each person in your family or group has a different goal. Or maybe each day of your trip has its own goal.

One of our first trips as a married couple was to French Polynesia on a cruise ship called the *Paul Gauguin*. The cruise offered introductory scuba diving courses. You do a few trials on deck pool dives and then a shallow open-water dive in the waters of Bora Bora.

This was very much outside my comfort zone at the time, but I had set a goal to do the dive in Bora Bora. The hardest part for me took place in the pool, where you have to take off your mask completely while breathing through your regulator and calmly put it back on. I was so nervous thinking I would swallow a bunch of water. Well, I didn't! It took all of my courage to be able to calmly focus on breathing and remove my mask. I got a bit of salt water in my nose and eyes, but I did it! And now, 14 years later, I've dived all around the world! But I'll always remember that very first pool dive.

A goal doesn't have to be huge. Last year, my immediate family had a reunion in Southern California. The girls all wanted to spend some special time together, so one morning, the dads took all the

We spent time with local communities in Guatemala during a service trip with the nonprofit Healing Waters (page 366).

kids to the beach so the ladies could have a nice brunch. My mom was 69, and for the first time in her life, she tried brussels sprouts—and she loved them! She has cooked and eaten many since! Even in the smallest of ways, travel can change your perspective.

So I encourage you to intentionally think about what you want to achieve on your next trip: Do you want to try a new activity? Sample local cuisine? See the world from a new perspective? Think about why you chose your destination, then purposefully plan the activities you're looking to experience.

BRING IN SOME SERVICE

Years ago, Garrett and I decided we wanted to do an act of service every single month. Sometimes we would choose someone we know and decide how we could best help them. Other times, we would do something for complete strangers, like pay for a young couple's meal at a restaurant. This tradition has continued throughout our marriage.

Before we first took off on our full-time travels, we thought through our values and decided to include service as a travel goal. An act of service can be as small as giving a little extra tip to a server or something larger, such as taking a day to volunteer at an orphanage or visit a senior center.

Usually, travel is a selfish endeavor. Taking the time to really look outside yourself and your own family and see who you could serve locally will be a huge blessing. It also allows you to look beyond the tourist curtain and get a sense of—and engage in—the local culture.

On our visit to Turks and Caicos in 2016, we found an after-school program that was looking for tutoring volunteers. We asked ahead of time if the program had any specific needs and learned they could use more shoes. We reached out to a company called Freshly Picked. They were thrilled to hear of our plans and sent us with a huge box of shoes and clothing for the kids. We were only there for about two hours, reading and going over some math homework with six kids, but hopefully our time and the items we brought helped those children in some way. It's important to us that our kids are exposed to children with different circumstances and know that there are valuable ways we can support and care for others. There's no greater way to teach love, kindness, and charity than by showing them firsthand.

While we understand we're in a unique situation where we can ask for help from companies, we encourage you to seek opportunities to give back wherever you can—and it doesn't have to mean taking a huge chunk of time out of your plans. Your service can include leaving books behind at local libraries, giving an extra tip to the cleaning staff at your hotel, or donating extra toiletries to a local shelter.

SET REALISTIC EXPECTATIONS

Remember that traveling with kids is difficult. Give yourself time and grace. You're not going to see it all, and you're not going to do it all. You might have to miss an activity for an unexpected nap or if a kid gets

Hluboká Castle in Czechia is one of many castles for families to explore in the region.

Český Krumlov is our favorite village in Czechia. You must try their traditional dessert, *trdelníks*, or chimney cakes.

sick. You might decide a day at the pool is a better option for your family than the tour you had intended to take that day. Sure, make plans; just remember that you need to go at your children's pace.

One time, we had a whole week in Vienna, Austria. Man, that city is gorgeous! There is so much history, art, and culture. Our kids were young at the time (ages two and four), and I knew they couldn't handle the tours and had zero interest in art. We spent the whole week at Stadtpark, a beautiful park in the heart of Vienna with a cute duck pond and playgrounds. I couldn't give you a single recommendation of tourist-related things to do in Vienna besides "Visit Stadtpark." But my whole family loved it, and I have no regrets going when they were so young.

Traveling doesn't mean that your kids will get a whole new personality. They're still your kids, and you're still their parents. Make your plans according to what you know they can handle and what routines you need to keep (mealtimes, naptimes, etc.). Choose age-appropriate activities that you know your kids will have an interest in. If there's something you want to see but know your kids can't handle (that beautiful art museum, a tour of historic buildings), consider booking childcare (see page 107) or having one parent stay with the kids by the pool while you cross that item off the bucket list. The trip will be better and more memorable if everyone is actually enjoying their time rather than melting down or bickering.

PLAN FOR THE UNEXPECTED

Sometimes a new opportunity comes up. Don't be so planned-to-the-minute that you aren't open to a potentially better experience. Leave time to meet new people and take suggestions from locals.

Adventure hard, snooze hard! The kids will take a nap wherever they need, even in the saddle of an ATV in the Costa Rican jungle (page 164).

Experiencing the world as a family has been a dream come true. (Homer, Alaska, page 310)

CAST A WIDE NET FOR RECOMMENDATIONS

You'd be surprised how many people are excited to talk about their hometowns or past travels. Even if you don't have a big following, social media is a great place to start. So go ahead and do a little post on Instagram or Facebook asking people for tips, suggestions, or help!

- Facebook searches: There are Facebook groups for all sorts of things. We recently joined a Facebook group for Bali ahead of a trip. We wanted up-to-date information on the health travel requirements and found that this group is more reliable than the government websites because it's full of other recent travelers and locals. People offered connections for airport transportation, information on visa requirements, and even specific tours.

- Instagram inspiration: My husband and I will use a geolocation search for a destination to see what sorts of things people are doing and sharing. We've found great suggestions for food, tours, and other must-dos just by seeing what people are posting in the area.

Big sister is ready to assist little brother as he looks for brown bears in Alaska (page 310).

• Bucket List Community: Garrett and I are working on building out our own app for our Bucket List Community that allows people from all over the world to connect with like-minded travelers. Our hope is to offer a wonderful, safe space for people to ask questions, get suggestions, and, ideally, make some lifelong friends.

The information online is endless, but don't forget to get out and do your own exploring once you get to your destination. Talk to locals! That includes the people at the front desk of your hotel, servers at restaurants, and Airbnb or Vrbo hosts. They will probably have better information than anyone on the internet.

ORGANIZE THE TIPS

However you choose to plan your trip, make sure you have a way of keeping your itinerary trackable. When we first started to travel, I had a giant Google Doc for our itineraries. It had flight details, confirmation numbers, rental car details and airport transfers, and the information for our accommodations. It was color coded, and I added links and my research for activities.

Of course, there's more than one way to keep your itinerary. Recently, I've enjoyed an app called TripIt, which stores all of my travel information and gives me updates on flight delays and changes. Use Google Maps as you're doing your research. You can save restaurants and shops that you want to go to right in the app. Then you can easily check how far one thing is from another.

Early in our travels we went to Australia. I naively thought we could easily go to Sydney, surf the Gold Coast, cage-dive with great whites, and scuba dive the Great Barrier Reef. I soon realized it was like planning to go to the United States and thinking it'd be easy to visit Houston, Florida, New York City, and Maine in the same trip. I was such a rookie! ≋

Sweet Manilla has always been a calm and patient traveler, even during long travel days and stressful flight delays.

We pack extra light: On one three-month trip to Africa we packed just one Bucket List backpack per family member and two large duffel bags.

CHAPTER FIVE

PACKING FOR ALL AGES

How to Pack No Matter Where You're Going

....

Travel has changed me in so many ways, including leading me toward a minimalist lifestyle. When we first left for four months of travel, I packed some things that I laugh about now—jarred spices, enough diapers and tampons to last a year, and a Magic Bullet blender. I thought I would have a very hard time living out of a suitcase. I couldn't imagine downsizing and not having a space of my own.

I now pride myself on being an efficient packer. Our family recently spent three months in Africa with only one backpack and one carry-on for each of us. I pack pretty much the same for three months in Africa as I do for two weeks of spring break.

When I come home, I find myself wanting to purge my house. I can easily function out of a small suitcase, so closets full of clothing and rooms full of *stuff* give me stress. At home, all of my clothes fit in four small drawers. Garrett's clothes fit in two. Our kids share one chest of toys. We focus on quality over quantity.

I mention this because I am so grateful for this way of life, and I would have never discovered it if I hadn't lived successfully out of a suitcase for months on end.

We have packed and unpacked more times than I can count. Remember when packing that *less is more*. The more stuff you bring with you on your travels, the more stress. Same with life.

Here are tips I've learned on the road to packing everything you need and nothing you don't.

PACKING FOR ADULTS

For us, travel is a lifestyle and not necessarily a vacation. So we might pack things that some people may not bring on a shorter trip. We keep up our health and fitness routines while traveling, so our suitcases include workout bands, protein powder, and supplements. We recently started to travel with a collapsible roller for stretching.

We also bring our own DaFiN fins and Cressi dive masks to tropical places. Our kids are braver and more confident in the water when they have their own familiar, good-quality masks and snorkels. These are heavy and take up space, but bringing them is a priority for Garrett. He likes to say, "Why would I ever go anywhere where I don't need a mask and fins?"

I pack clothes that work well together so I can breezily interchange tops and bottoms and make new outfits. Our clothes are also layerable so that we can add on or take off clothes as needed.

A note about laundry: I always plan to do a load or two along the way to help lighten what we need to pack. To that end, I pack a small laundry bag for dirty clothes. If I'm booking a rental home, I always look for one with a washer and dryer. Hotels will charge an arm and a leg for laundry services, so try to find a local laundromat. If you're in a big city, there are often laundry-service apps available. I recently used one in Boston that dropped our laundered clothes at our hotel within 24 hours.

If I don't have access to a washer and dryer, I'll use the good ol' trusty bathtub trick: Turn on the faucet, throw in a bunch of soap (laundry or bath soap both work), and then stomp around on the clothes for 10 minutes or so. Hand-scrub where needed. Drain the tub, then repeat two or three times until the water starts running clear. Then wring out everything and hang to dry. It gets the job done!

Another pro tip: Pack a small plastic bag of dryer sheets. If you add one or two sheets to your luggage, it keeps things smelling fresh.

I also pack a mini-pharmacy for our family. I keep this packed between trips (and restock it as needed) so it's easy to throw in a bag. I have some basic essential oils, Tylenol or Advil (for both adults and kids), allergy medicine, cold medicine, eye drops, and oral antibiotics (for adults and kids). I'll also pack extra toothbrushes, bandages, bug repellent, nail clippers, and tweezers. Some of these go in my carry-on toiletries bag (another bag I keep packed and at the ready), and the extras go in our luggage.

Garrett is in charge of all our camera and technical gear. He keeps all of that, along with our most valuable hard drives, in his backpack. He off-loads his photos and videos and backs up his hard drives every night. Of all our bags, my husband's backpack is the heaviest, and he makes sure it's all secure: Our computers, hard drives, wallets, and passports are kept in safes when we travel.

I'm in charge of passports and important documents while we're on the move. I keep documents in my backpack and then all passports either in my fanny pack or in the passport pocket of my backpack. I don't use passport holders. I found them to be a bigger hassle when checking five people into a flight. Airlines and gate agents usually take the passport out anyway. I have printed photocopies too—just in case. Finally, I have digital versions on my phone that can be accessed without Wi-Fi! I also have photocopies of birth certificates and our marriage license. In all our years of travel, the only time we've had to show any extra documentation was at South Africa immigration, when they asked for our children's birth certificates. Still, it's important to have records in case it comes up.

Every item has its proper place and someone in charge of it. When we get into rental cars and taxis, both my husband and I count the number of bags in the back. We had one minor incident where we showed up to a lodge in Vail, Colorado, with no bags. We had to turn around and drive two hours back to my parents' house in Denver to get them! It's a mistake we are determined never to make again.

Each of my children has a packing cube—yes, *one* packing cube—for their clothes. Then there is a shared cube for underwear, socks, and swimsuits. All the kids' cubes go into one large suitcase.

We keep the kids' packs light, like ours. No matter how long we'll be traveling, we only bring four or five shirts and three or four pairs of pants or shorts for each kid—all in similar styles and colors so they can swap things out for different variations. All their clothes also layer well for warmer and colder weather. For winter trips, we have a separate bag for ski gear. Coats and pants go together, and gloves and mittens, hats, scarves, and goggles each have their own packing cube. If we're tight on space, we'll wear coats on the plane.

Each kid has their own small backpack that we let them pack themselves starting at around two years old. They choose snacks and toys for the plane, which gets the kids even more excited for the journey to our destination. The kids carry their own bags. Whatever they want to pack they have to carry and track; that knowledge helps keep them from loading their bags with too much stuff.

Our kids have never had any sort of security object like blankets or stuffed animals. I know those can be tricky with travel—heaven forbid they get lost. But they also provide comfort they (and you) might need away from home. If you can leave it at home, do. If not, keep a close watch on it, and maybe have a backup. Our kids did use pacifiers as babies, and boy, did we have backups on backups of those!

Bring only what you need. This is most of what we packed when we had young babies.

PACKING FOR BABIES AND NURSING MOMS

Packing for babies is always the trickiest. Babies have so much gear, and so much of it is essential. But you have to remember what you're bringing and how many hands you have to carry things. The distance between the car and check-in can be long, and if you have multiple bags, a stroller, a car seat, a Pack 'n Play, and a kid (or kids) to look after, it's absolute *chaos*.

When we roll up to the airport, each person in our family has a job and their assigned bags. Garrett jumps out and tries to grab us a luggage trolley. (It's worth the $5 if you have a long walk or wait before check-in!) The kids get out of the car and know to stand on the curb. Each kid puts on their own backpack. My older kids pull a carry-on with wheels. Our toddler jumps in the stroller. Mom pushes the stroller and Dad pushes the trolley with all the bags. I'm usually the one in charge of check-in. Dad entertains the kids and keeps them contained throughout the check-in process. If there is curbside check-in, *use it!* Sometimes with lap children, the airlines will make you check in inside for their unique ticket, but definitely take advantage of curbside check-in if you've got lots of baggage. Remember to have a couple bucks per bag for a tip!

Here are some baby specifics:

• Car seats: When our third baby, Calihan, was born, I bought a lightweight car seat. There are safe options that weigh around six to nine pounds (3 to 4 kg); these are better for travel than seats that are 15 pounds (7 kg) or more.

When I had babies and checked in for a flight, I always asked if there was an open seat on the plane. Always. Many airline agents are happy to help a mother with a baby and give the extra space. Depending on your baby's age and how they do in a car seat, it can be so nice to bring your car seat on the plane. It's comfortable for the baby (especially for naps) and clears up your lap! It's always worth asking.

Depending on your travel plans, you may or may not need a car seat, so plan ahead. If you have some long drives ahead, then yes, bring a car seat. Some countries, like Germany, require all children to be in age-appropriate car seats (their taxis have baby seats available!). When we travel to places like Fiji, Tonga, or some countries in South America, we can get away with a baby on a lap for a short drive. Of course, consider your own comfort levels too.

• Strollers: The lighter the better! We fell in love with the BabyZen Yoyo+ stroller. It folds up easily (with one hand!) and fits in the overhead bin on an airplane. If I am asked to check the stroller, I just collapse it and show the flight attendant how tiny it gets. I'm always allowed to bring it on board. It makes such a difference not to have to wait for a stroller at the end of the jetway after the flight!

• Breast pumps: I've traveled with my Medela travel pump, and it's worked just fine. If you are going international, remember to have the proper power converters. For my last child, I was very happy with a hand pump that I could quietly use on a flight. It helped that it was much lighter and smaller and fit in my backpack.

With minimalist packing, we can easily take smaller flights in places that require them, like the Bahamas (page 294).

Our first few months we traveled with a huge double stroller. Rookie mistake. But I *do* recommend the dreamy North Island of New Zealand.

Manilla, at 17 months, having a preflight bottle. It must have been a stressful flight delay because I usually wait until takeoff to give babies their bottles (to help with ear pressure).

Speaking of pumping, if you're a nursing mom traveling without your baby, I know how tricky that can be. I have traveled without my babies when they were nine to 10 months old. You can carry on breast milk—liquid and frozen—in excess of the 3.4-ounce rule for other liquids. Freezer packs are also allowed for both breast milk and baby food. Just remember to tell a TSA agent ahead of putting bags through the x-ray machine; breast milk will need to be scanned separately.

• Diapers: Keep a good stash of diapers in your diaper bag or backpack and some in your checked luggage as well. But remember: You can buy diapers all over the world! You may not be able to find the nice organic kinds that you may be used to in the U.S.—so pack extras of those. But we've bought diapers all over. We've found that some countries only have the pull-up kind, even for infants, and we've asked strangers on planes for an extra diaper if they also have a kid.

I also (still, to this day!) have a stash of Munchkin Arm & Hammer Diaper Bag refills. They are necessary for the baby diapers (they help reduce odors), but I also love having extra trash bags for kids' messes on flights!

• Baby carriers: If you're bringing a baby carrier, make sure it's one you've used before that you and your baby like. There's nothing worse than spending 10 minutes figuring out how to strap on the carrier, only for your baby to not want to stay in it! If you don't use a baby carrier very much, don't bring one!

• Bottles: Bring your favorite baby bottles from home, and make sure you have some good bottle cleaners too. You may need to buy bottled water to clean baby bottles if you're in locations where the tap water is not drinkable.

• Backups: Have backups of *everything*. Backup binkies, backup bottles, backup diapers and wipes, and an extra set (or two!) of clothes. (For you and for them!) This goes for all kids until they are solidly potty-trained. We've walked off planes with a five-year-old wrapped in blankets because they'd soiled themselves.

LUGGAGE TIPS

• Tag your bags. If you can avoid checking bags, it's always a good idea. Learn to be a light packer so you can fit everything you need in carry-ons and backpacks. If you must check a bag, make sure it has a luggage tag with your name, phone number, and email address. You

It's music to a parent's ears to hear your kids laughing and chatting together. (Cape Town, South Africa, page 216)

can also add in a little tracking device, like an AirTag, to keep track of your luggage. Every time we check a bag, I take a quick picture of the luggage tag on my phone at the check-in desk, just in case the bag gets lost. This has been clutch on multiple occasions! Lastly, affix a brightly colored ribbon or sticker to your suitcase. So many bags look the same, and you don't want your bag to be taken accidentally.

- Double-check luggage restrictions. If you're going somewhere remote or to a smaller country, luggage restrictions can vary. Some countries have a 40-pound (18.1 kg) luggage limit instead of the 50-pound (22.7 kg) limit that is standard in the U.S. Some small planes limit you to 30 pounds (13.6 kg) or require soft-shelled luggage.

- Pack an extra duffel or small bag. When we check bags, we usually have a little duffel stuffed inside that's filled with either our workout gear or snorkel stuff. Whatever you place inside, it's nice to have another bag or backpack in case your main luggage is overweight. You can pull it out, fill it up, and check it separately.

- Carry on a change of clothes and toiletries. Each person in your party should have a spare change of clothes in a carry-on bag, along with essential toiletries. You never know what messes you'll make along the way (especially with kids!) or if your luggage will go missing! ≋

Don't skip the luggage cart! Take a load off your back and shoulders whenever you can.

Getting ready to kiss the plane as we board. It's a family tradition!

After three years of full-time family travel, we settled down in Hawaii and even bought a car! We restored a vintage Land Rover Defender 110.

PART TWO

EN ROUTE
AND ON THE
GROUND

Each kid is responsible for what goes into their backpack—then carrying it! If they complain about a heavy pack, it's their job to lighten the load.

CHAPTER SIX

GETTING THERE

Traveling With Kids

....

When we had children we decided we wouldn't stop living our lives. Instead, we would bring our kids along and show them the world; we'd make experiences as a family. It was a nice thought, but when it comes time to board a plane with a nine-month-old, it's easier said than done.

When we left for the South Pacific (our first few months of traveling), our daughter, Dorothy, was almost three, but Manilla was only 11 months old, which made for some difficult flights. I'll never forget when a stranger from one row back handed us little Manilla—he had crawled underneath the seats and ended up in the stranger's lap.

But frankly, I attribute much of our travel success to Manilla. He traveled full-time from 11 months to four years old. He literally grew up on the road. And he was a very good toddler. Whereas most busy 18-month-old boys would be running around an airport, Manilla would quietly stand by my side in an hour-long security line. Manilla was a very reserved little boy. Had our third child, Calihan, come second … well, I don't know if we would've kept traveling. Cali can be a handful!

I think the easiest time to fly with babies is from two to nine months. Young babies aren't yet set in their routines, aren't very mobile, and are happy to go along for the ride. A key to making traveling with babies easier: Invest in a good baby carrier and stroller—your child can sleep and eat on the go.

And then there's traveling with babies and toddlers from nine to 24 months. I'm not going to lie: It's tough! I suggest traveling with your baby as much as possible before they are really mobile. Hopefully, by the time they're a little older, travel will feel like routine and they may adapt more easily—but there will always be challenges.

After hundreds of hours in planes, trains, and automobiles with kiddos, I've collected our best tips for travel days with kids. But here's the biggest tip: Kids feed off your energy! If you're stressed out, tired, and high-strung, your kids will feel that. Buck up and fake it until you make it to your destination! There are a thousand things that can (and will) go wrong on a travel day. The journey to your destination is half the adventure, and if you enjoy it, your kids will too!

TIPS FOR FLYING WITH BABIES

- Arrive early! For domestic flights, give yourself at least 90 minutes, two hours if you are checking luggage. For international trips, two to three hours is necessary. If you breeze through check-in, immigration, and security, then great! Use the extra time to grab some food and get the wiggles out. I usually try to keep my babies awake until we get on the plane.
- Use curbside check-in. If curbside luggage check is available, take advantage of it, especially if you are bringing extra baby gear (car seats, strollers, etc.). Curbside check-in is typically a free service; you just tip the representative about $2 per bag. *Sometimes* you will still be asked to go inside to check in a lap child, so ask a rep before waiting in any lines.
- Check how full the flight is. At the check-in counter, the staff can let you know if there is extra space on the plane and if you can bring your car seat on or need to check it. Usually, if there are extra seats, the staff will be more than happy to adjust seat assignments to give you and your baby an extra seat—even if you didn't pay for it!
- Choose the right line. At check-in and customs, look for the lines for families, expectant mothers, or those with special needs. We see a lot of these lines outside the United States. You can often skip a long wait with children!
- Most people will offer a helping hand. Don't be afraid or shy to accept help—or ask for it. Many passengers have been in your shoes before and are compassionate. As for the one percent of people who are mean or roll their eyes over a struggling or crying child, well, I think karma will find them!
- Feed or nurse babies on takeoff and landing. Nursing helps reduce any ear pain. If they are sleeping, don't worry about waking them up, just let them sleep.

Small toys, snacks, and surprises—and special travel day screen time—can help make plane rides go smoother.

A little impromptu dance party to get our wiggles out before boarding a flight to Zambia

Traveling is all about
seeing life from a new
perspective.

- On international flights, look into booking bulkhead rows. Some planes have a bassinet for young infants to sleep in. The airlines often have specific weight and height requirements for those bassinets, but they can be such a blessing to give yourself some space. If you're not using the bassinet, I advise against bulkhead rows because the armrests can't be moved.
- Book a seat at the back of the plane. Toward the back, the engine is louder; that white noise can help babies fall asleep. Avoid a seat within the last two rows, because people coming into and out of the bathroom can wake up your kids.
- Consider a red-eye. With babies, I prefer red-eyes, especially for a 10- to 12-hour flight. Flying through the night makes it easier to keep the baby asleep rather than having to entertain them in a tiny airplane row for 10 hours on a daytime flight.
- Download good music or audiobooks. You can listen on your headphones while walking up and down the aisle to rock the baby to sleep. You need entertainment too!
- Bring a photocopy of your baby's birth certificate. Flight attendants and gate agents sometimes check birth certificates for security reasons and also to make sure a lap child is under two years old.
- Make friends with the flight attendants. We've been blessed with some incredible flight attendants over the years who have been absolute angels to us in times of need. One flight attendant, for instance, spent time mixing hot and cold water so Cali could have a warm bottle.
- Dress in layers. Some planes are hot and some are freezing—you never know which you'll get! When I had infants, I always brought a good swaddle wrap and blanket for the baby.
- Board early or board last? If you've got a lot of stuff, are feeling anxious, or just want extra time to settle in, take advantage of family boarding. But if you have assigned seats and don't need the time, use that extra 15 to 20 minutes of boarding to let the kids get more wiggles out. Or send one parent on board to get settled while the other does one final lap with the little ones.

TRAVELING WITH TODDLERS

This is the danger zone. I'm not going to lie. Traveling with toddlers can be very hard! We've seen it all: airport tantrums, can't-sit-still-on-the-plane fits, accidents, and more. On a completely full flight from Beijing to L.A., our toddler was sleeping on my husband and wet himself. Both Manilla and Garrett spent more than 11 hours in damp, stinky pee clothes. Garrett was in such a terrible mood. But I couldn't say anything, since I wasn't the one covered in pee.

Having traveled with toddlers for a collective eight years, I've learned a few tricks that might help you avoid some of the tougher travel days we've experienced:

- Book a seat for your toddler. If you can afford it, consider buying a seat for a wiggly baby under the age of two rather than opting for the lap infant route. Having the extra space gives toddlers room to move and play—and gives you a break from wrestling them onto your lap. Or if you're being more frugal, you can chance it by looking for flights with more open seats. When my kids were infants, I sometimes booked an emptier flight, knowing I could later ask the flight attendant for an extra seat.

Dorothy gives Manilla a squeeze as they watch a plane take off in Zurich, Switzerland. (Air travel is truly a miracle in itself!)

- Book your flight around naptime. Sometimes kids are overstimulated on a flight and they won't nap, but they may at least be a bit calmer at naptime than at the most active part of the day. We can usually get our kids to fall asleep if a flight is around their nap or bedtime. You feel like you've conquered the world when you get a kid to fall asleep on a flight.
- Use a collapsible stroller. We've had layovers in the middle of the night, and it's so nice to put a sleeping baby directly into the stroller to keep snoozing while we deplane.
- Activities! You can find great activity books or busy books online. Etsy sells some really great boxes. Activities can include anything from sticker books, doodle pads, water pens, sticky notes, Play-Doh, Wikki Stix, etc. Hit up a dollar store or the dollar section of Target before a flight and load up on cheap goodies that you can give to the kiddos as surprises or rewards.
- Snacks, snacks, and more snacks! But make them healthy! You don't need a sugar rush and a crash on a long flight. Pack food that takes a while to eat and can act as an activity—a box of raisins, string cheese, or sugar-free lollipops.
- Be prepared for mess. I always have an extra zipper-lock bag or trash bag that I keep with me for dirty diapers, trash, and those huge messes that always seem to happen on airplanes.

Manilla looks for tree frogs and cool bugs in Zimbabwe (page 372).

- Try melatonin to help them sleep. After the age of two, I'll give my kids melatonin for a long flight or red-eye. I suggest doing a trial run before a flight—and checking with your pediatrician. Sometimes it can backfire and make your kids extra groggy and emotional, so it's best to know if they can handle it before you're in the air. Another hot tip about melatonin: Give it to them no more than 30 minutes before takeoff. Too early and you might find yourself carrying three limp bodies on board with your luggage (true story!).

- Give yourself plenty of extra time during layovers. If you're traveling internationally, you will have to go through security again—and some airports are *huge* (Atlanta, Dubai, Denver, Los Angeles, and Hong Kong, to name a few). I never book a layover under 60 minutes domestically or 90 minutes internationally.

- Use the bathroom before you board. That goes for everyone in the family!

- Fill your reusable water bottles. Most airports have water stations (look near restrooms), or you can ask if you can fill your bottle at a café or restaurant before boarding.

- Get the wiggles out! Run a few laps, have a dance party, find hallways to race down, or find an airport playground or kids' area to burn off some energy.

- Reinforce potty training habits. For kids who are still potty training, make sure you take frequent bathroom breaks on the plane. Don't wait for the kids to tell you they need to go—airplane bathrooms might feel unfamiliar to them and they won't recognize the usual cues.

- Take advantage of family boarding. If you board early, use that time to get settled in. I get snacks and water bottles out and the kids' first activity ready. I put my "bathroom baggie" (my smaller version of a diaper bag, with changing pad, diapers, wipes, sanitation bags) in the seat-back pocket so I can take the kids to the bathroom at a moment's notice. And I make sure my backpack is easily accessible for anything else I may need. Don't put things in the overhead bin that you'll need on the flight!
- Take toddlers to the bathroom before landing. Somehow my kids always have to go potty right when we are landing. You never know how long that seatbelt sign will be on.

TRAVELING WITH OLDER KIDS

- Get the kids excited. Leading up to a trip, we make up bedtime stories to talk to our kids about the fun escape that lies ahead. This helps shift their perspective—from a grueling air travel day to taking off on a magical adventure!
- Save screen time for travel days. We have minimal electronic usage at home, so iPads are a huge treat when we travel. We let the kids pick out games and shows to play and watch on the flight. They are so excited for this extra screen time and aren't bored because it's novel to them. Our kids also know that any fighting or extremely bad behavior while we're traveling will mean their devices will get taken away.
- Take turns with your partner. Give each other time to rest or take a break. We know when to step in and help out to make sure the other one doesn't get too stressed or burned out. And if you need a moment, ask for it. Nothing is worse to a traveling kid than stressed-out parents!
- Get a pair of good kids' headphones. Some flights have the screens on the back of the seats that are loaded with great shows and games for kids, and you'll need headphones (with a jack) to take advantage of them. Other planes don't have seatback TVs but offer entertainment hubs on your own smart device—be sure to download the airline's app before takeoff!
- Have your kids pack their own backpack. They will know what games, activities, and snacks are awaiting them and will be extra excited for the travel day ahead. Here are some things our kids pack in their backpacks:
  - ✓ iPad—fully charged and loaded with new games and shows, plus a charger cord and a backup charger
  - ✓ Headphones
  - ✓ Small dolls, action figures, toy cars, Play-Doh, or other favorite toys
  - ✓ Sticker books and coloring books with colored pencils (crayons melt and break and markers dry up easily!)
  - ✓ One favorite book (books are bulky!)
  - ✓ Snacks like raisins, veggie straws, dried fruit, string cheese, and Goldfish

CARS

I'm the first to admit we are not frequent road-trippers! But I do believe a lot of the same tips for flights apply to drives. First of all, we travel with a travel booster seat called the mifold. It's for kids four years old and up, and it packs up super small—about the size of a box of tissues. We used a Nuna infant carrier, since it was only about five pounds (2.3 kg) and had compatible attachments with our travel stroller.

On road trips, the old saying "Find joy in the journey" very much applies. Make the long, potentially weary trip as fun as possible. Take turns choosing your favorite songs, find podcasts and short stories that the whole family can enjoy, get excited for everything—even for the next gas station. And make sure to get out at scenic spots and rest stops.

BOATS

Nothing can ruin a trip more than seasickness. Stock up on Dramamine and antinausea medicine before your trip. Dramamine Kids comes in easily chewable tablets, approved for kids two to 12 years old. Of course, check with your pediatrician before giving it to your kids. Dramamine is best taken the night before so that you'll sleep well and won't be as drowsy on the day of boating.

Open water, waves, and unexpected weather can be nerve-racking—even when your kids are strong swimmers. I have a constant high level of stress, and my mom brain always goes to the worst-case scenario. Be extra alert and attentive with kids on boats. If you charter a boat, follow rules about wearing life jackets. Or make your kids keep them on at all times on deck if you're nervous.

TRAINS

In Europe, trains are incredibly convenient and meant for everyday travel. There are no luggage limitations, no check-in lines or security, and now e-tickets are available on your phone. Kids under four to six (may vary by train) are typically able to ride free, and tickets for kids under 12 are often quite discounted. Some trains even have family-friendly coaches with baby-changing areas and dedicated space to play.

For longer distances, consider taking an overnight train. That's a *real* adventure! These trains have special sleeper cars with two, four, or six bunks per car. It's a bit extra in cost, but it'll save you a night in a hotel.

My biggest tip for traveling by train is to stay organized! Trains are on a very precise schedule. You need to be ready to get on and off quickly, so have all of your bags together well before your stop and be ready to move fast if needed. We've missed stops on bullet trains in Japan because we weren't ready with our bags. So check and double-check which stop you're getting off at.

EXPECTATIONS

We have high expectations of our kids, and they generally rise to the occasion. Our kids know how to sit for an hour-long meal at a restaurant without a phone or iPad. They know to be quiet and polite. But it wasn't always like this; we had to teach them how to be patient. Those toddler years were especially hard, but the kids learned along the way. You can't give up after one or two bad experiences. Kids will never learn how to do something if they don't have ample opportunity to try. The old adage is true: Practice makes perfect! (Or close to it.)

But practice has also helped us as parents. We expect tired and cranky kids if they've watched a lot of shows, eaten a lot of sugar, or are running low on sleep. A lot of those things are in our control as parents: If we do what we know we need to do (pack healthy snacks, encourage sleep when we can, etc.), the kids do just fine. ≣

When we moved to Hawaii in 2018, we committed to learning how to surf (notice our unwaxed boards!). Today, these boards are full of old wax, dents and dings, and so many waves.

We visited Ashford Castle in Ireland when I was six months pregnant with Calihan.

CHAPTER SEVEN

EXPECTATIONS WHILE EXPECTING

Traveling While Pregnant

. . . .

I clearly remember our discussion about having a third child. We were driving from northern Scotland to Liverpool, England, a long, gorgeous drive during which I convinced my husband that we needed three kids! We were still knee-deep in full-time travel and there were a lot of details to work out. Traveling with two young kids was already hard! We had to ask (and answer) a lot of questions: Would having a third child put an end to our traveling? (No!) Would I be able to travel late into my pregnancy (Yes!) Were there precautions we would have to take? (Of course!)

I found out I was pregnant with my third while we were in South Africa. We went on safari, and our guide told us that another vehicle spotted a lioness with three baby cubs. I quickly wrote my safari guide a note on my phone to help me tell my husband that we too were having "three baby cubs." It was so precious—and you can see this supersweet moment on our YouTube channel.

I had had two really great pregnancies and labors, so I pushed most of my worries aside and pressed on with full-time travel. Let me tell you, it was hard! Even if you're only going on a two-hour flight, travel takes such a physical toll on your body—especially while pregnant.

Of course, not every moment of traveling while pregnant with Cali was easy. During my first trimester, I suffered from nausea and fatigue while we traveled—so much so that I can't look at our pictures from Iceland and Norway without feeling a little queasy. Traveling in France at 30 weeks pregnant was difficult because of all the smells and the tobacco smoke. In Belgium, people are really protective of pregnant women. I had at least three trainers at the gym in Belgium tell me I shouldn't lift such heavy weights while pregnant.

We traveled full-time internationally until I was 32 weeks along. Then we settled down in a rental home in Utah to deliver our third baby, Calihan. Once he was eight weeks old, we took off again. His first trip was to Cuba.

TIPS FOR TRAVELING WHILE PREGNANT

• Consult with your doctor. Ask for the go-ahead for general travel and participation in activities. Most doctors will clear travel up to 36 weeks for a healthy pregnancy.

• Have a backup plan. Book stays within reasonable distance of a local hospital or medical care. Prepare for the worst-case scenario.

• Book an aisle seat on planes. This will be a godsend for frequent bathroom breaks and give you more room to stretch out your legs and belly.

• Take lots of breaks. For long flights or drives, make sure to frequently stretch and get your blood flowing. You may get a little swollen, but frequent walks, seated leg and foot exercises, and compression socks can help.

• Use early boarding. If you tell the gate agents that you're pregnant, they will often give you preboarding access. This is especially helpful on airlines without assigned seating, like Southwest, for scoring an aisle seat near the bathroom.

• Ask for a pat-down. TSA scanners are safe for pregnant women, but if you feel uncomfortable, tell a TSA agent you're carrying and prefer to opt out. This means you'll get a pat-down instead of going through the scanner.

• Pack by trimester. For the first 12 weeks, bring suckers, ginger chews, crackers, gum, and mints to help with nausea. For the second trimester, be mindful of eating foods that might increase heartburn and indigestion. Come third trimester, carry on a good pillow and pack extra-comfortable maternity pants. Throughout the pregnancy, make sure you have all your prenatal supplements, drink plenty of water, and pack lots of snacks. ≡

Traveling mama: We continued traveling until two months before my due date
and then were back at it when Calihan was exactly two months old.

Cali quickly joined the fun on the road—Belize was his second country, at 10 weeks old. (Cuba was his first!)

Every day is an opportunity to learn and grow. Garrett helps Dorothy capture the sights from the steps of a temple in Kathmandu, Nepal.

CHAPTER EIGHT

THE ART OF ADJUSTING

Tips and Tricks for Going International

....

Over the years, I've learned a lot about international travel—often the hard way! The following list is a random collection of tips and tricks—but really gets into the nitty-gritty of traveling abroad.

PASSPORTS AND VISAS

- Check your passport validity. Make sure your passport has not expired! And that it's not *about* to expire. Many countries will not take a passport that will expire within six months (to ensure it won't expire while you're in the country). Also, make sure you have at least one full blank page in your passport. We were almost barred from a flight from Qatar to South Africa because my husband had many spaces open but not one full page!

- Get and renew your passports early. It can take 10 to 13 weeks (or seven to nine with expedited processing) to get a new passport. You also have to send in your current passport when you are renewing, which means no international traveling during processing. There are 26 regional passport agencies in the U.S. that offer same-day passports, but you must have proof that you'll be traveling internationally within two weeks or have proof of a life-or-death situation to qualify for same-day processing.

- Have your baby and child photos ready. I love cute baby passport photos. It's easiest to take them at a local CVS, Walgreens, or post office with a scheduled appointment. These places know the restrictions on sizes, backgrounds, and more. The post office can also help you process your passport request.

- Use an agency. If you're like me, passport details cause a lot of stress. Thankfully, there are agencies that can help you with everything (including visas). We've used RushMyPassport .com in the past with great results.

For just a very short second, I let baby Calihan be in charge of the family passports!

- Set up quick access to passport details. I keep a small business card–size piece of paper in my backpack with all of our passport numbers and expiration dates. It's so nice to have on hand for filling out immigration forms without shuffling through everyone's booklets.
- Understand visas. Don't just expect to show up in a country—you might get turned away! Some countries don't require visas, some provide visas on arrival, some charge a fee, some allow you to get a visa online in advance, and others require a strict application process. To help figure this all out, we use an app called Atlys.

ARRIVALS AND DEPARTURES

Every country has different entry and exit policies, so it's important to be prepared *before* you take off for your destination. Here are some of the best tips for your international travel days:

- Know the immigration requirements. Double-check the vaccine requirements (and appropriate record forms), passport requirements, visa requirements, and fees. Some countries require cash for visas or national park entry fees—and some require that cash to be in the local currency. Some countries ask for birth certificates for minors.
- Have your departure flight booked. Some countries will not allow entry without proof of onward travel. You can't just go to Indonesia for an unknown period of time.

- Back up your important info. Have printed copies of important documents (passports, birth certificates, your itinerary, all hotel and transportation information). Also, have those documents downloaded to your phone so you can access them without the internet. Many immigration forms ask for the name, address, and phone number of your accommodations—keep that handy and somewhere easy to get to. Oh, and pack a pen!
- Use a travel app. We use an app called TripIt. It compiles all of our flights, rental cars, and reservations, and gives us flight updates and check-in notifications. I can easily share itineraries with family and friends.

LANGUAGE BARRIERS

"How do you navigate language barriers?" This is a question I get asked all the time. The answer is: It's never really been a problem!

I took six years of Spanish and I lived in Russia for two years. When someone speaks to me in Spanish or Russian, I understand them well, but my response is in a mumbo jumbo of both!

Dorothy and Manilla learn to make a fire from a member of the Maasai tribe at Chem Chem Lodge in Tanzania (page 348).

Grabbing some bananas as a road trip snack before the three-hour drive from Delhi to Agra, India (page 334)

My proficient high school Spanish gets me quite far in any country that speaks the Romance languages (such as Spanish, French, Italian, Portuguese). I can navigate us pretty well around cities and easily pick up a bunch of words. And for the most part, a lot of the world speaks English. Even if we meet someone who doesn't speak English, we always get by.

Here are a few things we've done that have helped:

- Take advantage of your hotel concierge or host. Most hotels have a concierge or front desk host who speaks English. You can get any information you need from them. If you're staying at a home rental, such as those booked through Airbnb or Vrbo, ask your host for help.
- Use technology. Download a language app like Google Translate to help with simple phrases. Apps like iTranslate use your phone camera to hover over text and translate it for you— super handy when it comes to street and building signs, as well as menus.
- Enjoy the cultural immersion. Don't stress about the language. It's a beautiful thing to try to communicate with another human being with minimal words. It adds to the adventure.

FOREIGN CURRENCY

Money can be a surprisingly confusing part of international travel. You have to know which currency is used, whether U.S. dollars are accepted, and conversion rates. Not all countries (or areas) are credit card friendly, and currency differences can still be complicated in those that are.

- Download a converter app. I don't just mean for currency—but for everything! Keep in mind most of the world uses the metric system, which means knowing the weather and how far

Markets are great places to find artisan crafts and support the locals.

We found the people in Fiji (page 178) to be some of the friendliest in the world! They especially love young kids.

it is from one place to another can be tricky. I use an app called Units+ to convert things like currency, speed, temperature, and distance. I use this app all the time!

• Get cash from an ATM. Before leaving your arrival airport, hit up an ATM. This is one of the easiest and cheapest methods to get cash while traveling. ATMs typically provide a better exchange rate than currency exchange stands or airport kiosks. Some ATMs or cards have a limit, so if you need more than $200 in local currency, bring additional cards for withdrawal. Also, it's always a great idea to have at least a couple hundred dollars in U.S. cash with you, just in case. (I usually keep $200 in my backpack, as does Garrett.) Almost every country will take U.S. dollars if absolutely necessary.

• Use a credit card with no foreign transaction fees. You might swipe a lot between meals, excursions, and your hotel—and those fees can really add up! If your card has a fee, consider opening a new one that doesn't, if you're planning a lot of international travel. While you're abroad, sometimes you'll be asked during a credit card charge if you would like to pay in local currency or in U.S. dollars. Always pay in local currency; it will save on any exchange or card fees.

• Learn to negotiate. I'm the absolute worst at this. I usually just pay whatever someone tells me, because I don't like confrontation. But there are many countries where haggling is part of everyday life. In countries where you shop at street and market vendors—places like Mexico, China, Turkey, India, and Egypt—sellers will tell you a higher price than what they expect to receive. Be prepared to go back and forth with a vendor; it might take a bit to get to the price you're looking for.

TECHNOLOGY, INTERNET, AND PHONES

While it's nice to consider disconnecting on a family vacation, we know that's not always a reality for everyone. Here are some things to keep in mind when it comes to tech:

- International phone plans: All phone carriers offer different international plans. Before you travel, find out which makes the most sense for you—a month-to-month plan, a "pay as you go," or an international day pass. Understand your carrier and plan in advance so you don't get nailed with major roaming and international feels.
- Hotspots: We love traveling with Wi-Fi hotspots. They cost $5 to $10 a day, and they work as well as the surrounding cell service. So if you're in Bangkok, they'll work great, but if you're in the rice fields of Thailand, they may not! Hotspots are great in case of an emergency or if you need to look up directions. Research the best options where you're going, based on cell connectivity and Wi-Fi availability.
- Power outlets: If you're traveling internationally, you'll likely need power outlet converters. You can buy an inexpensive set for less than $15. We like to travel with a multidevice charging station. That way we only need one outlet converter.
- Disconnection: We've enjoyed disconnecting as we adventure during the day and then reconnecting to service and the hotel Wi-Fi when we are back in our room. I highly recommend giving this a try to fully immerse yourself in what you are doing and seeing.

RENTAL CARS

Using public transportation is a great option, especially in a foreign country, but if you're staying for an extended period of time or need to rely on a car, here are some great tips for rentals abroad:

- Keep left! Be ready to drive on the opposite side of the road—and of the car—in many foreign countries. It's a bit of an adjustment, but you'll get used to it. I'm the designated driver in my family while my husband navigates. He continuously reminds me, "Keep left, keep left, keep left," especially when at intersections or turning.
- Consider an international driver's license. Some countries require an International Driving Permit (IDP) to rent a car. I got permits for us at AAA before we started traveling, and we renewed them annually. But I had never once been asked for it. So at some point we stopped renewing our licenses. Then, of course, we were asked for them in Greece when we tried to rent mopeds. We couldn't rent a scooter without an international license. Who knew?
- Take note of office hours. Car rental services aren't always available 24/7. So check the hours of the car rental place, and plan accordingly so you don't get stuck!
- Double-check your car before you leave the rental station. Take photos of the car when you pick it up and let a rental car attendant know of any previous damage. You don't want to get charged for something you didn't do.
- Make sure you specify manual or automatic. Most international rental cars are manual. If you can't drive a stick shift, specify in your reservation that you need an automatic. ≣

When we're in places like the Falkland Islands (a U.K. territory, page
306), Garrett has to constantly
remind me to stay left on the road!

A special family memory: celebrating the holidays at the Ritz-Carlton in New York City (page 276)

CHAPTER NINE

MAKING ANYWHERE HOME

Sink Into Your Surroundings and
Adjust to New Time Zones

....

As parents, we work really hard to help our babies get into a routine as soon as possible. Routines help provide stability and security. They help eliminate the guessing game. When you've pushed naptime back and your baby is crying, you know exactly why a routine matters!

My default happy place lies in routine and consistency. But I think as parents, we sometimes overdo it. We require black-out curtains, sound machines, a tight swaddle, and a minimum of 15 minutes of rocking just to get a kid to nap. Then when we take our little ones on a vacation and out of their routine, they lose all sense of security.

Many may disagree, but I think it can be helpful for kids to break out of the routine every once in a while. It's okay to let your babies nap on the go or stay up a little late, and—yes, I'm saying it!—it's okay to wake a sleeping baby. Of course, all of this comes with the ability to give your kids grace—and expect certain behaviors when they are tired or hungry. We try to keep our routines simple, like having bedtime stories after brushing teeth, so the routines we stick to are in our control no matter where we are in the world.

We began traveling when our son Manilla was 11 months old and our daughter, Dorothy, was almost three years old. Our kids basically grew up on the road. For them, the only constant in their lives is inconsistency. From a young age, they learned to sleep wherever and whenever. I can lay down a towel and a pillow for Manilla as a bed and he will fall right asleep. They find comfort in knowing that wherever we are as a family is home.

Obviously, our circumstances are unique, and most people don't travel to this extreme. But if you want to start traveling as a family, here are a few tips we've learned for helping kids adapt to life on the road—whether that means a weeklong vacation or a monthlong adventure.

HELPING KIDS ADJUST

- Start early and start small. Even when they're babies, you can take kids camping, for a stay-cation at a nearby hotel, or over to Grandma and Grandpa's house for the night. Let them experience what it's like to sleep somewhere different. Put your baby or toddler in a different room for the night just to let them feel what it's like to sleep in a different bed. The more you can practice in small ways, the easier it will be on big trips.

- Remember the best-laid plans ... Schedule flights as best you can around naptime and happy time. Just remember, sometimes things come up, delays happen, and you can't control everything. But the more you plan around your kids' usual behaviors, the better.

- Talk about your expectations. For kids older than three, you can set your expectations. Talk about your travel day, future adventures, and what you expect of them as you travel. That covers a lot of bases: not kicking the seat in front of them on an airplane, having them carry their own backpacks, reminding them they'll be sleeping somewhere new. When you help them prepare for the next adventure, they'll rise to the occasion, we've found.

- Keep some of your routine. Routine on the road will never be the same as it is at home. Still, you can take steps to have some semblance of your typical behaviors. That might include a morning walk, a sit-down breakfast, or pool time. If your kids are young, plan your day around naptime—whether that's a nap in the car or back at the hotel—because rested kids are happy kids!

No matter where we are, keeping some routines, like bedtime stories, helps our kids adjust to new places and time zones more easily.

Dorothy, Manilla, and I share an ice cream on the side of the road in Cuba. Desserts are a tasty way to experience new cultures!

- Don't overplan. At the end of the day, you'll need to go at the pace of your kids. If they are tired and miserable, you will be too. We usually pick one activity a day so that the kids have downtime and aren't constantly on the go. And make sure you have one activity that they are truly excited about, such as pool time, park time, or an ice cream stop.
- Remember, you won't see it all. With kids, you most likely won't be able to see everything. If your child is losing it, it's okay to call it quits for the day. Traveling as a family still means parenting—you're not just there on a vacation. Meet your kids where they are and adapt as you go.

COMBATING TIME CHANGES AND JET LAG

- Try adjusting a few days before your trip. Slowly adjust your family's schedule to either waking up earlier or going to bed earlier to push closer to what your new time zone will be. Shifting even an hour or two one way or the other can help adjust to a larger change.
- Try to avoid seats next to the bathroom on an airplane. People walk by constantly, and hearing those doors and extremely loud flushes can keep you awake all night!
- Drink water, avoid sugar, and stretch. Air travel takes a huge toll on you, and dehydration and sugary food will add to the stress. Bring a refillable water bottle that you can fill up at the airport and ask flight attendants to fill too. Choose healthier snacks, like pretzels, carrot sticks, and string cheese, over sugary options like granola bars and cookies.
- Use the plane time as a reset. If you're arriving at your destination at nighttime, try your hardest to stay awake on the plane. Then you'll crash hard when you get to your room. Or if you're arriving in the morning, try to sleep on the flight so that you're ready to go during the day.
- Don't nap! This is one of the hardest things to do when combating jet lag, but probably the most important. It's best to push through a long jet-lagged day and then go to bed at a normal hour. For babies and toddlers who still need a nap, try to get them on a schedule that's as similar to the new time zone as possible. Keep naps to their normal length (no more than two hours—set an alarm!) so the kids still go to bed on time.
- Use melatonin. If we arrive at night and are not tired, I'll give everyone in the family some melatonin gummies to help them fall asleep. I've found taking more than 5 milligrams makes me really groggy and restless. I wouldn't take more than 3 to 5 milligrams for adults and 1 to 3 milligrams for children. (Note: Talk to your doctor before giving your kids melatonin!)
- Don't stress if you can't sleep. If you find yourself awake at 3 a.m., get up, get some work done, read a book, or even go to the gym. Sometimes putting your mind into something other than trying to fall asleep helps your body relax.
- Give yourself a day to adjust. Don't plan anything too exciting or important during the first two days. You might just be a zombie. Your first few travel days should be low-key: Have a less-planned-out schedule, consider spending time at the pool or the beach if it's available, and take casual walks.
- Regulate your light. Sunlight influences how your body regulates the creation of melatonin. If it's light outside, your body will make less melatonin. If you're tired but it's still daytime, go outside! It will reset your mind and body. On the reverse, if you need to go to sleep, cut

Some proper R&R with my babies before dinner in Fiji (page 178)

out any sunlight. When it's time for sleep, I make sure curtains are blocking out all the light, and I put up the Do Not Disturb sign on the hotel room door.

- Quickly get on local mealtimes. If it's time for breakfast at your destination, go have breakfast, even if it's dinnertime back at home. Your body will start to tell itself that it's morning!

- Set an alarm. Don't let yourself sleep until noon when you need to adjust. Set your alarm for a reasonable time. Get up, get breakfast, and start your day.

- Explain time zones to your older kids. I think kids older than three can start to understand that it's time for breakfast in England and dinnertime at home. Teaching them about time zones will help them understand why their little bodies might feel off. (I can't promise it means they won't still be sleepy, though!)

- Keep the lights off. If your child wakes up in the middle of the night, keep the lights off and the blinds closed. If they're hungry, give them a small snack and help them go back to bed.

- Exercise and play outside! Being active and outside wakes your body up; then you're ready to crash at night. One time, we had just flown back home from a summer in Africa and we were so excited to see the new *Lion King* movie that we decided to go see it the day we arrived. Dumb idea. The whole family fell asleep in the theater. It was a good reminder that when you're adjusting to a time zone, you need to make sure you plan your activities outside! ≡

What a workout! Garrett and I take a breathtaking run on the grassy, sheep- and alpaca-dotted hills of New Zealand (page 182).

No shoes? No problem on
small island-hopper flights!

CHAPTER TEN

STAYING HEALTHY AND SAFE

Always Be Prepared

. . . .

Obviously, safety will be one of your main concerns as you travel with your kids. You hear horror stories, and these oftentimes straight up scare people off any sort of travel. I purposefully don't watch movies like *Taken, Jaws,* or *Snakes on a Plane* (ha!). Rest assured that I have every single fear that a mom could have—my mind always goes to the worst-case scenario when I don't see my kid for 0.5 seconds. Leaving your home and routine can be uncomfortable. But I've learned to live with these fears and discomfort rather than let them stop me and our family from life experiences.

STAYING SAFE

- Be aware of high-alert moments. My husband and I are on high alert at airports, train stations, touristy attractions, or in any large crowd. We are always holding hands with a child and are sure to have eyes on our kids at all times. We always communicate who is in charge and who has eyes on which children.

- Avoid stranger danger. We encourage our kids to be kind and friendly to strangers. But if Mom and Dad are not around, they know they don't need to respond to anyone—and they should *never* go off with anyone they don't know. Our kids know that if they can't see us, even for just a few moments, they should yell "Mom!" or "Dad!" really loudly. And if we yell their names, they must respond immediately. We remind them of this frequently.

- Only take rides in marked vehicles or with uniformed personnel. Don't take a ride at the airport with people who are just standing there hawking a lift. Use the designated taxi station or marked rideshare areas to make sure you're getting into a safe vehicle. People can be very pushy. Be confident in the way you speak and refuse. We also prefer arranging transportation ahead of time in foreign countries as an extra precaution.

- Beware of pickpockets. You have to be smart. Never carry your phone, wallet, or anything of value in a pocket. On crowded cities or buses, put your backpack on your front side. Don't leave cell phones or wallets on a table. And don't leave valuables inside your car.
- Follow your gut. If something feels off or suspicious, don't be afraid to leave or speak up.
- Delay your social media posting. We almost always post on a delay. It's just not a good idea to let people know your precise location or that your home is empty. While it's tempting to share your trip in the moment, it might be safer to wait until you're back home.
- Share your itinerary with family or friends. Make sure that someone not on your trip knows your exact location at all times. I use the "share my location" feature on my phone with a few of my family members. Before we take off, I also send some family members our detailed itinerary, including dates, arrival times, and key information about where we're staying.
- Locate the nearest U.S. Embassy. We've never had to do this, but if you lose a passport or get into a pickle, it's good to know where the nearest U.S. Embassy is and how to be in touch with them. It's also good to know where the closest embassy is should you need assistance getting out of the country quickly or in an emergency.
- Use a VPN. A VPN is a "virtual private network" that will help keep information on your computer private while on a shared or public network. Make sure to choose a VPN that is compatible with your device, has no hidden fees, and is available in as many countries as possible. ExpressVPN or NordVPN are solid choices.

It's always a good idea to have printed and digital copies of your boarding passes, visas, and itineraries.

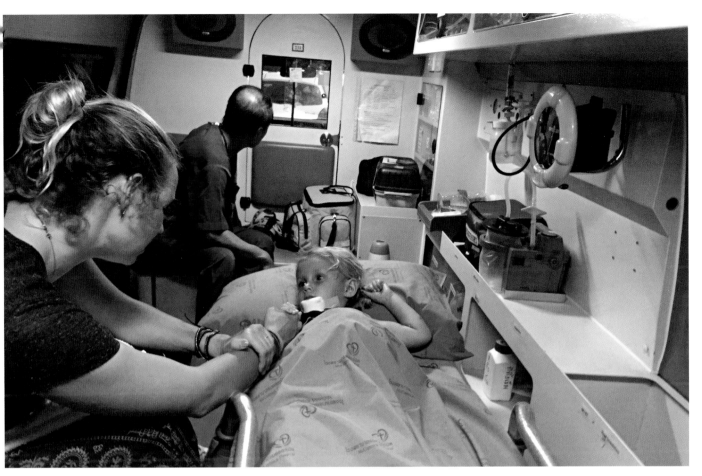

A sad but memorable experience: A slip in the shower sent Dorothy to the ER in Thailand for some stitches on her chin.

- Have a backup stash of cash. Always have some extra money in case of an emergency. Ideally, it should be enough money to get you home safely. Store the cash in the safe at your accommodations or keep it inside a zipped pocket of your backpack while out and about. I usually have a credit card and cash stuffed into my bra.

INSURANCE AND MEDICAL

We've been lucky to have very few medical problems during our travels. In all 90-plus locations, we've only had two ER visits (one in Thailand and one in Nepal). Each of these was a positive experience in an international hospital. It also helped that for both of those instances, we had a local with us. In Thailand, our hotel kindly sent someone from the concierge team to assist us with translations and the whole process. In Nepal, a local from our service trip went along with us to help.

Aside from some normal tummy bugs and standard flus, I once had a severe ear infection in the Maldives, Garrett got the Zika virus in Dominica, and Manilla got impetigo in India. In each case, we either had natural remedies or the medication we needed on hand or were able to get it at a local pharmacy. Foreign pharmacies work differently than in the U.S.: You can often get things over the counter that would require a prescription at home. In Tonga, we had no problems getting Manilla antibiotics for impetigo. In Cape Town, a pharmacist kindly provided a local version of Zofran for my prenatal nausea.

Some curious zebras check out Dorothy and Manilla in Tanzania (page 348).

Here some tips for dealing with medical needs abroad:

- Get traveler's insurance. We always purchase traveler's insurance. We use a company called Travel Guard by AIG. It covers travel delays or cancellations, lost luggage, medical emergencies, and evacuation. It's not that expensive, and when it's your once-in-a-lifetime bucket list trip, you'll want to have this just in case. Things can go wrong, and you don't want to be out a lot of money! You need to buy travel insurance before leaving for your trip, and you can add multiple legs of a trip onto one policy.

- Pack a small pharmacy. My doctor put together a "travel pharmacy" for us that we take wherever we go. We have prescription-strength antibiotics for adults and kids, plus medicines for a UTI, swimmer's ear, and nausea. We also have some natural insect repellent, reef-friendly sunscreen, a small first aid kit, and medicines for the flu or common cold.

- Have your vaccination cards on hand. Keep your vaccination records and always have a digital version you can access without Wi-Fi. Before we left the U.S. in 2015, we went to the CDC's website and looked up the countries we were visiting. The site has a list of suggested vaccines for every country. We made sure we were up to date on the typical vaccines and then tacked on what we all needed for specific destinations. For example, if you're traveling to certain parts of Africa, you will need a yellow fever card. If you're not clear on what you might need, it's always a good idea to talk to your doctor; they can look up recommendations and make suggestions for you. Since 2020, countries have implemented various COVID-19 vaccine requirements, so double-check before traveling!

- Get malaria medications. If you're traveling to sub-Saharan Africa, parts of South America, or other malaria zones, make sure to talk to your lodge, hotel, or Airbnb or Vrbo host and ask them about the current risk. Some areas are not actually high risk or are only high malaria zones during specific times of the year. Then consult with your doctor to determine if you should take malaria medications.

- Find a medical concierge. There are so many wonderful telehealth platforms to use nowadays, and many are covered by insurance. Before you travel, you can set up an account with a telemed service to have 24/7 worldwide medical assistance! You can also ask your doctor if they offer telemed services or have a patient portal where you can email questions—or if they'd be willing to take emails (or calls) from you directly while you travel.

STAYING HEALTHY ON THE ROAD

Travel isn't easy on your body, and being tired is the quickest way to get sick. So it's important to take some steps to stay healthy along the way.

- Ask about the water. There are so many countries where the tap water doesn't agree with tourists' bodies. If you don't know beforehand, ask your hotel or host if the tap water is okay to drink and brush your teeth with. If it's not, make sure you have a good stock of bottled water or a water-filtration system. Use that water for drinking, brushing teeth, taking medicines, etc.

- Eat good food. Be wary of where your food comes from and how long it may have been sitting out. In some places, it's best to not eat raw food (that includes veggies and fruits!) if it

One of my favorite ways to get around is by bike, especially when the basket has such precious cargo!

Cute photo idea: Have the kids race toward the camera on burst mode! (Maldives)

Garrett and I make an effort to continue our daily workout routines no matter where we are, be it Cannon Beach, Oregon (page 258), or somewhere across the pond.

might not have been washed properly or with safe water. When it comes to fresh fruit, stick to oranges or bananas or other fruit with peels.

• Pack vitamins and supplements. Bring your normal vitamins and supplements with you on the road. We have a good stash of vitamins C and E, elderberry supplements, and antioxidants that we take on travel days to help our immune systems.

• Exercise. Not all people like to exercise on vacation, but we start our days with movement, even if it's short. It's a way for us to have a little bit of routine in our day and feel way better. Even a short walk can help—and exercise is a good way to keep healthy.

• Stretch. My husband and I are in the habit of stretching a little before we get on a long flight. Mid-flight, I'll go to the back of the plane and do some light stretching as well. This wards off aches and pains from long hours on a flight.

• Drink plenty of water. It's easy to get dehydrated on travel days. Drinking plenty of water will keep you hydrated, help you avoid constipation, and help you overcome jet lag.

• Wash your hands. Make sure you're extra vigilant with your and your kids' hands. Sinks and hand soap aren't always readily available, so I keep a stash of antibacterial wipes and spray in my bag. ≋

Garrett and I took a kidless trip to Bora Bora. These special vacations aren't to escape our kids. We believe a happy marriage equals happy kids.

CHAPTER ELEVEN

HOW TO HAVE ADULT TIME

Finding Childcare While You're Away

....

When you're traveling, especially on longer trips, it's nice for parents to get some alone time. Nothing is better than a date night in Paris or spending the day doing an adult activity like scuba diving. But it can be hard and—I'm not going to lie—a little scary to find and trust childcare in a new place.

Your concerns are valid, but take it from me: We've found childcare we've been confident in around the globe so we could make room for Mom and Dad days and nights.

There are a few options when you're traveling and looking for childcare, and we've tried them all!

BRING A NANNY

When we first left for our full-time travels in 2015, we brought along a nanny. We wanted someone to help with our kids so that Garrett and I could go on some big adventures like scuba diving and surfing.

After about four weeks, we realized that it wasn't a good fit for us. While we liked our nanny, we decided we really wanted to have special family time as a little unit—alone.

A full-time nanny wasn't right for us, but we still might bring someone on a weeklong trip if we feel we need an extra set of hands. For example, we brought someone to Tonga and Rwanda to help with the kiddos because they couldn't fully participate in various activities. We also brought a nanny to the Galápagos Islands so we could have an extra set of eyes on the kids while we lived on a boat. Sometimes the person we bring along is a longtime babysitter. Other times it is a friend or family member.

Nannies might be a good idea for your family if you have a familiar babysitter who feels like part of the family or a longtime nanny already in place. But keep in mind, if you bring a nanny, that's another person's travel expenses you'll have to cover, including room, food, transportation, and activity costs. You'll likely also have to pay for their childcare services on top of the trip costs.

USE CAREGIVING WEBSITES

Care.com is available in 20-plus countries around the world. This is a great website that allows you to screen potential sitters and put in your specific needs. Another bonus: All caregivers available on the site go through a background and security check—and you can check references to feel extra safe.

ASK THE HOTEL

Nice hotels often offer babysitting services with vetted and qualified people—especially when the hotel or resort bills itself as family friendly. We've used these types of services many times at the Four Seasons, Ritz-Carlton, and various Disney resorts.

FIND A KIDS' CLUB

If you want to go on some grown-up daytime adventures, book a hotel that has a kids' club. Often, this service is included in your stay. The clubs usually have a team of "counselors" who will watch your kiddos for specific hours and offer lots of activities, from arts and crafts to pool time to outdoor sports.

ASK THE COMMUNITY

We're trusting people—probably more trusting than most. The key here is listening to your gut. We often attend church when we travel, and on a few occasions, we've met people at services who have then watched our kids. If you find yourself immersing your family in the community (be it through visiting a recreation center or meeting other families at a local playground), consider asking for help from those you make real connections with. ≣

We don't regularly travel with a nanny, but occasionally we do bring along someone, like our good friend Elizabeth, who spent a couple weeks with us in Africa so Garrett and I could go gorilla-trekking.

We used to bring childcare to Tonga (page 342) so Garrett and I could go out on diving excursions. Now that the kids are older, they come out with us!

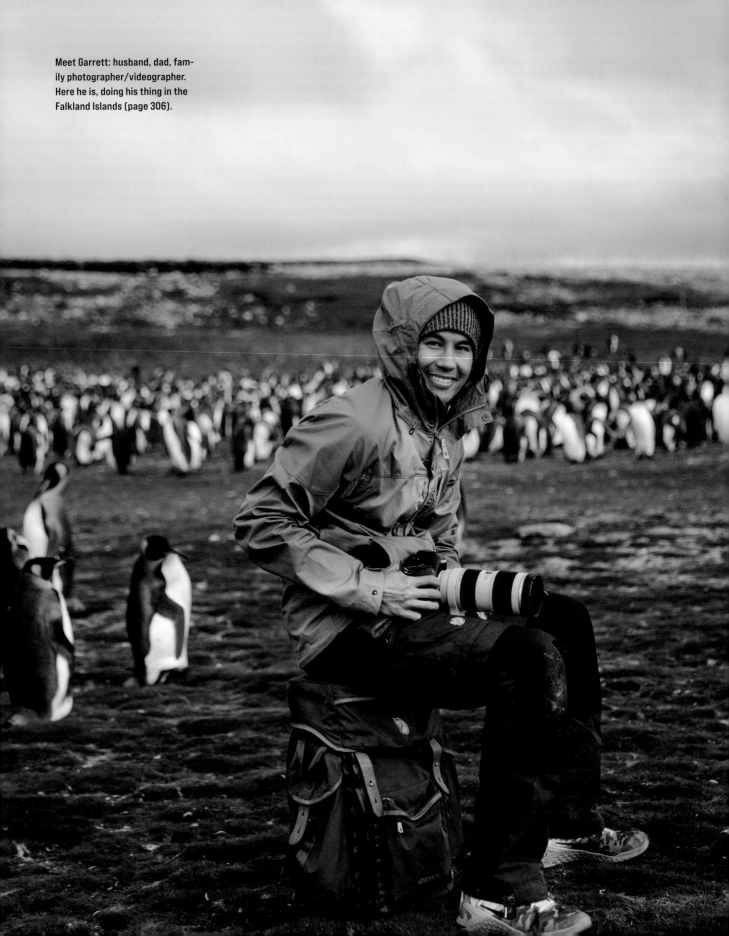

Meet Garrett: husband, dad, family photographer/videographer. Here he is, doing his thing in the Falkland Islands (page 306).

CHAPTER TWELVE

CAPTURING MEMORIES

Documenting Your Travels

....

My husband has always been an avid journal keeper. When we got engaged, he surprised me with a large book of journal entries and photos of our relationship. It's the full story of our courtship, straight from his personal journal. I love it so much. So it was no surprise that when social media came along, Garrett embraced this new, simpler way to document our family. The day our daughter was born, he created an Instagram account for her and began posting a photo a day.

When we decided to start traveling, Garrett quickly set up our Instagram and YouTube accounts. He wanted them to be, first and foremost, family journals. Second, his posts were a great way for friends and family back home to follow along on our adventures.

I feel endless gratitude to Garrett for taking the time to preserve our family memories. Sometimes all the gear, the setup, and the time he takes editing our photos and videos drives me nuts, but at the end of the day, I'm so happy to have all of these precious days and adventures preserved. They are my absolute treasure.

More important than Garrett's eye as a photographer and videographer: He is a fantastic story-teller. He does a great job documenting the prettiest parts of each trip and editing those moments into a 20-minute video that tells the whole story.

If you go back into the archives of our YouTube channel, you can see by the first few videos that we were rookies—but I love them! They're a time capsule from the start of our journey. Over the years, Garrett has gotten better about how he shoots, what he shoots, and how he edits. He prefers videography because he wants to keep the memories of hearing our kids speak rather than just still photos.

You don't have to have a YouTube channel or even care about social media to document the special memories of your family's adventures at home and abroad. If you're looking to capture these moments together, here are a few tips from Garrett on how to document your travels:

I'm forever grateful that Garrett has captured our family memories, like Dorothy, age five, running on the beach in Zanzibar, Tanzania (page 348).

Garrett beautifully captures
the candid, simple moments,
even when we're not traveling,
like a typical beach Saturday
near our home in Hawaii.

- Remember, the best camera is the one you have! People often ask what camera is the best, and while we could suggest you go spend thousands of dollars on a very nice, expensive DSLR camera, the most important thing is that you have your camera handy. Oftentimes, that means your smartphone. Probably 85 percent of all of our family footage is shot on an iPhone. We maybe shoot 5 percent on our Canon DSLR and 10 percent on our GoPro. (Note: Having a GoPro is great for the more active parts of your trip when you don't want to wreck your camera or phone. We use ours for surfing, scuba diving, and skiing.)

- Take a photography class. It's a good idea to have a basic understanding of how a camera works, as well as the dynamics of lighting and shooting. There are tons of resources online on Udemy, Skillshare, and YouTube, and you can learn and practice at your own pace.

- Buy some presets. For less than $50, you can buy presets (many photographers and creators sell them, including us!) that filter even the poorest-quality image. There are also video presets that will take your editing to the next level.

- Edit your own videos. Garrett only became better at shooting after spending hours editing bad footage. He saw what he was doing wrong while shooting and started to correct those behaviors. Over time and through experimentation, he learned how to hold the camera more still and how to improve camera setup and lighting. We use After Effects and iMovie to edit our videos. Both are really user friendly, and there are plenty of tutorials online.

- Set a deadline. Think about what you want to make: A video? A scrapbook? A blog? Whatever it is, set a deadline. Otherwise, those photos and videos will just sit in a camera memory card or on hard drives forever. Deadlines help you get motivated to work toward the goal.

- Tell a story. Document every piece of your entire journey, including the prep, travel, arrival, adventures, funny moments, stressful times, and departure. It'll mean so much more to you if you can see the full picture. (You can't believe how much watching someone pack can generate that feeling of excitement before your next trip!)

OUR GEAR

We travel with the bare necessities that enable us to capture our memories from sky, land, and underwater. Here's a list of all the tech (as of 2023) we pack for our adventures:

✓ 2 GoPros (GoPro Hero11 and GoPro MAX 360)
✓ Canon EOS R5
✓ Battery charger(s) for the above
✓ Canon RF 24-70mm f/2.8 L lens for landscapes, portraits, and videos
✓ Canon RF 70-200mm f/2.8 L lens as a zoom lens for portraits, wildlife, and sports
✓ DJI Mavic 2 Zoom drone (check the drone restrictions in the countries you visit)
✓ LaCie hard drives (always back them up)
✓ Adapter station to keep your gear together, charged, and organized. ≣

Dorothy walking in her father's footsteps on her first safari in South Africa (page 216)

CHAPTER THIRTEEN

ADVENTURES BIG AND SMALL

Seek New Experiences—Wherever You Are

....

If you've watched any of our YouTube videos, you may know that a key theme for our family is *bravery*. We teach our children the importance of trying new things. I hope that on every trip you take, you'll venture a little outside your comfort zone. It doesn't have to be wakesurfing or zip-lining either—it can be trying a new dish or snorkeling for the first time. This world is so beautiful and has so much to offer. So get out there and be brave!

TRYING NEW FOODS

We have a family motto when it comes to food: You just have to try it once. If you don't like it, you don't have to eat it all. But you have to at least try it. That goes for the adults too.

Many large chain hotels cater to kids—for better or for worse! There have been many trips when Dorothy, Manilla, and Cali relied on the kids' menu to get by and ate nothing but chicken nuggets, pizza, and hamburgers. When I can, I try to remember to have my kids order from the adult menu—or at least make sure they try a few bites of my and Garrett's meals.

We don't often make our kids eat unusual things like insects or risky street food. But we do want them to try the local cuisine. Our kids have learned to love foods like sushi, quiche, artichokes, and curry because we encouraged them to try something new. They may not have finished a whole plate (or even had a second bite!), but they've sampled *poisson cru,* octopus, caviar, and escargot—among other regional cuisines around the world.

My kids aren't perfect eaters. More often than not, they'll still order the mac 'n' cheese, but they do know they have to adhere to the family rule: Try it once! (And adults—you have to set the example!)

SWIMMING WITH KIDS

There's something you need to remember when it comes to helping your kids get outside their comfort zone: *trust!* This means you trusting them, but most important, them having trust in you.

Water sports have been an ever evolving skill in our family, starting from a young age. We've worked hard to teach our kids to be strong and confident swimmers, snorkelers, divers, and now surfers! Kids and water can be scary for parents, but if you work hard to make your kids skilled and confident, a lot of that fear can be managed.

We have a deep love and respect for the ocean, and many of our family travels and hobbies are connected to water. We taught our kids how to swim at a young age. When they were babies, we started by showing them how to put their head underwater and get comfortable being splashed. We then moved to showing them how to hold their breath and blow out bubbles. Over time, we bring in new challenges. They might start by jumping into the pool or swimming from the wall a short distance to us. As they build up their skills, the challenges get harder, like swimming from one end of the pool to the other in one breath or diving down six-plus feet (2 m) to pick up a toy. Throughout this process, the number one thing we teach them is *trust.* We push them to try new and hard things, but they are confident that we are always there to help them. So no matter the challenge, they're safe!

Having kids who are comfortable and confident swimmers has opened up experiences like free diving with humpback whales in Tonga, cage-diving with great whites in multiple locations, wakesurfing in Lake Tahoe, and surfing at home and all over the world. This year, we are excited to introduce our oldest to the world of scuba diving!

But maybe you're not as into water sports—that's totally fine. Instead, ask yourself: What's your dream adventure that pushes you a little outside your comfort zone? Is it biking across the United States? Is it hiking for days without cell service in Denali National Park? Is it snorkeling with sharks

Families that mermaid together ... (Four Seasons Resort Seychelles at Desroches Island, page 356)

We took our confident water babies cage-diving with great white sharks.

Some adventures are grander than others, like a safari in Tanzania (page 348). Cali did his first one at six months!

and stingrays in Tahiti? Follow that instinct and put in the practice you need to get the whole family feeling safe, confident, and comfortable.

GOING DEEP ON WILDLIFE AND CONSERVATION

In all our adventures, my absolute favorite thing is to see a new creature for the very first time. I'll never forget the first humpback whale I saw in Tonga. The whale came within 20 feet (6 m) of me, and I was completely humbled and awestruck to be so close to such an incredible creature. Witnessing it firsthand brought tears to my eyes.

My experience with this whale, along with all the other wildlife we've seen on safari or diving, has been life-changing. There's a saying in conservation that you have to experience something firsthand in order to truly act to protect it. I can vouch for that. I have become a huge ocean and wildlife advocate, and I strive to make decisions in my life to protect our planet, including bringing reusable water bottles and reef-friendly sunscreen on our trips. More than never leaving anything behind, as a family we try to leave places better than we found them by picking up trash we see along the way. We also strive to book eco-friendly hotels or those that have sustainability in mind.

If you are not a water person, you should still consider a wildlife experience for your next adventure. We loved our trip to the Falkland Islands, where we watched giant elephant seals fighting, saw gorgeous albatrosses, and learned about five different kinds of penguins. And, of course, I can't neglect to mention my all-time favorite: an African safari!

Even on our domestic trips, we seek out wildlife. We loved the grizzly bears in Alaska, the nesting sea turtles in South Carolina, and the giant buffalo in Yellowstone. We feel it's important to teach our kids about wildlife, and we hope they will forever be advocates for our beautiful planet.

WILDLIFE DISCLAIMER

We encourage you to seek wildlife experiences to get a better appreciation for the world, but be sure you do your research on companies, organizations, and tours. We've learned some of this the hard way.

I'm obsessed with dolphins and dreamed of the day when I could pet one. When I finally had the chance to touch, swim with, and even ride a dolphin, I was thrilled! But about five seconds into the experience, I could see that it wasn't right. It wasn't good for the dolphins, which were not being properly cared for. When we visited Thailand, I was so excited to see elephants that I went along with our hotel's suggestion to go to an "elephant park." You could pay extra money to ride an elephant, while a guide sat on the elephant's head and poked the elephant with a spear to direct it along a trail. I'm embarrassed to say that we did this. It wasn't right, and I'll never ride an elephant again. These negative experiences led us to avoid organizations that don't properly care for their animals.

Unfortunately, there are plenty of experiences around the world in which animals are mistreated and abused solely to entertain tourists. It's our jobs as travelers to avoid these traps and to seek out humane and conservation-focused wildlife experiences.

When booking wildlife tours (and even zoo visits), look for those making efforts in animal conservation. Choose places that don't interfere with wild animals' natural instincts or habitats, or sanctuaries that are doing their best to rehabilitate animals and reintroduce them into the wild. ≡

Wildlife-viewing has become a family passion. Many of our travels now revolve around seeing animals in their natural habitat.

We spent 10 days in Bali (page 226) teaching English, playing games, and making crafts with children at an orphanage. It was Dorothy's first experience at a school.

CHAPTER FOURTEEN

BE OF SERVICE

Find Ways to Get Involved

....

About a year before we left for our travels, we came up with a goal as a family. The first Sunday of each month, we would thoughtfully and prayerfully think of whom we could serve that month. We had been blessed financially and wanted to show our gratitude by paying it forward.

Sometimes we would give gifts of considerable size, like sending a family whose dad was battling brain cancer to Disneyland. Another time we dropped off an envelope of gift cards for a struggling newly married couple so they could go on nice date nights. We helped family members pay for their kids to play competitive sports, which they couldn't have afforded otherwise. Other times, it was smaller: watching friends' kids so they could have a date night or helping design and build a family member's new company website.

We stuck to that tradition when we began traveling. One time we left an extra nice tip for a waitress in Malta after she'd mentioned that she had moved there to follow a dream but had found it difficult to make rent once she arrived. In Berlin, we joined the staff of our hotel in buying and bringing winter clothing to Syrian refugees at a local shelter, where we then spent an evening playing games with families.

We always try to be generous during our travels, but as a family, we make it a goal to be extra thoughtful in our giving. And there are loads of ways you can do so while on the road.

CONSIDER YOUR TALENTS AND SKILLS

Giving your time can often be more valuable than giving money. What are your talents and hobbies? How can you share those with the world?

My husband is a tech entrepreneur and loves trying to help other aspiring entrepreneurs. In places like Rwanda, New Zealand, and Greece, we have sought out tech and founder hubs where he could give talks. These opportunities have been an incredible way to connect with like-minded people around the world and help foster new generations of talent.

I grew up speaking Spanish in school, and then I spent two years living in Russia. I never thought those two languages would ever cross paths, but when I woke up one morning and saw on the news that Ukrainian refugees were at the Mexican border, I immediately jumped at the opportunity to help. I flew to San Diego and spent the weekend driving refugees to a hospital in Tijuana, organizing medical donations, dropping off meals, helping to translate for families filling out paperwork, getting medical aid, and more.

Giving back doesn't always mean working in a soup kitchen or donating clothes or money. You can help nurture families, people, and careers by using your own talents and skills. I'm sure there are many around the world who could benefit!

FIND ORGANIZED SERVICE OPPORTUNITIES

Many hotels or tour companies work with local programs that would be happy to have an extra set of hands. Reach out before your trip and ask about these sorts of opportunities.

If you can't find an organization through your host, I've found Facebook groups to be a great place to look. Many small organizations don't have a budget for a fancy website, but they do have a Facebook group page.

Note that some organizations require background checks or applications. We learned that when we were unable to do service in Australia and New Zealand. Turns out we needed to plan far ahead of our trip to volunteer there because of the strict vetting done by organizations in those countries.

Every time we go the extra mile to plan a service aspect into our travels, it ends up being the highlight of the whole trip! ≋

Our group expedition to the Galápagos Islands (page 246) started with a service day in
Guayaquil at the Hogar Inés Chambers Home.

Even young Manilla got involved in sprucing up the Hogar Inés Chambers Home in Ecuador (page 246).

You can make anywhere a home, even somewhere as far away as Bora Bora.

CHAPTER FIFTEEN

LIVING LIKE A LOCAL

How to Encourage Cultural Experiences

. . . .

I'm so grateful for the opportunity to travel. I love being able to show my children that there is no one way or right way to live. There are people all over the world who live so differently from us, and that is truly a beautiful thing.

I always pay special attention to the way other little kids live their lives. I remember on our first visit to Japan, in June 2016, we took a train around Tokyo. Four of the most adorable little girls, no more than a day over five years old, were on their way to school—alone!—on these crowded trains. I watched them in their matching blue school uniforms navigate their way around the bustling city. Meanwhile, I don't let my kids walk around the corner to a friend's house alone in our hometown.

When a boy turns five years old in Tanzania, he begins to spend all day herding and protecting the sheep and goats. Livestock is basically their family's money, and these little boys are in charge of it all. Five years old! I wouldn't trust my five-year-old with a five-dollar bill, let alone my livestock.

That's the beauty of sharing the world with our kids. We all see a different way of life. It inspires us, teaches us, and shows us there is more than one way to live. It's an important life lesson to share with our children. So how do you help them experience and truly understand other cultures? Here are some of my favorite tips.

LEAVE THE BUBBLE

Even if you're traveling in a "bubble," like a cruise or an all-inclusive resort, make sure you take a day to go experience a more local, "real-life" situation.

We've been to Tahiti nine times. (Wild, I know.) One of our favorite places in the whole wide world is Bora Bora, which is home to some of the most luxurious resorts in the world. We usually spend our time around the bungalow and pool, and we pepper in some scuba diving excursions. But one of my favorite memories of all of our Tahiti trips is leaving the resort and cruising around on bikes on a Friday night. We found local food trucks and ate the best bites. Then we spent the evening playing soccer with locals in a game we stumbled across.

Another one of our family's all-time favorite countries is Tonga, which we visit to swim with humpback whales. Tonga as a country honors the Sabbath and completely shuts down on Sundays. Hardly any stores or restaurants are open. On Sundays, you can walk around and hear the most beautiful sound of hymns from the various churches. There are no pianos, organs, or instruments—only the beautiful harmonizing of voices. We love going to church in Tonga!

Having a local experience doesn't have to mean embedding yourself in the community for months at a time. You can find plenty of cultural experiences in little moments, from walking around a neighborhood to shopping at a local market to simply talking to strangers.

LEARN ABOUT THE HISTORY

My mom has a huge love of history that she inherited from her father. When I was about 10 years old, she took me on a trip without my siblings to Washington, D.C. My mom took me everywhere—the White House, Mount Vernon, Ford's Theatre. To this day, I can tell you about Abraham Lincoln's assassination in Ford's Theatre and the experiences of the enslaved people at George Washington's Mount Vernon, just from that one trip with my mom. My mom was passionate about history, which in turn got 10-year-old me excited to visit what could have been boring attractions to a little girl.

We share pieces of history with our kids at any age. Dorothy, Manilla, and Garrett take in the Acropolis in Athens, Greece (page 250).

Even sensitive subjects can be addressed appropriately with youngsters. We felt it was important for ours to visit the 9/11 Memorial in New York City (page 276).

We were glad we got to see the Azure Window in Malta during our 2016 visit; it collapsed in a storm in 2017.

It's difficult to retain the attention of a three- and five-year-old, let alone get them to understand the history of a site like the Acropolis in Greece or the Colosseum in Rome. But the kids will feel *your* excitement to learn and appreciate history—so it's still worth bringing them to historical monuments and places. I hope one day Dorothy will study ancient Greek mythology in school and her vague recollection of visiting Athens will make it a little more meaningful.

Our kids have visited the 9/11 Memorial in New York City twice now. It was an interesting exercise to try to explain what happened on that day in 2001 to our young kids. It's not a simple or easy task. Lots of history around the world is hard for even adults to fathom or understand. But I'm grateful for these teaching moments to help my kids gain compassion, understanding, and knowledge.

Don't shy away from important historical places because you think your kids are "too young." Bring them along, but remember to meet them where they are. (For instance, we took our children to the Kigali Genocide Memorial in Rwanda but didn't take them inside because of graphic content.) Explain things in a context that is appropriate for their age—if you need to, find a book or website that might help you teach them about what they've seen. But at the same time, don't feel the need to belabor the point or spend more time than they can handle in a place. Exposure is half the battle!

FIND LOCAL EXPERIENCES

Check out websites such as Airbnb's Experiences page to find more local and authentic outings—like a cooking class in Thailand, a wheel-throwing class in Cappadocia, Turkey, or a textile-making course in South Africa. If you're staying at a resort, ask what cultural experiences they offer.

Social media is an incredible way to connect with people from all over the world. We've used Instagram to connect with local photographers who take us out on adventures. One time, we connected with photographer Kurt Arrigo and met up in person in Malta. He took us out on his boat and showed us his favorite spots. He even took some pictures for us! We're very grateful Kurt took us to see the famous Azure Window, which has since collapsed.

You'd be surprised how many small communities there are online for very specific niches. I joined a Bali Travel Facebook group in advance of a recent trip to help navigate travel restrictions and to get suggestions for an itinerary. People can be so helpful, and you might want to schedule some meetups.

We even have a community of our own! On our app, Bucket List, you can connect with other like-minded individuals and families and share intel about travel.

MAKE FRIENDS IN FOREIGN PLACES

One of the great things about traveling with kids is that they tend to break down barriers. We speak to so many more people when we are with our kids, and we've made many friends this way.

Once, on a beach in the Bahamas, we met a French-Canadian family with kids who were similar ages to ours. We stayed in touch and reconnected with them when we both ended up in Turks and Caicos. In Italy, we stayed in an apartment outside Rome for a week. Our neighbors invited us over for dinner and introduced us to their friends. They gave us a ton of suggestions for restaurants around the city, told us where to park at tourist attractions, and even taught me how to make authentic Italian carbonara. We met another young family at a waterfall in Dominica. Six years later, at home in Hawaii, we ran into them at a kids' surf competition. It truly is a small world! ≋

There are going to be obstacles and stumbling blocks wherever you go, but you can always pick yourself right back up!

CHAPTER SIXTEEN

WHEN THINGS GO WRONG

Expect the Unexpected

....

When I was a moody teenager growing up in Denver, Colorado, my dad would wake me up every morning. He'd ask me questions and want to have a full conversation before 7 a.m. I'd make incoherent grunts and give him all the glares. He'd ask, "Jessica, are you happy?" I would grunt out, "Yes." And he would reply, "Then tell your face." He would proceed to tell me, "You choose your attitude." Every day he said that to me. "You choose your attitude."

This isn't just good travel advice; it's good life advice. Travel can be stressful, exhausting, intimidating, and overwhelming. But always remember: *You choose your attitude.*

We've had our fair share of travel disasters. We had our travel plans completely rerouted due to volcanic eruptions in Bali. I've worn the same clothes for five days straight when the Tongan airline pulled our suitcase off the plane because the cargo was too heavy. And we've had not just one but *three* doctor visits for stitches in foreign countries. But no matter what is thrown our way, we try to keep up a good attitude. And some of our "worst" trips taught us lessons we turn to again and again.

TAKE TURNS FREAKING OUT

Garrett and I try not to freak out at the same time. Knowing your partner—and their triggers—is key. Garrett can see when I'm starting to lose it, which happens frequently on travel days! He's quick to step in and take the kids while I handle whatever the situation is. I do the same for him. Garrett is often concerned about our ocean wildlife encounters. He wants to make sure the kids are safe and have a good experience so that we can continue to do these activities. He wants snorkels cleared, baby soap on hand to clean masks, good wet suits, and the kids in a good mood. I make sure to stay positive and rally the troops. And I keep the kids busy while he preps and packs the gear.

SUPPORT ONE ANOTHER

In June 2017, we were flying from the Maldives to South Africa, with a layover in Doha, Qatar. While at the airport in the Maldives, Manilla tripped while running and split his lip. We could tell he definitely needed stitches. The airport had a first aid center that offered to stitch him up. We could've gone to the hospital, but that would've meant a missed flight and a very expensive layover and reroute. My mommy heart couldn't handle watching as the medical clinic stitched him up with a big needle and no pain meds. Garrett is way better than I am in those situations and stepped in to hold Manilla through the stitches. Manilla was an absolute trooper!

We arrived in Doha five hours later in the middle of the night. The kids crashed on the floor of the airport for a few hours. As we boarded our flight to Johannesburg, they stopped Garrett because his passport didn't have an entire open page—a requirement in the country. They weren't going to let him board. Manilla had the fattest lip, we had tired and cranky kids, and we were dealing with a super-strict gate agent. Quick-thinking Garrett was able to convince the apprehensive gate agent to let us on the plane, and we made it safe and sound to South Africa.

Of course, it didn't end there. In South Africa, Garrett and Dorothy were wrestling. Dorothy had a pillow in her mouth that Garrett pulled out. With the pillow came one of her front baby teeth. It was so sad. She was fine, it was a clean pull, but he felt awful. I called my friend who is a pediatric dentist, and he assured me (and Garrett!) that everything would be okay.

We do our best to step in to help one another when one of us needs it. Sometimes that means a call to a doctor or a friend, sometimes it means being the shoulder to cry on or the arms to provide comfort, and sometimes it means some creative thinking!

A golden sunrise memory in Rio de Janeiro, Brazil

There's no safer place than in Mommy's arms.

All of us improved our surfing through lessons with Tropic-surf on Desroches Island in Seychelles (page 356).

COUNT YOUR BLESSINGS

We were robbed in South Africa. They stole all my clothes and the kids' clothes from our rental car after I'd run inside our Airbnb to grab another suitcase. If you've ever been robbed, you know how horrible this feels: You feel vulnerable and victimized. And we don't own much, so it felt even more bitter losing literally everything.

Luckily, we were in Cape Town and had access to a good mall—and the means to buy what we needed. It helped to put things into perspective: We were all safe; things are just things. We were reminded of what's important and were able to get past the disaster by counting our blessings.

Another time, we were en route to the Caribbean with a one-night layover in Miami. We were flying out at around 9 a.m. and arrived at the airport our typical two hours early. At that time, Manilla was under two years old. Some airlines require you to check in with a gate agent rather than at a kiosk when you have a "lap infant." By the time we got to the front of the line, we had less than an hour before the plane was scheduled to leave and the gate agent wouldn't let us check our bags. It was airline policy, no matter whose fault it was that we were so close to departure time. They told us that we'd have to stay the night in Miami (again) and could fly out the next day. I was furious. They sent us to the even longer customer service line to change our flights.

While I dealt with the airline, Garrett was trying to entertain both our kids. While they were playing, Manilla fell down and split his lip (this time it didn't require stitches, thankfully), and he

We stopped to pet Icelandic horses on the side of the road (page 316). (P.S., this picture was taken after 10 p.m.—the sun never sets in the summer in Iceland.)

Three little rascals on the lookout for wildlife at the famous Giraffe Manor in Nairobi, Kenya

was sobbing. I stood there crying, tired and frustrated, and told my husband I just wanted to go home. But we didn't have a home! I cried even harder. As I stood in the Miami airport crying, I looked at my whimpering, fat-lipped toddler, at my daughter, who was trying to help him, and at my husband, carrying all of our belongings. I realized that this *was* home. Family is home. And it's all that matters.

The hard moments can be just that, hard. They can be exhausting. They can bring you to tears or anger. It's easy enough to remind you to count your blessings when you're past a moment and not in the thick of things. But while you're traveling, when the tough moments happen (because we promise, they will happen), try developing tools to remind you what truly matters, whether that's taking an appreciative look around at your family, practicing a gratitude mantra, or just taking a few deep breaths. You'll get through the moment and go on to make wonderful memories.

A must-do experience: Take a selfie with the quokkas of Rottnest Island in Western Australia (page 330).

LAUGH IT OUT

Fast-forward to summer 2021. We were in Tanzania, where we'd rented out our favorite lodge, TAASA, and brought some of our closest family and friends. We spent the day at the Mara River, inside the famous Serengeti Reserve. It's an incredible experience to see the wildebeest crossings here, but it requires a very long drive and day.

It took us about five hours to get to the river, and by the time we arrived, all of the kids were spent. So they hopped right back into one of the safari vehicles and headed back to camp, which turned out to be a huge blessing. They were all safe.

In the Serengeti they often do what are called "controlled burns," in which they burn the grass to stimulate growth and kill off parasitic ticks, flies, and specific plants. Turns out, there was a controlled burn planned the day we visited, and when the wind picked up, the fires started blowing everywhere.

During our long drive back to camp—a few hours after the kids had gone back—the smoke was so heavy we could hardly breathe. We drove right along the burning brush with the escaping bugs pelting us the whole time. We came across some hungry lions also fleeing the fires. We could have moaned and groaned—even panicked—but quickly, we all just started laughing at the circumstances. One thing after another seemed to go wrong: Our guide got our vehicle stuck in some mud about 200 yards (180 m) from a large fire. We feared black mambas and other snakes would be making their way out from the flames too. Two other safari vehicles tried to get our truck out of the mud for about an hour. No luck. We had to squeeze 18 people into one safari Jeep. Oh, and we were rushing to get out of the Serengeti by 6 p.m. before the park closed. The car was swerving, trying not to get stuck, and I thought we would surely tip over. We got stuck again, but our guide wouldn't let us walk out because a nearby water buffalo bull was acting aggressive.

It was absolute chaos. We were all terrified and wanted to cry. Instead, we laughed. We laughed and laughed. It was either cry and freak out—or laugh. We made it out safe and on time. And that day is one of my favorite memories ever. I wouldn't trade those special moments with my friends and family for anything!

Travels are bound to have mishaps, mistakes, and actual disasters. It's part of the journey. Don't let it tear you or your trip down! Let these moments build up your resilience—and teach you valuable lessons for your next adventure. ≡

We have grown so much from our travels and through lessons learned from each culture we experience together.

CHAPTER SEVENTEEN

PERSONALITY TRAITS

Life Lessons From Years Living Abroad

· ·

After all these years and all these travels, I've changed very much as a human. Travel has brought out and highlighted some crucial personality traits of mine—some sweet, some salty! When we were in Rome, we signed up for a gym for the week, and they tried to charge me hundreds of dollars. I went berserk. I knew we were being taken advantage of, and I was not going to stand for it. I was so blunt and direct in calling them out—which I am not necessarily comfortable doing in my normal life. Garrett still refers to this side of me as "Italian Jess." It rarely comes out, but when it does, watch out!

While "Italian Jess" is an anomaly, I do think there are some personality traits everyone should cultivate to enhance their travel experience.

• Be patient. After all these years of travel, I've learned that I choose my attitude. Remember the Serenity Prayer: "Accept the things I cannot change." I can control only myself. Even the best-laid plans can blow up in your face. Long lines, missed flights, toddler tantrums, and botched reservations are just part of the adventure. Sure, things can get crazy and incredibly frustrating. Take a deep breath, and give others a break too. Your gate agent can't control when your plane takes off. You'll get further by being kind than by snapping.

One time our flight from Phoenix to Salt Lake City was oversold, and Garrett was the last to check in. He and another passenger were about to miss the cut for the flight. The other guy was yelling at the gate agent. Garrett, meanwhile, remained calm, kind, and patient. There was one seat left. Guess who they gave it to. We went home, and Cranky Man got left in Phoenix. In an infuriating situation, how is losing it on a stranger going to help?

Also keep in mind things run differently in foreign countries (there's truth behind the phrase "island time"), so patience and understanding truly are virtues.

• Be open-minded. I admit that when we first started traveling, I thought the United States was the best place on Earth. I thought it was better than every other country. I was quickly proven wrong, and can see now that I had a very immature and closed-off view of the world. Each place you visit has a different culture and a different flavor. Who's to say there's one way to live correctly? Who's to say the way *you* find happiness is the only way? We've learned that there is no "best" country and that every place has its own wonderful features. Be open-minded to new experiences, new foods, and new cultures. Be quick to accept invitations and slow to judge.

• Be outgoing. When you travel with an outgoing friend or family member, you quickly learn how much more enriching travel can be. You can meet people from all over the world and learn about how they live. It's one thing to quietly walk around a city and shop, but it's a whole other experience when you talk to restaurant servers, store clerks, or strangers on the street. Be brave, be curious, and be social—even if that's not generally how you move about in your normal life. Ask your taxi or rideshare driver about their family and their dreams. Meeting people opens up doors for new opportunities and experiences. It also builds acceptance, tolerance, open-mindedness, and love.

Early in our travels, Garrett and I would try to pass the buck when it came to talking to strangers. "You ask him!" "No. You ask!" But then we've had experiences like when we asked a young couple in Mexico for tips in the area, only to be offered a tour with their family's catamaran company. A year later, the couple offered my sister-in-law the same kindness when we sent her to Mexico on vacation. Now, we rarely shy away from talking to locals!

• Be assertive. I've learned that the United States is one of the few countries in the world where people will always beat around the bush. Americans tend to be polite instead of direct. It's not a bad thing, but I feel like I've learned from other countries how to be direct and bold. (This is where Italian Jess comes in.) And in turn, I don't take offense when someone speaks in a direct way right back to me.

• Be detail oriented. If you pay attention to the details *before* your trip, you can relax a bit once you're actually traveling. When you book a flight, hotel, or rental car, check and double-check your dates, times, and pick-up locations. (I learned this the hard way when I showed up in Los Angeles to pick up a rental car booked in San Francisco.) ≋

Our good friend Brooks snapped one of my all-time favorite photos: Garrett and I looking at chimpanzees in Uganda.

We often recommend Belize to U.S. travelers looking to go abroad for the first time. It's nearby, safe, English-speaking, and even accepts the U.S. dollar.

CHAPTER EIGHTEEN

HOW WE TRAVELED FULL-TIME

Living Life on the Road

. . . .

I realize that our situation is unique. Most people don't take off one day and make a life (and career) out of traveling. When we first left in August 2015, our plan was to travel for four months. We planned to come back in December for the holidays and make a decision about where we wanted to settle down.

Much to my surprise, Garrett and I agreed that we loved our life on the road and wanted to keep going! We had spent about 80 percent of the initial $45,000 that we had budgeted for our travels. Garrett wanted to see how far we could go by leveraging our social media. And so we agreed that we wouldn't dip into our savings—once the money was gone, we would stop.

Long story short: We worked very hard and ended up turning our travels into a career! For about a year we were able to break even. Then we began to earn a bit of a salary. Our full-time travel turned into our full-time jobs. It's not for everyone, but here's a little look into how we made it happen for us.

BECOMING TRAVEL INFLUENCERS

Garrett's and my skills very much complement each other. It's our teamwork that has made The Bucket List Family quite successful.

I studied advertising in college. I had planned to do product placement in movies and television. While I haven't placed products into movies, I have placed them into my own life! We partner with brands and tourism boards by highlighting destinations, experiences, and products we love on social media as part of our family journey. In doing so, we often get discounted rates or products and services for free in exchange for the exposure. That college degree did come in handy!

Garrett is a designer with a great eye. He honed his photography and videography skills while we traveled (see chapter 12). He's also an incredible storyteller. I'm a proficient web developer, and I built our website—but he put the design touches on it and developed our branding.

The term "influencer" didn't really exist back in 2015 when we started The Bucket List Family. Garrett liked to call us "family travel journalists." And that's what we did—we journaled and shared our family's adventures online. We were fortunate with our timing. We broke into the space early, before it became crowded with people actively seeking the influencer lifestyle. And we also worked extremely hard! I attribute our success to our backgrounds in marketing, skills in photography, Garrett's brilliant ability to tell a story, really cute kids, lots of hard work and persistence, and *really good timing!*

While this route of becoming a "travel influencer" is now super difficult and quite honestly overcrowded, if you can figure out a way to live on the road while working, I think it's a beautiful lifestyle!

WORKING ON THE ROAD

We've met some incredible people over the years who are full-time travelers. Many of them are not travel influencers but have set up their lives so that they can work from almost anywhere in the world.

We have friends who live internationally who are remote piano teachers, counselors, and life coaches. Others are freelancers or own e-commerce sites. They homeschool their kids to enable a family lifestyle that includes travel. Some stay in a country for a few months and then move on. Others have set up shop in Europe and then travel with their kids on weekends.

Living on the road means working on the road too, such as uploading a weekly YouTube video on the cripplingly slow internet in Tonga (page 342).

We flew in this small chopper to explore Iguazú Falls from the air (page 290), an epic memory.

We're just an ordinary family doing ordinary things in extraordinary places, like having breakfast and air-drying laundry on a tiny private island in Norway (page 396)!

A giraffe roams the Serengeti in Tanzania (page 348).

Anyone who is serious about making travel a full-time gig has to deal with some major obstacles: living situations; managing residences, work, and relationships back home; getting accustomed to new cultures; working in extreme time zone differences; and navigating the logistics of insurance, taxes, and banking. Kudos to those who can make it work!

In 2018, we stopped traveling full-time, but if we ever go back to that life, I'd love to spend months in a country to truly get to know the place and the culture. Or when my kids are older, I'd love to do a year abroad and put them in an international school. There's no better learning experience than immersing yourself in a new place and community.

There are so many ways to achieve a nomadic lifestyle—you just have to find the balance that works for you!

WORLD SCHOOLING

I personally don't have the capacity to homeschool—it takes a lot of planning and energy. But I think homeschooling is a great option for anyone looking to travel full-time if it suits the parent and the child. There are so many different homeschooling programs to choose from and online communities that help guide you and provide support.

When our oldest was about to start kindergarten, we slowed down traveling and bought a home in Hawaii. We wanted consistency and a steady community for our family. Our kids attend a private school that's very open to our travels. We do our best to schedule trips around school holidays, and we

I love to see our kids be curious and respectful around wildlife, like with the giant tortoises in Seychelles (page 356).

Though we've made Hawaii our home base, we still travel often: sometimes to far-off countries, sometimes just to the other parts of the island.

add on a few extra days to breaks. The long summer break is a big deal for us. Our kids' elementary school values travel (it's why we chose it!), and the teachers are excited to hear about our trips when we return. I do my best to make sure my kids are up to speed in their classes, and we bring any necessary homework with us on the road. As the kids have gotten older, they have gained more of a desire to be home for school activities, sports, and friends, so we schedule around their lives now too. At home, we slow down on social media and document only those moments we want to remember most—family surf sessions, soccer games, and simple family gatherings.

I also go out of my way to make sure the kids are learning during our travels. One summer, we spent about 50 days traveling around Africa. We called it "Summer Semester on Safari." Each week we would have the kids pick an animal that we had seen on a safari. We'd ask our safari guides all about that animal and throughout the week grill our kids about what they had learned. At the end of the week, the kids would sit down in front of a camera (for our YouTube channel) and share everything they knew about that animal. This was such a fun way for the kids to learn and also be held accountable for sharing their new knowledge. It also helped instill one of our core values: a love for nature and conservation.

IS IT FOR YOU?

It surprised me how much I enjoyed full-time travel. I'm a traditional and routine-oriented person, so it felt out of left field to live this adventure. Yet I found I loved a minimalist lifestyle. I loved the special time with my husband and kids, and I loved experiencing new parts of this world with them.

But after three years of full-time travel, we agreed that it was time to set up a home base. We wanted our kids to go to school and have consistent friends. We missed having a community.

Travel is hard! A week or two away from your home, friends, work, routine, and bed is exhausting and can really take a toll. But I still prefer our long summers of three months of travel over a 10-day holiday. It feels good to get into a routine on the road and have a home away from home, even if it's not the same home the whole time. It's a complete mental shift. I don't think about home while I travel. I don't let myself miss my bed or friends or community. I try to enjoy the life right in front of me. If I don't, I get homesick.

So many people say, "I don't know how you do it! I'm always so excited to get home after a vacation." Trust me, I feel the same way! That's why I love extended travel. It's a chance to immerse yourself somewhere new and then return to the comforts of friends, family, and home.

Full-time travel is not for everyone! We've had a few friends take off for full-time travel, only to return home a month later. But I think it's a great thing to try. You'll immerse yourself in new places and cultures in a way that you just can't on a short vacation. And you don't have to make travel your life or career to do it "full-time." If you can afford to do so, take a month or a summer away from school or work and give it a try. You might surprise yourself, like I did.

You can also get creative to make full-time travel more affordable. See if you can work remotely for a short period of time so you aren't sacrificing your paycheck (and be sure to check that tax laws won't prohibit you from working away from home long term). Instead of booking a hotel or expensive rental home, try swapping homes with someone in another state or country—or rent an RV! Maybe you'll love it, maybe you'll hate it, but time spent with family is never wasted. ≋

One of our favorite national parks is Zion in southern Utah (page 264).

PART THREE

WHERE TO GO

ARCTIC OCEAN

Alaska

Iceland

NORTH

AMERICA

AREA ENLARGED

Scottish
Highlands

Osl

Banff

Amsterdam
London

Cannon Beach

Paris

E

Florenc

Lake Tahoe

New York

PACIFIC OCEAN

Zion National Park

ATLANTIC OCEAN

Lisbon

Hilton Head Island

Baja California

Walt Disney World, Orlando

Bermuda

Marrakech

North Shore, Oahu

Exuma

Antigua

Dominica

A   F

Santa Teresa

Galápagos
Islands

SOUTH

AMERICA

Cook Islands

Iguazú
Falls

ATLANTIC OCEAN

PACIFIC OCEAN

Chilean Patagonia

Falkland Islands
(Islas Malvinas)

SOUTHERN OCEAN

We've visited the Galápagos Islands (page 246) twice now, and we still can't get enough of the untouched wildlife and nature!

CHAPTER NINETEEN

START YOUR OWN BUCKET LIST

50 Destinations to Start Your Family's Adventure

....

When we started traveling, we had no idea what countries would be most welcoming to families, how long a flight our children could manage, or how we'd get through jet lag and missed naptimes. But nine years and more than 90 countries later, we're pretty seasoned travelers—as are our three kids. And that means we are in a unique position to make recommendations to other families of travelers. In fact, it's probably one of the things we're asked most: "Where should we go next?"

The 50 destinations that follow are some of our favorite spots. They topped our list for this book because they each hold a special memory, be it a holiday favorite (see the Christmas markets in Berlin, page 240), a life-changing experience learning local history (Rwanda, page 236), a one-of-a-kind adventure (swimming with whale sharks in Tonga, page 342), or just an amazing family getaway (Lake Tahoe, Nevada, U.S.A., page 362).

These itineraries come in all shapes and sizes. There are U.S. destinations for long-weekend get-aways and road trips (see Zion, Utah, page 264). Overseas, you'll find recommendations for adventures big (diving with sharks in Fiji, page 178) and small (swimming with pigs off the coast of Exuma, page 294). There are easy-to-get-to destinations (the Scottish Highlands, page 198) and those off the beaten path (Bhutan, page 320). My hope is there is something for everyone, no matter what kind of traveler you may be.

In each destination, I recommend activities for both adults and kids, plus where to stay (including where we stayed, as well as luxury, mid-range—what I call "comfort"—and budget options), what to eat, and how to get there. I hope this is just the start of your own bucket list—and that these 50 itineraries inspire you to pack your bags and go. ☰

SANTA TERESA, COSTA RICA

Zip-line Through the Jungle

Santa Teresa has a laid-back, surfy vibe and is surrounded by lush greenery and mountains.

often suggest Costa Rica as a great place to take one of your first international trips—especially with kids. We visited when Manilla was four, Dorothy six, and Cali just five months. There are a lot of direct flights to and from the U.S., even with low-cost airlines like Southwest and Spirit Airlines. Once you're there, Costa Rica is very easy to navigate, and a huge bonus is having both the beach and the jungle to explore! One of our favorite spots is the cute western beach of Santa Teresa. Smaller and less developed than other westside towns (such as Tamarindo or Manuel Antonio), Santa Teresa has exactly what we need: It's great

for all surf levels, has wonderful restaurants, and is super kid friendly.

If you're in Costa Rica, there's no doubt you'll hear *pura vida* as a greeting wherever you go. Meaning "pure or simple life," it's more than just a phrase—it's a reminder to focus on the good life and appreciate your surroundings.

HOW TO GET THERE

There are a few different ways to get to Santa Teresa. We flew into San Jose's Juan Santamaria Airport and then to Tambor Airport. From there, it's only a 45-minute drive to

Santa Teresa. We rented an SUV and definitely recommend you do as well. The roads are bumpy and have lots of potholes. Alternatively, you could rent a car in San Jose and head to Puntarenas, where you drive right onto a ferry to Paquera, which is a short drive to Santa Teresa. In its entirety, this takes about five hours; six if you skip the ferry and drive various highways and back roads.

WHAT TO DO

• Adventure: **Zip-lining:** Costa Rica, and particularly Santa Teresa, truly boasts some of the best zip-lining in the world, where you'll find yourselves sailing high above the jungle. We booked the Mal Pais canopy ride with Zuma Tours: Eight different cables soar over a national park—one is 800 feet (240 m) up! After our first tour, we immediately booked it again for a few days later! A staffer helped Manilla, then just shy of five years old, do the zip lines; he absolutely loved it. **Surfing:** Santa Teresa is a great place to learn how to surf. There are

Don't Miss
....

Costa Rica is *alive!* In May, thousands of land crabs travel to the beach to lay their eggs. They were everywhere during our visit!

plenty of local instructors if you need lessons. The break near us was family friendly, with a sandy shore break and roller waves. But there are different levels of breaks all along the coast. (We visited with friends in May and could find a break for both the kiddos and the more experienced dads.) The kids could surf and play in these waves for hours. I suggest you rent boards for your entire stay. Double-check with your surf instructor that you'll be getting a lesson at a good time of day—the waves change significantly depending on the tides. **Four-wheeling:** There are multiple rental shops to pick up ATVs at the edge of town. Santa Teresa caters to tourists—which I love, don't get me wrong—but make sure you get out

Just trying to keep up with my rock star surfing kiddos. This may be my biggest wave to date!

of town to explore the villages. On your ATV ride you can try out the local restaurants and shops, buy fruit on the side of the road, and meet locals.

WHEN TO VISIT

Santa Teresa is a great year-round destination! Because Costa Rica is close to the Equator, the temperature is pretty much always mild. Rainy season is from May to November, but it's actually a nice time to visit: The landscape is even more green than it is the rest of the year, and you can also see whales and dolphins. December to April is best for beginner surfers, May to October for intermediate surfers.

WHERE TO STAY

We stayed in one of Joya Villa's two stunning properties, perched up above the trees and overlooking the ocean just off the beach. In this part of Costa Rica you can find a villa or rental home that is pretty luxurious for a reasonable price.

• **Comfort:** The House of Somos hotel has a very cool surfer vibe, with butterfly chairs by the pool and a café inside a little Airstream trailer.
• **Budget:** Santa Teresa Surf Vista Villas, set atop a private hilltop, offers simple but comfy accommodations, with lots of hammocks to lounge in and a pool to swim in.

WHAT TO EAT

Costa Rica is not necessarily known for its food, but that's not to say it's not good! Traditional Costa Rican fare includes a lot of rice and beans (and hot sauce), plus superfresh fruits and vegetables such as pineapple and hearts of palm. Santa Teresa takes a more modern, healthy approach to cuisine, and the food vibe is more "hippie surf town" than traditional Costa Rican fare, so it has loads of restaurants that cater to vegan and gluten-free diets. Some of our favorites include Cafe Social for breakfast, The Bakery for lunch, Eat Street (an open marketplace), and Koji's Restaurant for fresh sushi.

We found ourselves in Costa Rica during the crab migration (when they all head to the beach to mate). They were everywhere—even our bathroom!

Brave like a dolphin: Dorothy gets ready to go zip-lining in the Costa Rican jungle.

CAPPADOCIA, TURKEY

Ride a Hot-Air Balloon

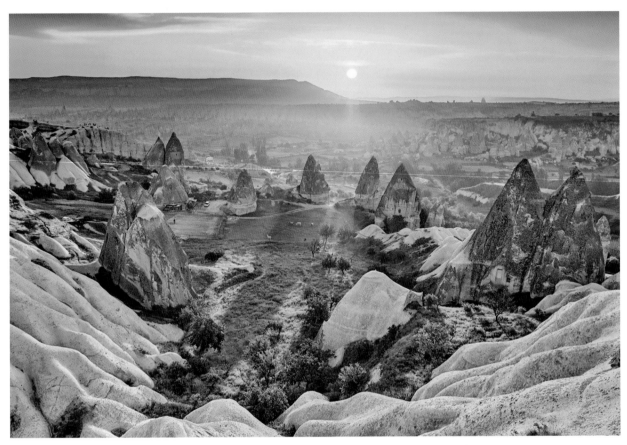

Cappadocia is known for its rock formations, often called "fairy chimneys."

Turkey is one of my all-time favorite countries. Throughout the country, from beautiful Istanbul to the smaller towns, the people of Turkey (Türkiye) are what really make this place so lovely. They were so welcoming everywhere we went—especially to children. Beyond its friendly citizenry, Turkey has an incredible culture and history. There is so much to experience in Istanbul, but the highlight of our trip was a visit to the Cappadocia region.

When we arrived in Cappadocia, we were surprised that it looked familiar: The long desert plains and red mountain vistas look like Utah, where Garrett and I went to college. You may have seen pictures of Cappadocia, most likely of its famous sunrise hot-air balloon rides over unique "fairy chimney" rock formations and vast mountain cave dwellings. Every morning at sunrise, dozens of hot-air balloons fly over the city. It's magical.

Speaking of those cave dwellings: From a distance, you see mountains with holes in them. When you get closer, you realize those holes are doorways and windows. There is so much beautiful history across the region, including

UNESCO-protected cathedrals with scripture etched on the walls from 5000 B.C.

HOW TO GET THERE

Fly into either Kayseri or Nevşehir airport: From either one, Cappadocia is a 30- to 40-minute drive away.

WHAT TO DO

• Adventure: **Hot-air ballooning:** This is a bucket list *must!* Every morning in Cappadocia, dozens of hot-air balloons launch just before sunrise. Most outfitters provide a snack and coffee before you board and finish with a champagne toast and light breakfast. The morning light and the multitude of other balloons in the sky make for some absolutely stunning photos. We were lucky enough to witness a marriage proposal during our ride! There is an age requirement for these rides, so ask your hotel about childcare—ours offered it—if the kids aren't old enough. Don't worry! The kids can still experience the magic: One morning Garrett woke up Dorothy—four years old at the time— early and took her to watch the balloons over the city from our hotel.

• Culture: **Kaymakli Underground City:** Christians hiding from Persian and Arab invaders lived in a fully underground city, Kaymakli, in the early sixth and seventh centuries. The city is a maze of pathways and rooms, preserved enough that you can still see where these people lived, cooked, and stored weapons. Four of the eight levels can be explored by visitors, but beware to those who get a little (or a lot) claustrophobic—like myself: These spaces can get dark and tight! **Open-air museums:** Multiple museums in the Cappadocia area are fascinating, UNESCO-protected sites, including monasteries cut out of the rocks, some containing incredible Christian frescoes.

Get a Guide
·····································
In Turkey, I highly suggest hiring a tour guide or agency. We rarely use guides, but in Turkey we felt safer with a local by our side. On top of feeling safe, we got to know a local person who shared so much about the culture and history that we wouldn't have learned otherwise. We hired our guide through BarefootPlus Travel.

WHEN TO VISIT

Cappadocia is extra busy (and hot) in the summer months. The best times to visit are March and April or September and October, when the temperatures are mild. Winter months can be chilly. We visited in October.

You can sleep inside a cave hotel in Cappadocia.

We loved taking the kids to explore the rock formations with ancient dwellings built right into them.

WHERE TO STAY

I highly suggest staying in one of the cave hotels! The experience of sleeping inside a cave is surreal—and you'll also have breathtaking views. We stayed at Argos in Cappadocia, a small boutique hotel built into the mountain rock. It overlooks the city and gives you a great view of the hot-air balloons every morning. The staff treats you like family, and they were so lovely to our children. All the cave hotels are a little dark and borderline claustrophobic—but unique and incredible! It's amazing what's been built into the rock.

• **Comfort:** The rooms at Hanzade Suites are on the bigger side, for a cave hotel, and your stay includes a lovely buffet breakfast. They even have a family-friendly suite with two bedrooms that you can book for the whole gang.

• **Budget:** The family-run Naturels Cave House is small but incredibly cozy, with comfy rugs and furnishings. The boutique inn sits in a restored 300-year-old stone house close to town.

WHAT TO EAT

We hired a guide in Cappadocia who took us to authentic restaurants where the whole family enjoyed kebabs, *kofte* (little meatballs), *lokum* (Turkish delight), *kebap* (grilled meats with salad or veggies, my favorite), and baklava, of course. I wish I could remember the names of our favorite restaurants, but, honestly, our guide always took us to very small, local spots with maybe five tables max. Ask your hotel or guide for suggestions.

Don't miss the tasty sweets, like baklava, in Turkey!

A must-do: Take a hot-air balloon ride over the fairy chimneys in Cappadocia at sunrise.

KYOTO, JAPAN

Hike to the Fushimi Inari Taisha Shrine

Kyoto is beautiful in the fall when the leaves change colors around its bountiful parks.

Japan, as a whole, feels so different from the U.S. It has such a unique blend of tradition and modernity. It's my daughter's favorite country in the whole world. She fell in love with Japanese food, specifically udon noodles and sushi. Dorothy was three years old at the time we visited and loved Tokyo, especially the abundance of Hello Kitty, the Harajuku girl culture, and how the city was very high-tech, flashy, pink, and full of bright lights.

We all absolutely love Tokyo (and we have a lot of other spots in Japan still on our bucket list), but Kyoto is one of our favorite places. Kyoto represents quintessential Japan to me. It's small, quaint, and has beautiful history and Japanese culture packed into a walkable city. Because it's right along the Kamo River, we found Kyoto was the perfect place to explore by bicycle. We biked to the numerous shrines and Zen gardens along the river and visited the Nishiki Market every day.

HOW TO GET THERE

Kyoto is only a few hours away from Tokyo by bullet train and about an hour from Osaka. Manilla, only one year old at the time, loved the bullet train. It feels like you're on a plane; the ride is that smooth. But you can tell how fast you're going when you're flying through the countryside. Beware: Those bullet trains are on a schedule, and they wait for no one! We learned that lesson the hard way and missed our stop!

WHAT TO DO

• Culture: **Fushimi Inari Taisha shrine:** This is perhaps the most iconic place in Kyoto. It's a one- to three-hour hike up a beautiful mountain framed with thousands of bright orange gates. Called torii, they symbolize the passage from our world to the sacred world. Once you reach the shrine, you'll find a small town and market at its base. I highly recommend packing snacks and water for the kids and a carrier for little babies, since the path is not stroller friendly. To be honest, the hike isn't the friendliest for super-young ones because it's long and steep—we only made it about a mile (1.6 km) with our littles.

But go as far as you can—the views and experience are worth every step. **Nishiki Market:** We spent part of each day of our visit strolling through this giant market lined with artisans' stalls filled with clothes and textiles. It's like the Grand Bazaar of Kyoto. The market also has amazing restaurants, treats, and ceramics. Garrett and I even got a massage there on a night we arranged for a babysitter back at the hotel! **Arashiyama:** This bamboo forest is absolutely stunning. It's free to visit and open 24 hours a day—but it's popular and can get crowded. Still, I could have stayed there and walked around for hours. My littles, though, didn't find it as exciting, so we were sure to stop for ice cream at one of the shops on the way out of the forest.

WHEN TO VISIT

Kyoto is best in the spring and fall. In the springtime, you can catch the amazing cherry trees in full bloom. And in the fall,

LEFT: Garrett and Manilla at the Yasaka shrine RIGHT: Most *ryokans* have beautiful courtyards and greenery.

岸和田市本町四一 日信建設㈱ 河村憲亮

岸和田市本町四ノ一 日信建設㈱ 代表取締役 河村 幸志

京都市中京区 (有)井上パッケージ 井上章一

西宮市 福中和正 家族一同 中村正雪

名古屋市中川区五女子町

We carried our kids a good chunk of the way to the Fushimi Inari Taisha shrine. We didn't make it all the way, but we loved this iconic spot.

We were mesmerized strolling through the Arashiyama bamboo forest.

you can witness the vibrant hues of the leaves as they change colors. Summer can be humid, and winter can be quite cold.

WHERE TO STAY

Next time we visit Kyoto, we will be sure to stay in a *ryokan*—one of the traditional Japanese inns peppered throughout the country. Ryokans are more than just a place to sleep; they're a unique cultural experience, with tatami-covered floors, futon beds, and Japanese-style baths, and most offer local food. There are ryokans of all shapes, sizes, and costs.

We stayed at the Ritz-Carlton, Kyoto, which backs up to the Kamo River. It has a Zen vibe, and they accommodate children with a cute in-room tent, books, and toys, plus a bracelet that grants them a free scoop of ice cream each day.

The hotel also helped arrange bike rentals for our stay, which was mostly how we got around.

- **Comfort:** Hoshinoya Kyoto is only accessible by boat, which sets the slow pace you'll live by here. Enjoy soaking in cedar tubs and lounging in silk robes.
- **Budget:** Onsen Kadensho is a larger ryokan that boasts hot springs (both communal and private). It's located right near the train station.

WHAT TO EAT

In Japan you can't skip the ramen, soba, and udon noodle dishes. You also won't be able to miss green tea–flavored *everything!* I'm not a huge sushi person, but those little conveyor belt sushi spots are popular—and fun. So is teppanyaki. Kids love to watch that fire!

FIJI

Go Diving With Sharks

We love the people and culture of Fiji—and its stunning and healthy coral reefs.

Fiji ranks super high on our family's list for multiple reasons. First, it has some of the most crystal clear water and beautiful reefs for snorkeling and diving, plus some amazing wildlife to see, including sharks! But most important, Fijians are the *nicest* people on the planet. They are incredibly welcoming—especially to little kids and babies. This is a hot take, but while I really enjoyed (arguably more popular) Tahiti, I would take Fiji over it any day. It's probably a little cheaper to visit too.

I consider Fiji a triple threat: a place where you can get in adventure, culture, and service in one trip!

HOW TO GET THERE

Fiji has two great international airports, Suva (also known as Nausori) and Nadi. Suva is on the windward side of the island, which is generally rainier (but very green!). Nadi is drier. Major airlines that fly from North America into Nadi include Fiji Airways and Air New Zealand.

WHAT TO DO

• Adventure: **Scuba dive with sharks:** Beqa Lagoon's Shark Reef Marine Reserve is a protected reef with eight different species of sharks and hundreds of species of fish. Dive guides will instruct you on proper execution and safety. This is not a cage dive! We dropped below the surface with a rope and took a short swim to a large, human-made coral barrier, which we waited behind. The guides, dressed in armor, fed sharks from a giant trash bin of chum. We were able to see some of the largest ocean predators very close-up. I was impressed by the respect all the locals and dive staff had for the reef and the sharks. They made sure that everyone understood the rules for participating in such a unique experience (remain calm; move slowly), as well the incredible conservation efforts that go hand in hand with the shark dives. Participants must be at least 15 years old and have open-water diving certification. **Hop aboard a seaplane:** Fiji is a great place to try out this bucket list experience. There's a small water runway about 10 minutes from the Nadi airport. Our pilot flew us to our resort, and before he turned around he jumped right into the ocean to cool off! Our pilot also let two-year-old Manilla sit on my lap in the front seat for a full view of the cockpit—and ocean—while we flew.

• Culture: **Participate in a kava ceremony:** If you are lucky enough to be invited to a kava ceremony, do it! Be sure to look into the suggested etiquette as far as how to dress, what to bring, and the proper way to show respect to the village and village chief. **Enjoy the music:** Whether you are arriving at the airport, or coming from or going to your hotel, you'll most likely be serenaded by locals. Music is a big part of Fijian life!

• Service: **Visit a village:** Many resorts partner with local villages to facilitate tourist visits. We love that Fiji and its resorts have a massive focus on sustainability and local outreach programs. If you plan to participate in a village visit, reach out

"Yes-man" Garrett is always open to unique opportunities. Here he is participating in a fire-lighting ceremony at Nanuku Resort.

to your resort in advance and ask if you can bring anything that local villagers need, such as toothbrushes or little toys.

WHEN TO VISIT

Things get hot, rainy, and humid from January through March. The cooler, drier times of the year (May through October) are more ideal.

WHERE TO STAY

We've been to Fiji twice and have stayed at six different resorts, so I have a handful of recommendations at various price points and locations.

Kokomo Fiji is top of the line. The resort's seaplane or helicopter picks you up from Nadi and transports you to the private island. While the price is steep, stays at villas and residences include meals, water sports, a spa treatment, kids' club access, nanny services (one nanny per child!), and more.

Nanuku Resort is another luxury property we loved. It's about 90 minutes from the Suva airport and is a quick drive to a scuba shop that offers a *must-do* shark dive. Aside from its wonderful location, the resort's villas were stunning—and the whole place smelled amazing. I later learned it's a scent from Pure Fiji, which I now use at home.

Tides Reach Fiji offers a blend of luxury and comfort on the island of Taveuni. It has such a cozy and welcoming feeling. The staff takes great care of you at all meals, and you have access to a boat and Jet Skis for unlimited water fun! This is a great place to bring a large group or family.

Paradise Cove is a wonderful comfort option. There were many families at the resort who had stayed there before; I always take that as a good sign!

WHAT TO EAT

Enjoy all the fresh seafood Fiji has to offer! Their most popular dish is *kokoda,* which is similar to ceviche—fresh-caught fish marinated in citrus juices and coconut milk and served with veggies. There's a huge Indian influence in Fiji, so you'll find great curries too.

Most resorts in Fiji help support a local village. We played with some schoolkids on an island near our resort.

You bet Dorothy and Manilla were thrilled to ride in (and play off of) a seaplane. The planes are surprisingly smooth at takeoff and landing.

QUEENSTOWN, NEW ZEALAND

Boat Through Milford Sound

There's a postcard-worthy shot everywhere you look in Queenstown.

New Zealand is my favorite. There, I said it. It's my favorite country to visit, and if I were going to live anywhere else in the world, I'd move to New Zealand. In fact, we actually applied for work visas a few years back and were accepted, but we had to change our plans when we got pregnant with Calihan. Maybe some day in the future I'll fulfill that dream!

You can't travel all the way to New Zealand and not see both the North and South Islands. We spent a few weeks in rental homes on the North Island, then spent another 10 days in Queenstown on the South Island. It'd be amaz-ing to rent an RV and tour the country. Perhaps for our next visit!

It is so hard for me to say this, but if I *had* to choose between the two, I'd pick the South Island. Around every corner is a postcard-perfect setting. Drive around the out-skirts of Queenstown and you'll go from amazing lake country to rolling hills to majestic mountains. It's otherworldly.

New Zealand is incredible, but it is very, very far away from the United States! Maybe God did that on purpose? Otherwise everyone would live there!

HOW TO GET THERE

Queenstown has an international airport with incoming direct flights from multiple cities in Australia. It is an easy flight from Auckland, Wellington, or Christchurch. The descent into Queenstown is absolutely breathtaking: You fly over a mountain range called the Remarkables that are, in fact, remarkable.

WHAT TO DO

• Adventure: **Milford Sound:** There are a handful of ways to get to Milford Sound—car, plane, or helicopter. I highly suggest driving from Queenstown. It's a great way to take in the beautiful scenery along the way. Factor in time for your trip: Without stopping, the route takes just under four hours. But you'll want to pull over frequently, not just for bathroom and food breaks but also for numerous photo ops. And along the way, you'll usually find a very sarcastic Kiwi telling you all about the area and spots where they filmed *The Lord of the Rings*. Once you get to Milford Sound, book a ferryboat. You can take a ferry around the sound for a few hours or overnight. We've done both and especially loved the overnight cruise. On your ride around the sound, you'll get a tour of the surrounding giant cliffs and majestic waterfalls. If you're lucky, you'll even see some fur seals, bottlenose dolphins, and penguins! Did I already say this is my favorite place on the entire planet? **Rafting:** If you have older kids, rafting is such a fun experience! Guides help you navigate the Shotover and Kawarau Rivers. We went without the kids and felt very safe, even after almost flipping our raft. Kiwis have a great sense of humor, and there was no shortage of laughter on this day. **Bungee jumping:** Queenstown is ground zero for bungee jumping—literally: It's where the sport was invented. There are a handful of places around Queenstown to bungee jump, including AJ Hackett Bungy, named

Take Your Teens
....

This town was made for older kids and teens who'd be excited (and able) to do some of the more extreme activities, including rafting and bungee jumping.

after the man who popularized bungee. You can choose your position to jump—swan dive, backflip, upside down, and many other creative ways! We opted for the swing on one of our visits—the kids stayed home with a sitter. (Jumpers must be 10 years old and weigh at least 35 kilograms, about 77 pounds).

• Culture: **Arrowtown:** Twenty minutes from Queenstown is Arrowtown, an old mining town with candy shops and restaurants. You can also mine for gold, which the kids loved. **Rugby:** The New Zealand All Blacks are New Zealand's national rugby team and the pride and joy of the country. The

We road-tripped to the Blue Pools to see Garrett bungee jump off this bridge!

Bungee jumping where the terrifying sport was invented: You can see Garrett holding on to me like his life depended on it!

All Blacks are famous for being one of the (if not *the*) best rugby teams in the world. To get a real feel for New Zealand culture, definitely hit up a game in person, or watch one on television at a local bar or restaurant.

WHEN TO VISIT

Queenstown is great year-round, depending on what you are looking for. Summer months (December to February) are perfect for hiking, rafting, and getting outdoors. Spring and fall are mild, with fewer crowds. And then there's great skiing in the winter (June to August).

WHERE TO STAY

Go with a rental home in New Zealand. We stayed in rentals in the countryside among the majestic rolling hills. Driving around New Zealand is a joy since everywhere you go is so beautiful. There are really great family-friendly homes and condos in Queenstown and in the nearby areas.

WHAT TO EAT

Because New Zealand is relatively remote, almost everything there is locally sourced. We found that even small gas stations had some quality (real) food, including fresh meat pies. New Zealand also has some of the happiest cows I've ever seen. They roam the countryside, looking like they are living their best life. So definitely try the locally sourced beef and dairy—New Zealand has some of the best ice cream!

In Queenstown proper, don't miss Fergburger, famous for their big ol' juicy burgers. You'll spot the long line from a ways off. The Cookie Time Cookie Bar is a personal favorite, as I'm an absolute sucker for a warm, freshly baked cookie. (They also have cookie ice cream sandwiches and cookie milkshakes!)

Of course, one of my favorite things about New Zealand is how family friendly it is. In almost every restaurant, there is a kids' corner or activities offered for kids to do during the meal (beyond the standard coloring page menu common in the U.S.). Brilliant!

My favorite place in the whole wide world: Milford Sound

DESTINATIONS FOR INFANTS

In my book, this is the time to rock and roll! Infants (babies two to nine months) already sleep and eat around the clock, and parents of an infant are zombies anyway, so swapping time zones isn't going to mess you up that badly. Pick destinations where activities are more or less walking around or doing easy hikes where you can wear your baby in a carrier. Here are a few of our top destinations for traveling with a baby.

Banff, Canada: Banff is amazing in all seasons, but a summertime outdoor trip is incredible and easy with a young one. Take the gondola up for some gorgeous views, and put your carrier to good use on some hikes. (See page 254 for more.)

Switzerland: Known for its stunning scenery, Switzerland is easy to explore by train or car. You can take a boat trip across one of its many lakes. Beautiful hikes are endless, and you can enjoy walking around some of the quaint Swiss towns—Interlaken and Lucerne are two of my favorites.

Boston, Massachusetts, U.S.A.: If you're looking for a walkable city, think about Boston. With a stroller or baby carrier, you can easily walk the Freedom Trail and see all the sights. A great add-on is a relaxing few days on Cape Cod afterward. We really enjoyed our stay at the Chatham Bars Inn, and they also have childcare available.

Paris, France: My favorite baby stroller (the BabyZen Yoyo+) originated in Paris. You can see why! Parisians have city life with a baby down to an art. You can cruise around the city with a stroller or carrier and enjoy hours in the Louvre or walking around Versailles. (See page 192 for more.)

Marrakech, Morocco: We found that Moroccan people were so happy to have babies around. Bringing an infant with you to explore the vibrant city is easy and safe. (See page 230 for more.)

Vienna, Austria: For a beautiful city with incredible history, art, and museums, turn to Vienna. It's easily accessible with a stroller or with a baby strapped to you. They also have family-friendly Kinderhotels throughout the country. (These can also be found in Germany, Croatia, Italy, and Portugal.)

Antigua, Guatemala: I can clearly picture the many Guatemalan women who went about their entire day with a baby strapped to them. It's an inspiration and a great way to see this beautiful, vibrant country! Hiking and exploring colorful Antigua makes for a great trip with an infant. We took Cali to Guatemala when he was four months old. So many locals asked to hold and love on him. (See page 366 for more.)

Rome, Italy: Walk and eat your way through Rome with a young baby. If your baby is good on the go, this is a great place to visit. Maybe just don't go in the heat of the summer.

Prague, Czechia: Prague is one of my favorite European cities. It's so picturesque and doesn't quite have the craziness of Paris or Rome. It's a great stop with an infant. In fact, visiting Prague, Vienna, and Budapest on one European trip (by car or train) is totally doable with a baby!

Barcelona, Spain: Spanish people tend to love babies, and that is definitely the case in Barcelona. You'll see a lot of babies out and about in various places, from tapas bars to galleries. The majority of the city is stroller friendly, making for nice walks along the beach or through the picturesque streets.

Cali's third country, at 10 weeks old, was Guatemala.

DUBAI, UNITED ARAB EMIRATES

Off-road on Sand Dunes

Dubai is an epic city that has tons to do for the whole family, including indoor skiing.

Our first visit to Dubai happened when a 2017 coup attempt in Turkey changed our flight plans between Asia and Europe. We landed in Dubai in June, aka in an oven. I wouldn't recommend visiting in the summer! But I do recommend visiting. Dubai is a huge city built in the middle of a desert. Everything you see has been imported—except oil, which is cheaper than water. It is incredible to see what humans can do. In Dubai, they've built the tallest building in the world (the Burj Khalifa), created palm-shaped islands, introduced seven-star hotels, and put ski slopes indoors. In short, Dubai is always push-ing the limits and working on the next biggest, tallest, brightest, and coolest thing.

On the other hand, there is little natural beauty within the city. To get that, you have to travel just outside, to the gorgeous sand dunes of the desert.

Dubai has a huge international airport and is a gateway to literally everywhere! When we're traveling to the other side of the world, I'll gladly take a 24-hour-plus layover in Dubai to acclimate to the time change. A night or two in Dubai beats spending extra money on a pricey lodge in our final destination.

HOW TO GET THERE

Emirates is one of our favorite airlines, especially for kids. They start each flight by giving kiddos a little travel activity bag that includes coloring and activity pages and a plush toy. They also have kid-friendly meal options and loads of in-flight games and entertainment.

Dubai International Airport is large, and it can take a while to move between terminals. So, if you have a short layover in Dubai, I suggest you move quickly! But they try to make it easy for families: The airport offers free strollers, and there are multiple kids' areas and playgrounds.

WHAT TO DO

• Adventure: **Off-roading:** "Dune bashing," as the locals call it, was one of our favorite adventures in Dubai. Ask your hotel to recommend an outfitter. A private SUV picks you up from your

Follow Your Interests
....
Dubai has just about anything you can think of—skydiving, fishing, skiing, art galleries, water parks, amusement parks, gardens, shopping—so let your imagination run wild here.

hotel and drives about 45 minutes outside the city. They stop to let some air out of the tires, then you are on your own private roller coaster through beautiful red sand dunes. We took our tour at sunset, and after the sun went down, we stopped to join other tours for a tented dinner complete with henna tattoo artists, music, and belly dancers. **Indoor skiing:** Dorothy (then four) and Manilla's (then two) first ever ski experience was indoors in Dubai! Unconventional, I know. Ski Dubai is a giant indoor arena with an indoor chair lift, a ski slope that reaches 280 feet high (85 m), and a ski park with tubing and

Dorothy checks out her fresh catch off the coast.

ice structures. They provide all the winter gear (because who brings their parkas to Dubai?!), and you get suited up for an indoor temperature of 30°F (-1°C). They also have gentoo and king penguins! **Burj Khalifa:** The tallest building in the world is half a mile (0.8 km) high, and you can go up to its 124th floor. We did that to enjoy the views, and afterward, at the base of the building, we enjoyed the Dubai Fountain, which has one of the world's largest choreographed fountain shows. The Burj Khalifa is next to the Dubai Mall, so you can pair your visit with a trip to the Dubai Aquarium and Underwater Zoo, a visit to KidZania (an interactive children's experience), ice-skating, and access to loads of shopping and restaurants.

WHEN TO VISIT

Winter is beautiful and busy in Dubai. Spring and fall are great times to visit to beat the crowds. But definitely avoid summer! It's an absolute furnace there. You can't be outside after 7 a.m.—and if you do leave the air-conditioned hotel, you'll have to sprint to the car! However, Dubai does have loads of fun indoor and air-conditioned activities if you find yourself there in the summer.

WHERE TO STAY

The Ritz-Carlton, Dubai, sits on Jumeirah Beach. Our children love their kids' club, and the hotel is used to taking in guests at all hours of the day and night thanks to those long Dubai layovers.
• **Comfort:** If you're looking for endless family fun, book a room at Atlantis Dubai, which offers complimentary access to the Aquaventure Waterpark and Lost Chambers Aquarium.
• **Budget:** Rove Downtown is close to the Burj Khalifa and the Dubai Mall. It features a nice outdoor swimming pool and sundeck, and there are many interconnecting rooms, which are great for families.

WHAT TO EAT

Middle Eastern cuisine is one of my favorites! I love the fresh salads, spreads, and grilled meats. We even took some cooking classes to learn how to make tabbouleh (a salad of parsley, tomatoes, mint, onion, and bulgur) and *kofta* (balls or loaves of minced meat). Dubai is an international city, so you can find incredible food from any country.

There is no shortage of luxury accommodations in Dubai.

If you're ever in Dubai, don't miss catching a sunset from the dunes.

PARIS, FRANCE

Live Like a Parisian

I suggest an autumn visit to Paris. Crowds are low, the weather is still nice, and the foliage is stunning!

I n my dream world, we could travel to destinations for a month at a time to really get a feel for what it is like to live in different places around the world. Paris is definitely one of those cities! Although it's super tempting to play tourist with so many things to see in Paris, it's also nice to relax and try to settle in and live like a Parisian.

Personally, I love to do things like tour the Louvre and see the Moulin Rouge, but my husband and kids don't. So during our week in Paris in the fall of 2017, we rented a flat and bought all our groceries at the local bakeries, fruit stands, cheese shops, and butchers. I'm not a coffee drinker, but if I were, I would've definitely had a croissant and coffee at a local café every morning. We rented bikes for the week, rode along the Seine, and visited local playgrounds.

Be a smart traveler in Paris. Avoid scammers, tourist traps, and buying from large, fancy cafés—you'll get ripped off! Instead choose smaller, more local shops for pastries and coffee. Oh, and watch for pickpockets! The city is unfortunately known for them. Keep your phones and wallets in a safe place, and don't leave them sitting on your table or in your back pocket.

HOW TO GET THERE

There are three major airports in Paris. We usually use Charles de Gaulle and have a shuttle pick us up from the airport. (It's about 75 euros for a one-way private transfer.) It's so nice to have someone waiting for you when you land.

You can also travel via the "Chunnel" from London—riding a high-speed Eurostar train through the Channel Tunnel. It takes a little over two hours and costs around $65 (although prices are higher on weekends). The Eurostar rail system also stops in Paris with connections all across Europe.

Once you arrive, Paris Métro, the city's subway system, is simple to use and fun to learn. Ridesharing is also easy to book in Paris. We rented bikes for our stay and found it easy to navigate the city on two wheels as well. We rented our bikes from Fat Tire Tours, which offers both daily bike rentals and guided tour opportunities.

WHAT TO DO

• Culture: **Picnic at an iconic site:** Grab a baguette and some fruit and cheese from one of the many cafés or local markets and enjoy a picnic by the Eiffel Tower. We did this almost every day! There's a large grassy area right by the tower, and in warmer months kids can splash in the pool area at the adjacent Trocadéro gardens. **Visit the Eiffel Tower after dark:** The Eiffel Tower twinkles for the first five minutes of every hour from dusk until 11 p.m. or 2 a.m., depending on the time of year. We took our kids to the top of the tower (you need a reservation to do so) by elevator—climbing the stairs takes 30 to 45 minutes *without kids*—for the sparkles and nighttime views. You can book a tour or explore on your own. We opted to do it on our own since I didn't think our young kids would be too interested in the history of the Eiffel Tower. **Use the hop-on/hop-off bus:** Sometimes in big cities, the easiest way to see more is by bus. We used one of Paris's hop-on/hop-off buses to get around. These buses stop at many of the big tourist spots, including the Arc de Triomphe, Notre-Dame Cathedral, and the Montmartre area. The kids loved sitting on the double-decker bus, and we got a small taste of the sights without losing the kids' attention.

Don't Forget to Stroll

Our favorite stroller company, BabyZen, was actually founded in France, and our stroller, the Yoyo+, was a lifesaver throughout Paris. We walked a lot, and our little one needed a rest here and there. It was so handy because it folds up small and is easy to carry down subway stairs.

WHEN TO VISIT

Visiting Paris in shoulder season (April and May or mid-September to November) will help you avoid the crowds. We visited in October and spent the majority of our time outside. The summer can get very hot, and air-conditioning is not as common as it is in the U.S. Paris is also beautiful around Christmastime.

There are tons of tasty treats throughout the city, including fresh croissants.

Showing Dorothy the beautiful architecture inside Notre-Dame Cathedral was a special moment. The cathedral was devastated by a fire in 2019, and we look forward to seeing its restored structure.

WHERE TO STAY

I recommend renting a charming flat. It's so nice to feel more like a local in Paris. For our Paris visit, we worked with Paris Perfect, which has dozens of gorgeous properties. Each home is carefully chosen and vetted to ensure high standards for quality, location, and comfort.

Paris does offer some adorable hotels, though. If a hotel is your preference, I suggest finding boutique accommodations in a neighborhood like Le Marais or Saint-Germain-des-Prés, which are beautiful, central, intimate, and popular among both tourists and locals.

• **Comfort:** Les Jardins du Marais is a chic spot within walking distance of museums and a Métro station.

• **Budget:** Hotel Royal Saint Germain is kid friendly and only a 10-minute walk from the Jardin du Luxembourg (a great spot to get wiggles out). It's also within walking distance of Notre-Dame Cathedral.

WHAT TO EAT

I don't even know where to begin with the food in Paris. You could literally eat all day long! French cuisine is a whole *thing,* and I won't pretend that I'm an expert. I do know that the breads, cheeses, pastries, and meats are all heavenly. Manilla's favorite foods are French: macarons, crepes, *chouquettes,* and meringues.

Try a French cooking class or a pastry class. That way, you can take a small taste of France home with you with the skills you develop.

We visited Paris with friends and took a bike ride along the Seine. 10/10 recommend!

Dorothy, Manilla, and I lit a prayer candle inside Notre-Dame Cathedral.

SCOTTISH HIGHLANDS, UNITED KINGDOM

Castles, Clans, and Cliffs

On our trip to Scotland, I explored my roots as part of the Graham clan.

My maternal family hails from Scotland. Oddly enough, I had a sense of "home" when we visited in 2016. If you're of Scottish descent like me and want to explore your roots, Scotland is really set up to help you discover your genealogy, starting with which clan you're in. I am in the Graham clan.

A clan is a group of people united by a common surname—blood relation or not. Scottish clans have a chief and a coat of arms, and people express devout loyalty to their own clan. There are well-documented intense rivalries between clans.

My parents have been to Scotland and visited the churches and graveyards of our ancestors. My mother stood on the porch of the church where my ancestors petitioned for food during the Potato Famine in 1846. It can be truly a powerful and emotional experience to stand where your ancestors once stood.

On our trip to Inverness, in the Scottish Highlands, we found old shops where you can buy books, photos, and even keychains bearing your clan's coat of arms. There are genealogists to tell you about your clan too. We were traveling with my friend Anna, who also has Scottish ties; she is a Campbell. The Campbell clan was known to be one of the largest and most powerful families, which means Anna had so much to read and learn about her family history. The Graham clan was a lot smaller, but I was still happy to learn a bit about my rough-and-tough heritage.

I suggest a visit to Scotland regardless of your roots. Anyone will love the fairy-tale landscape of green rolling hills with a beautiful stone castle off in the distance. Our kids certainly loved this trip: We spent a lot of time walking along the banks of Loch Ness looking for the famous Nessie.

HOW TO GET THERE

There are regular, direct flights to Inverness from London and a few other European cities, such as Amsterdam and Dublin. You can also take a train from other parts of the United Kingdom; it's about a three-and-a-half-hour ride from Edinburgh.

Just Ask

English is the national language of Scotland, but most residents have a *thick* accent. You may need to ask someone (politely, of course!) to slow down so you can understand.

WHAT TO DO

• Adventure: **Isle of Skye:** The Isle of Skye offers an absolutely breathtaking landscape, with green hills, vast mountains, and cliffside waterfalls that cascade into the ocean. It's worth taking a day (or two) to drive around, hike, and explore! We took a drive to the Fairy Pools, a beautiful waterfall with a frigid aquamarine pool, and took a quick dip. **Golfing:** Scotland is the birthplace of golf, and there are beautiful courses (often called "links") throughout the country. **Highland games:** We haven't been lucky enough to make it to the Highland games

The kids loved spotting the "furry cows" in the Scottish countryside.

A special memory: learning about falconry at the Gleneagles hotel. Fun fact: Garrett grew up raising falcons and hawks—his dad was a falconer by hobby!

We could play on a giant chess board in the courtyard of our Airbnb at Fort Augustus Abbey.

yet, but it's next on my Scottish bucket list! Each summer, local areas hold competitions that consist of dancing, axe throwing, tug-of-war, and much more!

• Culture: **Eilean Donan Castle:** Of all the castles to visit in the Scottish Highlands, Eilean Donan Castle is more than worth the detour. Located near the small town of Dornie in the northeastern Highlands, the 13th-century castle is believed to have been built by Alexander II. Eilean Donan is considered an icon among locals for its rich history and picturesque placement at the junction of three different lochs.

WHEN TO VISIT

Summer months in northern Scotland are absolutely beautiful. We visited in October, and it was chilly, but we were still able to spend a good amount of time outdoors.

WHERE TO STAY

We hit the jackpot of Airbnbs when we found an old restored abbey, Fort Augustus Abbey, on the banks of Loch Ness. It's now called the Highland Club Scotland. The building looks like a mini-Hogwarts on the outside, but on the inside there are 109 luxury one- to three-bedroom apartments. The property also has a giant outdoor chess set, indoor pool, gym, tennis courts, and playground.

There are a number of castle hotels in the area, including the five-star Inverlochy Castle in the foothills and Tulloch Castle, a four-star option passed down from old clans.

WHAT TO EAT

Scotland offers delicious homestyle cooking. You'll find lots of yummy stews and mashed potatoes. You have to taste the national dish, haggis, which is like a crumbly sausage made with sheep organs and oats. I don't love it, but it's a rite of passage every visitor must experience.

Garrett ordered a Scottish breakfast that was one of the biggest meals I've ever seen: eggs, bacon, sausage, beans, haggis, tomatoes, mushrooms, and toast. A hearty meal for hearty people!

LONDON, UNITED KINGDOM

Go to an English Premier League Football Game

London is full of history, culture, and beautiful parks—perfect for families.

I went to England with my family when I was about 12—the only international trip we ever took. I remember visiting the Tower of London, walking into Harrods, and eating fish-and-chips. People seemed very confused by our large family of six!

Our family's visit to London with our young kids (Dorothy was almost four and Manilla was two at the time) was more of an extended stay. Friends offered us their flat for three weeks while they were out of the country. I was thrilled to live like a local after 15 months of traveling full-time. The apartment was in Wimbledon, where we shopped at local grocery stores, cooked our own food, and spent time at local parks. We learned the London Tube (subway) system, took day trips nearby, and had date nights in the city.

London is full of touristy and nontouristy options for families. You'll see locals and tourists alike enjoying the day at Hyde Park or the Natural History Museum. But a major highlight for us was going to a proper football match. (A soccer game, to us Americans!) We went to a national game at Wembley Stadium, where we watched England vs. Malta. We also journeyed up to Liverpool to see a rivalry match between Manchester United and Liverpool. Man, I thought I knew sports and what it meant to be a fan, but you haven't experienced soccer, I mean, football, until you've been to a rivalry match between two English Premier League teams! The fans were singing and chanting for the *whole entire game*. I don't know how they knew what to say or sing next, but they were all on board and in unison. The match was so heated, and emotions ran so high for both the players and fans. It's a bucket list experience to see this in person!

HOW TO GET THERE

London is so easy to access, with six airports to choose from—City, Gatwick, Heathrow, Luton, Stansted, and Southend.

Getting around London via the Tube is a fun task. We had a car for our stay, but taking a train was much easier. Driving

Movie Night

There are so many kid-friendly movies that make a great preview ahead of a trip to London. We got our kids excited for our visit by watching *Peter Pan, Paddington,* and *Mary Poppins.*

on the left-hand side of the road and learning to navigate the multilane roundabouts can be intimidating.

WHAT TO DO

• Culture: **Teatime:** Around 4 p.m., you can order afternoon tea at any number of hotels or pubs. Tea is served with finger sandwiches, scones, and pastries. My daughter and I enjoyed a special mommy/daughter teatime date at the Knightsbridge Lounge. Harrods Tea Room also offers a quintessential experience. **Tower of London:** I was so happy to bring my kids

LEFT: Big Ben at night RIGHT: Don't miss taking your littles (here I am with two-year-old Manilla) on the London Eye.

to the Tower of London because I had memories of visiting there when I was a kid. It's a historical icon that even little kids can enjoy. We loved seeing the guards and trying our hardest to get them to smile or break character. Spoiler alert: They never did. **Playground hopping:** There are multiple children's playgrounds all over the city. Our favorite was the Diana Memorial Playground in Kensington Gardens because it has a giant pirate ship. **Sightseeing:** Other highlights from our trip included the Natural History Museum, the Warner Bros. Studio Tour London: The Making of Harry Potter (you'll see Platform 9¾, among other filming locations), Buckingham Palace, the London Eye, King's Cross, and seeing *Wicked* on the West End (London's alternative to Broadway).

WHEN TO VISIT

London is a year-round destination. It gets cold in the winter, but if you celebrate Christmas, there's no better place. Go whenever you can—and don't believe the myths about dreary London weather. You can find really beautiful days!

WHERE TO STAY

London is one of those cities where it's so nice to feel like a local and go the home-rental route. We did this for weeks. If you don't have a friend with a place to borrow, consider Airbnb, Vrbo, or homestay websites; there are tons of options.

At the end of our stay, we did spend a few nights downtown at the Knightsbridge Hotel. Knightsbridge, right in the heart of the city, has quintessential London vibes and old Victorian buildings.

WHAT TO EAT

Start your day with a proper English breakfast—eggs, beans, sausage, bacon, mushrooms, roasted tomatoes, and toast. For lunch, you gotta have some fish-and-chips. I'm not a fish-and-chips person, but my kids are! Make sure you have your afternoon English tea around 4 p.m. London is such a melting pot that it has almost every type of world cuisine. We found some incredible Indian (Dishoom), Japanese (Wagamama), and Italian (Pizza Pilgrims) food there.

Our kids love fish-and-chips; it's a staple in any place with British heritage.

We play a lot of "I Spy" during our travels. In London, the kids loved "spying" as many classic phone booths as possible.

Garrett and Dorothy share so much in common—even the same birthday!

BUDAPEST, HUNGARY

Spend a Day at the Baths

The Széchenyi Chain Bridge, the oldest bridge in Budapest, links Buda and Pest.

In the summer of 2016, when Manilla was almost 20 months and Dorothy three years, we spent about two weeks driving from city to city in Europe. We rented a car in Prague and drove to Vienna and Budapest. Europe is awesome because everything is so close, but that proximity can also be super stressful! I was overwhelmed knowing that Switzerland, Poland, Italy, and Germany were all just hours away—I wanted to do it all! I had to get over the stress of trying to do everything so that I could enjoy the few cities we did have time for. And Budapest, Hungary, was the perfect choice!

Budapest is a highly underrated European city, in my opinion: It's not too touristy and has a lot of authentic culture. It's renowned for its rich history, beautiful architecture, and thermal spas, which are known to have healing properties from the minerals in the water. The Danube River splits the city into two parts, Buda and Pest. Buda is the quieter and more historic part of the city, with buildings that look like they came out of a fairy tale. Pest, on the other hand, is young, vibrant, and known for its thriving nightlife. Although our young family was in bed by 8 p.m., I could tell that Pest lived up to its reputation!

HOW TO GET THERE

We rented a car and really enjoyed our time driving through the European countryside. However, in Europe it's worth taking advantage of the convenient train system. Eurostar (consider a Eurail Pass if you'll be in Europe for an extended period) and other lines get you almost anywhere!

In Budapest, we didn't drive anywhere. We either walked or jumped into a quick, convenient taxi.

WHAT TO DO

• Culture: **Szechenyi Baths:** Thermal baths, fed by mineral springs, have been essential to Budapest's culture since the third century. Szechenyi is the most iconic, most picturesque, and largest thermal bath in Budapest (it's also among the largest in all of Europe). Built in 1913, the complex is home to 18 different baths (15 indoor and three outdoor). You can also schedule massages and other spa services. Book your tickets online (kids are welcome!) and bring your swimsuit! I suggest getting there early to beat the crowds. **Danube River cruise:** Garrett and Dorothy had a special "daddy date" on a sunset dinner cruise on the Danube. They enjoyed a nice meal while learning more about the city and watching the sunset. You can book a cruise with the help of your hotel.

WHEN TO VISIT

Summer is absolutely beautiful in Budapest, although that's when it's also a bit more crowded as tourists flock to the city. It's still nice and warm in September and October.

Some pretty special Christmas markets are held in December. Many parts of Europe, including Budapest, are known for these spectacular markets. You can book a river cruise that takes you to markets in multiple cities along the Danube River, including Budapest, Vienna, and cities in Germany.

Mind Twist
....

Buy a Rubik's Cube! We learned that the Rubik's Cube was invented in Hungary, and we spent several days watching videos online learning how to master it! (Rubik's Cubes also make for great plane activities!)

WHERE TO STAY

We stayed at the Ritz-Carlton, Budapest. The highlight of our stay was when the staff surprised our kids with a princess gown and knight costume. We spent one morning at the Buda Castle learning to slay dragons in all our garb.

Budapest is very family friendly. The town square is lovely, and there are many parks.

The baths in Budapest
are a popular attrac-
tion—and well worth a
visit. We've never seen
anything like them.

- **Comfort:** Hotel Rum Budapest has a cool, modern, Ace Hotel–like vibe with a breakfast buffet at the hotel's rooftop bar. The unique and modern hotel was created entirely by local architects and designers and bills itself as perfect for urban explorers, in large part thanks to its location within walking distance of many attractions.

- **Budget:** The stylish four-star Hotel Collect Budapest has all the creature comforts of a high-end hotel—fluffy beds, nice bathrooms—at an affordable price. It's less than a 15-minute walk to the baths and the Hungarian National Museum. The hotel courtyard is a great place to enjoy a drink after a day of exploring.

WHAT TO EAT

Hungary is known for yummy goulash and *lángos,* a deep-fried doughy flatbread to which you can add toppings like sour cream, garlic butter, or cheese. Our favorite treat was *kürtőskalács,* or chimney cakes, a treat we also found in Czechia. Chimney cakes are sugary dough wrapped around wooden dowels and roasted over charcoal. You can eat them plain or with ice cream, Oreos, strawberries, whipped cream, or Nutella inside. They taste like fire-roasted cinnamon rolls!

One day, our hotel gave Manilla a knight's costume—he had a blast wearing it while exploring Buda Castle.

AMSTERDAM, NETHERLANDS

Cycle Like the Dutch

We rode bicycles from Amsterdam to Zaanse Schans, less than two hours away, to see the windmills.

Amsterdam—known for its beautiful canals, gorgeous architecture, and unique bike culture—is our favorite European city. It's just so cool.

As soon as we arrived in Amsterdam, we secured bikes for our family for the week. Our kids were young at the time, so we rented one of those cute bucket bikes where kids can sit in the front together. We quickly learned that biking in Amsterdam is no joke! You have to adhere to the proper etiquette: Stay in the bike lanes, move quickly, and don't go the wrong way.

But once we got the hang of it, biking was such a great way to explore this city and the endlessly interesting streets. Bonus: You can bike to nearby areas (such as Muiden to visit the famous Amsterdam Castle Muiderslot and Zaanse Schans to see windmills) and take your bike on the train if you're too beat for the journey back.

Amsterdam gets a lot of attention for legal sex work and marijuana, but those definitely aren't the whole story. We spent a week there and barely saw any of that. Instead, we saw that Amsterdam is young, vibrant, and creative. Everyone was tall, and English was spoken throughout. We shopped in the boutiques and found some lovely parks too.

A highlight of our week was finding out that the U.S. Women's National Soccer team was visiting. Garrett took Dorothy to the game, and it was so fun for them to experience how much Europeans love their soccer.

HOW TO GET THERE

We flew into Amsterdam Airport Schiphol, an easy airport to navigate and one to which a lot of international flights fly directly. You can grab a taxi or rideshare at the airport to get where you need to go.

WHAT TO DO

• Adventure: **Vondelpark:** This 19th-century urban park in the Amsterdam-Zuid neighborhood is vast and stunning—and it has *six* playgrounds. Pack a picnic and bike over for the day!

• Culture: **Anne Frank House:** The Anne Frank House is an

iconic part of Amsterdam (and world) history. Don't be scared: Even little kids can grasp the lessons here while trying to understand the Holocaust. You'll be surprised by the conversations a visit can spark. Make sure you buy your tickets online to reserve your spot—it sells out quickly. And take note that there are a lot of steep and narrow stairs to navigate. **Art museums:** Our family doesn't visit many art museums (Garrett and the kids aren't fans), but I'd be remiss if I didn't mention the incredible art that lives in Amsterdam. If you have a budding artist in the family or just a passing interest in the arts, there's

Amsterdam is a biker's city. We loved carting Dorothy and Manilla around on two wheels to go to the market, the gym, or sightseeing.

The Rijksmuseum, in Museum Square, is dedicated to Dutch art and history.

Skip standard hotels and consider staying on a houseboat on one of Amsterdam's famous canals.

the Rijksmuseum, which holds 22 Rembrandt paintings and six Vermeers, and, of course, the Van Gogh Museum, which houses hundreds of his works. **Boat canal tour:** We booked a canal tour one warm afternoon. The kids loved driving with the boat captain, eating *stroopwafels,* and ducking under the low canal bridges. Group tours start around 30 euros per person. I suggest booking a private canal boat (around 250 euros) to have a more intimate experience, if your family can swing it.

WHEN TO VISIT

Amsterdam is quite nice between April and October. Summer brings crowds, so the shoulder seasons (March, or September through November) are better. A very popular yet worthwhile time to visit is during tulip season, which starts at the end of March and goes through mid-May.

WHERE TO STAY

Rentals are a great option here, and our place in Amsterdam was one of my all-time favorites. We rented a houseboat on

a canal, and it was absolutely perfect! It was a small two-bedroom, but it had plenty of space and everything we needed, including a washer and dryer! Our host stocked our boat with eggs, milk, fruit, and some delicious pastries.

It's easy to rent a houseboat in Amsterdam on sites like Airbnb, Vrbo, or through local websites.

WHAT TO EAT

We would make our own breakfast in the houseboat, then spend the majority of the day out on our bikes exploring the city and trying new foods. Amsterdam felt very international in terms of cuisine. We appreciated the quality of food throughout the city and found so many delicious bakeries, fruit and veggie stands, and another Amsterdam staple, flower shops.

De Hallen, an indoor food market with around 20 unique street food stalls, was a favorite. They had everything from wood-fired pizza to artisan burgers to Vietnamese soups and dumplings to ice cream. I think we ate there three or four times in one week!

CAPE TOWN, SOUTH AFRICA

Walk With Penguins at Boulders Beach

South Africa was the first country we visited in Africa. It was a great introduction to the absolutely incredible continent.

South Africa was the first country we ever visited in Africa. We stayed in Cape Town for a few weeks in June 2017 when I was pregnant with Cali.

Cape Town is a gorgeous city. The iconic Table Mountain overlooks the ocean, and along the coast you'll see great promenades and a nice harbor area with amazing restaurants and shops. The whole city felt very active and engaged in the outdoors. It's also inexpensive. Our meals cost around $10 to $12 per person.

You will certainly see signs of heartbreaking poverty, reflective of the country's long history of apartheid. About five minutes into our drive from the airport, we saw homes made out of pieces of wood, cardboard, and sheet metal. Then just 10 minutes down the freeway, there were gorgeous modern homes perched along the mountain and beaches. The dichotomy between classes was very clear here, unlike other places we'd been before—and the juxtaposition was shocking.

Even though apartheid ended more than 25 years ago, there is still a clear and defined separation of race and class in South Africa. Our kids were two and four at the time of our visit, and it was their first real introduction to racism.

As they've grown older, we have had more conversations with them, and our BIPOC friends, about the inequalities we've seen all over the world. Our travels help us teach our kids about the importance of equality, love, and respect—and open doors to deeper conversations.

HOW TO GET THERE

Cape Town International Airport receives airlines from all over the world. In all our travels, South Africa is the one place where they've asked to see our children's birth certificates (to prove our relationship) at immigration.

WHAT TO DO

• Adventure: **Table Mountain:** Visiting Table Mountain is a must-do in Cape Town. To get to the top, you can take advantage of the cable car that spins for 360-degree views as it rises up the mountain. It's a great option for young kids who don't have a hike in them. Alternatively, for older kids and parents, you can take one of the trails to the top—there are a

Be Aware

....

Petty theft is common. We got robbed in Cape Town when we were loading our car with luggage. Keep your car empty and locked, and keep an eye on your valuables.

few different options with varying levels of difficulty. The views of the city and ocean from above are beautiful. **Great white shark cage-diving:** This was a highlight of our visit. Cape Town is home to great whites, and there are a few different types of shark tours you can do. We had a babysitter stay behind with three-year-old Manilla, but five-year-old Dorothy came along for the fun. We drove about two hours from Cape Town to Gansbaai to board a charter. We all geared up in wet suits to cage-dive and see the sharks. I'll admit, the water was freezing, and the visibility was minimal. But we still enjoyed the experience. If you don't want to get in the cage, the view from above on the boat is just as good! There are also boat tours from Cape Town where you can watch sharks breaching the

African red-billed hornbills (aka Zazu from *The Lion King*). Careful: They like to steal your breakfast muffins!

water, rather than getting in the water with them. That's definitely on my list if we hit South Africa at the right time of year! **Penguin-watching:** Take a nice drive about an hour from Cape Town to Boulders Beach, where you can see penguins. We did this a few times because we enjoyed it so much. There's a small conservation fee to pay on entry. On the beach you'll find lookout posts and some nice walking paths. Or you can go down to the water to get a closer look. Just make sure to give the penguins their due respect and space. **Safari:** There are some private game reserves near Cape Town, though I have never been. If this is your only stop in Africa, take the time to get up to Kruger National Park.

WHEN TO VISIT

Cape Town has a nice, temperate climate year-round. The summer months are drier and the winter months are a little more chilly and rainy. The shoulder months (March to May or September to November) are best to save some money and skip the crowds.

WHERE TO STAY

We stayed at a very nice ocean-view home on Clifton Beach. There are many luxury homes right along the coast for way more reasonable prices than you see at other beachfront destinations. All homes come with heavy-duty security measures—gates, cameras, and multiple locked doors to get through.

WHAT TO EAT

Cape Town restaurants are filled with cuisines from around the world. Our kids ate a lot of fish-and-chips. For local food, biltong is a dried, cured beef (similar to beef jerky) that is a really popular snack. A lot of wild game is also popular—kudu, ostrich (my favorite, which I had grilled in a stir-fry), springbok, and warthog.

Take a cable car (or hike) to the summit of Table Mountain for breathtaking views.

Numerous sharks make their home in South Africa's cold but lively waters. Here, Garrett was documenting the annual sardine run off the coast of Durban when this shark swam by.

A must-do experience: Walk with penguins at Boulders Beach near Cape Town!

CHIANG MAI, THAILAND

Celebrate Yi Peng—the Lantern Festival

Chiang Mai is a bustling city with peaceful rice fields in the countryside right beyond its walls.

When we first embarked on our world travels, we knew we wanted to visit Tonga in September for whale season and Thailand in November for the lantern festival. We filled out the rest of our itinerary with places in between (Australia, New Zealand, Fiji, and Singapore).

It was the photos and videos I had seen of the lantern festival in Chiang Mai that had me interested in Thailand. As soon as I saw a photo of hundreds of lanterns floating in the sky, I began doing my research.

There are actually two major Thai celebrations in the fall, and they generally overlap. There's Yi Peng, the floating lantern festival that honors the transition from rainy season to cool season, and Loy Krathong, during which locals place small candles and flowers on banana leaf boats, then sail them down the river in respect and thanks for Phrae Mae Khongkha, the goddess of water. Both festivals are meant to give thanks, release problems, and bring good fortune.

We made sure to visit Chiang Mai when these two holidays overlapped. One evening we took a taxi downtown to the lantern festival. We arrived around 5 p.m., which was way too early—the lantern and river launches didn't go off until sundown, but we had young kids! We spent the evening walking through markets and trying out some fair rides.

When the sun did go down, the lanterns were released into the sky and the offerings were sent down the river; it was an absolutely beautiful sight. We wrote a little family prayer on our lantern and sent it off into the sky. You really could see those lights from all over the city!

HOW TO GET THERE

It's easy to get to Chiang Mai from anywhere in Southeast Asia. You can fly into Chiang Mai International Airport from other international hubs, including Bangkok, Phuket, or Krabi. Domestic flights in Thailand are easy and relatively cheap.

WHAT TO DO

• Adventure: **Try Muay Thai lessons:** Garrett and I had the opportunity to take Muay Thai (or Thai boxing) lessons at our hotel with an expert. Our instructor was highly trained, and let me tell you, it was difficult! I'd done a bit of boxing before, but with Muay Thai you don't just punch; you also use your elbows, knees, and shins. We have so much respect for Muay Thai athletes!

• Culture: **Check out the night markets:** Thailand is also known for its night markets, which are held once or twice a week in different cities. In Chiang Mai, the Sunday night market and the Chang Puak (North Gate) market are among the most popular. Each market boasts amazing food vendors, craftspeople, and artists. We loved trying all the street food and spending our evening immersed in Thai culture.

• Service: **Visit an elephant orphanage:** We learned the hard way about elephant

parks in Thailand. While there are a few great places that focus on conservation and protecting Asian elephants, there are also many parks that abuse the animals. It's these parks that also heavily advertise to lure tourists. Make sure you do your research and find a legit place that treats the animals humanely. Elephant Nature Park, opened in the 1990s by Lek Chailert, is well known as one of the most ethical elephant parks in Thailand. The elephants there were once put to work as performers or logging workers. Visitors are allowed to feed the elephants from an observation platform, but you are not allowed to ride the animals. Volunteers are welcome to work and live at Elephant Nature Park. Most day visits include lunch on the property.

We visited Chiang Mai specifically for its annual lantern festival.

The stunning entrance
to the Dhara Dhevi Hotel
Chiang Mai

WHEN TO VISIT

The lantern festival generally happens in November, which is also the beginning of the dry season, which lasts through April. The climate changes throughout the country, so there's never really a bad time to visit.

WHERE TO STAY

• **Luxury:** The concept for Raya Heritage comes from the northern Thai culture's simple and elegant approach to life and art. This resort is situated along the banks of the Ping River and offers a tranquil and serene environment.

• **Comfort:** Thai Akara is within the old town part of Chiang Mai, which makes it super easy to get to many tourist attractions.

Being in the heart of town also allows guests to easily try a variety of cuisines at the local restaurants not far from the hotel.

• **Budget:** Phor Liang Meun features traditional hand-carved sculptures and is within walking distance of Wua Lai Walking Street—a bustling open-air market with food stalls.

WHAT TO EAT

Thailand has some of the absolute best food in the world! And it's so cheap! We could get a meal with appetizers, mains, smoothies, and desserts for our entire family for less than $15. Our favorites are pad Thai, pad see ew, and mango sticky rice. We found some of the best food from street vendors at the Thai night markets.

Dorothy does some yoga and meditation at the Dhara Dhevi Hotel Chiang Mai.

BALI, INDONESIA

Do Yoga Every Morning—the Kids Too

Rent a scooter and ride through the endless hills of rice fields in Ubud.

ndonesia was one of our first stops when we began traveling in 2015. It was at the top of my list for its beaches, jungles, and culture. We flew into Denpasar and spent a few days in Nusa Dua, a supermanicured area in southern Bali with a ton of hotel chains. Our next stop was Ubud, about an hour's drive north, where we found a lovely boutique hotel to spend the next few weeks.

Ubud is a laid-back town surrounded by rice fields. You can find your fair share of yogis and health-conscious people here. We got into a really nice routine spending our mornings at the Yoga Barn while the kids played back at the hotel with a babysitter. (Now that our kids are a little older, we would take them with us to yoga each morning if we go back!) After lunch, we went (as a family) to teach English at a local school and orphanage. In the evening we explored the streets of Ubud.

HOW TO GET THERE

To get to Ubud, fly into Ngurah Rai International Airport. Check with your hotel or villa before you arrive—a lot of them provide transportation to and from the airport. Otherwise, it's easy to get a cab. There are also a lot of little scooters around to rent, but beware: The traffic can be hectic!

WHAT TO DO

• Adventure: **Canyoneering:** Adventure and Spirit picked us up at 7 a.m. for a two-hour scenic drive through the island to the north shore, where they had a yummy breakfast prepared. Tours often fill up fast, but ours turned out to be only Garrett, me, and our two guides! They took us up a mountain and guided us through rappelling, rock sliding, cliff jumping, and zip-lining. This is definitely a fun adventure—and perfect for older kids, eight years and up. **Monkey forest:** The Sacred Monkey Forest Sanctuary, in the village of Padangtegal, is a must-do in Ubud. And it's also something you can do quickly to check it off your list. Kids will love seeing the monkeys up close, but beware: They can be cheeky and very aggressive, so follow the rules! **Tegenungan Waterfall:** This was an easy waterfall to get to in the village of Tegenungan Kemenuh. It was gorgeous and really family friendly—with some space to relax, play, and swim. You can even stand right underneath the falling water.

• Culture: **See craft making:** Each area of Bali is home to a unique craft. There are woodworkers in Gianyar, silversmiths in the village of Celuk, fabric weavers in Tenganan, and more. Our first stop in Bali was at a silversmith. We worked with them to design some custom jewelry for me. I had a black pearl from Tahiti and they helped me make a ring for it!

• Service: **Volunteer at a school/orphanage:** We were thrilled to connect with the WINS Foundation, run by a lovely Dutch gentleman who has helped create multiple education centers for orphans and at-risk children. We spent our afternoons teaching English and playing games with a group of 16 or so kids at the Yayasan Widya Sari center in Tianyar, just outside Ubud.

Two of my favorite things in Bali: the fresh fruit and smoothie bowls (left) and visiting the Monkey Forest (right). Careful, the monkeys get handsy!

Tegenungan Waterfall is stunning, with natural pools where you and the kids can cool off after a light hike.

I celebrated my 30th birthday in Bali with our family and the kids at the orphanage where we volunteered. It was so special.

We really got to know the kids since we were there for a few weeks. This was also Dorothy's first experience at a school—something we will always remember!

WHEN TO VISIT

The best time to visit Bali is June through September, when it's drier and less humid. November through January is the rainy season, and you can expect some heavy downpours!

WHERE TO STAY

A small villa rental is the way to go in Bali, and you can book one from various rental sites. You can find some great ones for cheap! We stayed at Pandawa Villas, which has four large units. We just so happened to be the only guests on the property! Our villa included a nice pool, daily breakfast, a driver, and a babysitter upon request. We grew very close to the people who worked there.

- **Luxury:** Six Senses Uluwatu has amazing views of the Indian Ocean. It is on the southernmost tip of Bali near one of its most sacred temples. It stays true to its sustainable ethos by giving food waste to the free-roaming resident chickens and converting kitchen oil to biodiesel.
- **Budget:** Ubud Village Hotel offers a series of experiences meant to help you delve deeper into Bali's culture. For example, you can create the daily temple offerings you see each morning or cook Balinese cuisine. The spa is great too.

WHAT TO EAT

Ubud is known for its hippie, healthy spots. You can find a lot of vegan or vegetarian options as well as your fair share of smoothies and bowls. Balinese food is delicious. Try plates of tropical fruit like mangosteen with bowls of rice porridge for breakfast and fried rice and grilled meats with *sambal* (chili sauce) for dinner.

MARRAKECH, MOROCCO

Explore the Souks

The Jemaa el-Fnaa souk is full of handicrafts and very tasty foods.

With its bright, vibrant colors and patterns, Marrakech feels like one giant Instagram feed. Between the *riads* (houses built around gardens or courtyards) and the souks (marketplaces), it's all so creatively inspiring. We were actually just starting to decorate our home in Hawaii when we visited Marrakech in 2018—it was perfect timing. You can't help but want to take everything home in your suitcase. We were especially intrigued by the incredible mosaics all over the city. Those mosaics ended up being inspiration for our primary bathroom.

Outside Marrakech there is the beautiful desert tucked beneath the Atlas Mountains. I highly suggest you make a trip into the desert area part of your visit. The landscapes are absolutely stunning—and there are great adventure experiences you can book too.

HOW TO GET THERE

Flying into Marrakech Menara Airport via Paris was easy for us. As of this writing, there are no direct flights from the U.S. to Marrakech, but you can fly directly to Casablanca and then take a short domestic flight into Marrakech.

The Marrakech airport has strict customs laws, and airport staffers confiscated Garrett's drone. We got it back before we flew out, but take note: Drones are not allowed in Morocco!

WHAT TO DO

• Adventure: **Explore the desert by camel:** You can explore the Atlas Mountains by camel and sleep in a tent under the stars. Your hotel can recommend a reputable tour, or look into Airbnb Experiences, which supports locals and offers more intimate excursions. We were picked up from our hotel and brought to an oasis camp with a pool to relax by in the afternoon. Then we rode camels through the dunes at sunset.

• Culture: **Visit Jemaa el-Fnaa:** Jemaa el-Fnaa is Marrakech's largest and most popular souk, visited by both tourists and locals. Throughout the souk, you'll see lots of performers doing acrobatics and playing traditional music. The kids loved watching each display. Bring cash to tip the performers. You can easily spend the whole day (or multiple days!) walking the souk. In the center square there are dozens of food vendors

Ship It!
....

Lots of vendors at souks provide international shipping, and the pricing isn't too crazy. So you can buy those amazing light fixtures, rugs, or pottery and they'll be waiting for you when you get home!

selling everything from grilled meats to flavorful and colorful spices. In the evenings, which are especially vibrant, we saw lots of locals gathering at their favorite vendors for a meal.

Take a class from a craftsperson: Tap into your creative side and learn from some of the best artists and craftspeople in the world. Marrakech offers loads of firsthand experiences: Take a pottery class or learn leatherworking. A cooking class would be great too!

WHEN TO VISIT

Shoulder seasons (spring and fall) are best, to avoid extreme temperatures and the summer crowds.

We let Cali take a little dip in a desert oasis.

WHERE TO STAY

We stayed at the absolutely lovely Four Seasons Resort Marrakech. It's located between the city's ancient medina and its cosmopolitan neighborhoods, which was convenient for getting to the largest souks or the city center. The resort had an especially lovely pool, and the kids' club was one of the nicest we've experienced. I remember picking up the kids to find they had learned how to make Moroccan flatbread!

• **Comfort:** Dar Seven is a five-room boutique hotel in the old part of Marrakech that serves a traditional Moroccan breakfast each morning with fresh mint tea, included in your stay.

• **Budget:** Riad Adore has the charm of a traditional riad with a plunge pool in the center of the courtyard. It's a short walk from the historic souks and the main square.

WHAT TO EAT

I absolutely love the food in this region of the world—especially the flavorful roasted meats, veggies, and couscous. You'll also find some wonderful juices and teas. I picked up a bunch of unique herbal teas and brought them home as gifts. If you love to cook at home, definitely pick up some of the beautiful spices at one of the markets!

One of the most traditional Moroccan dishes is tagine, which is popular throughout North Africa. Tagine is typically made with chicken (or other meats, such as lamb) and is braised in an earthenware pot—called a tagine—along with spices, onions, garlic, olives, and lemons. It's flavorful and absolutely a must-try if you're in Morocco!

Take a camel ride in the desert outside Marrakech, with the Atlas Mountains for views.

The markets of Marrakech are super colorful and vibrant, with arrays of spices and treats.

DESTINATIONS FOR BABIES

As soon as a baby (nine to 18 months) is mobile, it's a whole new ball game. Getting a busy crawling or walking toddler to stay still on a long flight is hard. *However,* I believe this is the perfect time to start teaching your kids good habits outside the home. Here are a few great destinations for the pre-toddler stage.

Fiji: I think Fiji is the most family-friendly destination. Fijians *love* children. As I mention on page 178, we found multiple resorts with kids' clubs and a childcare staffer for *each* child! No need to bring a nanny to this country—you can find incredible childcare locally.

Kona, Hawaii, U.S.A.: There are some great, kid-friendly beaches in Kona and fantastic hikes if your baby is good in a carrier. I also love taking my kids out on a boat. Babies love the wind in their face, and hopefully they'll be able to see some whales and dolphins. Book a shorter tour (two to three hours).

Tokyo, Japan: Even though Tokyo is a busy city, it's orderly and convenient, which makes it ideal for babies and toddlers. The parks are adorable and have clean family restrooms. Just make sure you have a good stroller—jet lag can hit hard in Tokyo, and babies will fall asleep at random times throughout the day. My toddler loved all the bright city lights, bullet trains, and anime.

North Island, New Zealand: New Zealand, as a whole, is super family friendly. Most restaurants have a little kids' corner or a few books and toys for the little ones. Additionally, there are great short hikes, zoos, parks, beaches, and nature walks throughout the North Island.

Belize: One of Cali's first countries was Belize. My favorite thing about Belize is how convenient it is (especially if it's your first trip outside the U.S.). It's easy to get to, people speak English, and they accept the U.S. dollar. For babies, you can take in the jungle scene on easy hikes or enjoy the very calm, sandy beaches.

Amsterdam, Netherlands: Amsterdam attracts young families because there are loads of beautiful parks, playgrounds, and indoor children's museums. You can also rent a bike with a child seat to explore the canals and streets. (See more on page 212.)

Krabi, Thailand: A short 90-minute flight from Bangkok, Krabi has a nice slower, beachy vibe. We rented a long-tail boat and enjoyed the islands for a day. Most restaurants have high chairs and will bring books or puzzles to the table. Our youngsters loved all the fresh fruit and smoothies on the beach.

Singapore: We traveled to Singapore when my son was 14 months, and we loved exploring the beautiful gardens and parks. Even if it's really hot, there are so many activities to do (see page 324) indoors and outdoors.

Dubai, U.A.E.: Dubai is a really popular family destination in the winter, but there is also so much to do indoors during the hot summer! The zoo, aquarium, and water parks are great for traveling with mobile babies. (See more on page 188.)

Turks and Caicos: Some of the most baby-friendly beaches I've ever seen are in Turks and Caicos. With supersoft sand and crystal clear water, it's a great place to relax as a family. There are loads of really nice home rentals, or you can stay at the family-friendly Beaches all-inclusive.

We hired a long-tail boat in Krabi to take us to some of Thailand's outer islands. Here I am bringing 14-month-old Manilla into the water.

KIGALI, RWANDA

Understand Important History

Kigali was not just a beautiful place to visit; its story of resilience and forgiveness changed my life forever.

Rwanda is one of my absolute favorite countries in the world. Most people are surprised when I tell them this, and I get it. I went into Rwanda with some major nerves—my only point of reference was having watched *Hotel Rwanda* in college. But Rwanda is the country that changed me the most, mainly because of what I learned about their recent history of genocide, which happened in *my* lifetime.

We spent our visit in Kigali, a lush, mountainous region known for its agriculture. While most people would assume seeing gorillas was the highlight of our trip, the most memorable experience was actually a visit to the Kigali Genocide Memorial. Due to the nature of the museum, a friend waited with the kids outside—the visuals inside are very disturbing, and I wouldn't bring a kid under the age of 12. The 1994 Rwandan genocide targeting the Tutsi killed 800,000 people in 100 days—it's often referred to as "100 days of slaughter." It devastated me to take in the horrifying photos and videos—but it's an important part of history that should not be overlooked.

I walked through the museum with my jaw dropped low and tears in my eyes. When the genocide ended, the war between the Hutu and Tutsi ended. Everyone put down their weapons and Rwanda picked up the pieces. Near the end of our visit, I watched a short video in which one man said something I'll never forget: "You can either cultivate love or cultivate hate. We chose love. We chose forgiveness." After remarkable devastation, Rwanda was pieced back together with love and forgiveness. What a testament to a nation's character and resilience.

HOW TO GET THERE

Most people add Rwanda to a multicountry visit to Africa. A handful of flights from Kilimanjaro, Lusaka, Nairobi, and Harare are available to Kigali International Airport. We flew in on a smaller airplane from Kilimanjaro. Long-haul direct flights arrive via Amsterdam, London, Brussels, Istanbul, Dubai, and Johannesburg.

WHAT TO DO

• Adventure: **Trek to see gorillas:** The volcanic Virunga Mountains are home to one of the most incredible creatures in the world: the gorilla! Each morning, trekkers meet in Volcanoes National Park and are assigned a family or troop to visit. You will join one of six groups, determined by your trekking ability. Note that kids under 15 aren't allowed; we had a nanny who watched ours. Rwanda has a great structure in place to allow people to visit each gorilla troop for just one hour per day. Fewer than 100 permits are available each day, so you must book far in advance. It's quite pricey ($1,500 per person per day), but I really respect how Rwanda protects these animals, and the price goes toward conservation efforts. It's important to know that these animals live in the wild, and spotting a gorilla isn't always guaranteed (though guides know the gorillas' patterns, and you'll almost always find them). One day, Garrett

Memorials and museums throughout the country educate visitors about the Rwandan genocide.

and I saw a family of about 10 gorillas, including babies. It was a beautiful experience. We were especially taken aback by the majesty of the celebrated silverback gorilla.

• Culture: **Go to a genocide memorial:** We visited the largest Rwandan genocide memorial, in Kigali, but there are many memorials throughout the country. Don't go to Rwanda without visiting one. Sometimes, a visit to a new place means facing hard truths about our world. Our experience was just that, but also a reminder of the resilience and goodness of people, as we saw in how the country has rebounded from this tragedy. **Enjoy a cup of coffee:** Rwanda has become known for its unique coffee, which has been a huge economic boon for the country. We're not coffee drinkers ourselves, but there were a ton of cute coffee shops all over Kigali—with bags of coffee to bring home for friends and family. Question Coffee offers a specialty coffee master class and a woman-led farm trek.

• Service: **Participate in Rwanda Service Day:** Rwanda has one of the coolest national holidays, called Umuganda. Umuganda means "coming together in oneness." On the last Saturday of each month, Rwandans perform mandatory community service from 8 to 11 a.m. Rwandan president Paul Kagame reintroduced this long-standing tradition in 1998 to rebuild the broken country after the war, and it continues to this day.

WHEN TO VISIT

June to September are the best months to see the gorillas. March to May is the rainy season and a better time to go south to see the chimpanzees.

WHERE TO STAY

We stayed at the beautiful Kigali Serena hotel. It was really big and had a great gym, pool, and breakfast buffet. For our gorilla trek, we worked with Volcano Safaris and stayed at the incredible Virunga Lodge, which overlooks the Virunga volcanoes.

WHAT TO EAT

Most food in Rwanda is locally sourced and so fresh. Meals here typically feature a lot of potatoes, plantains, and rice, along with some delicious grilled or roasted meats and lots of stews.

We trekked to look for the famous mountain gorillas in the Virunga Mountains, their natural habitat.

Dorothy, Manilla, and Calihan joined in drumming during a traditional musical performance.

BERLIN, GERMANY

Visit the German Christmas Markets

I love the holidays, and nothing can beat the European Christmas markets, which are spectacular in Berlin and throughout Germany.

Germany has great things to offer year-round—unique culture, history, and food, and lots of natural beauty—but what initially drew me in were the Christmas markets, and they absolutely did not disappoint. Most towns throughout Germany have their own Christmas market, each full of cute decorations, jewelry, pottery, toys, and so much delicious food. The whole town center smells of cinnamon candied nuts—and you have to get some! There are also crepes, bratwursts, hot chocolate, and the popular German mulled wine.

Most German Christmas markets open the last week of November and run through December 23. A lot of cities in Europe have nice Christmas markets, but Germany takes the cake for the best, and we experienced some of the best of all in Berlin!

HOW TO GET THERE

You can fly into so many great international hubs in Germany—Frankfurt, Munich, Dusseldorf, Berlin, and Hamburg, to name just a few. You can also hop on the Eurostar and arrive from many cities throughout Europe. We used the Berlin U-Bahn train system to get around the city. We also rented a car in a town called Wolfsburg and drove from city to city to experience different Christmas markets.

WHAT TO DO

• Culture: **A guided tour of Berlin:** I knew our young kids wouldn't love a guided tour through Berlin, so we didn't do one. But man, I would love to go back and take one when they're older or by myself. The city seems so young and free-spirited, and there are so many layers of history and signs of World War II throughout the streets that a guided tour would help you take a deeper dive into Berlin's past. **A picnic in the park:** If you're in Berlin in the summer, have a picnic in the park. It's a very German thing to do. You'll have your pick of 2,500 parks in the city to choose from! **Festivals:** Germany is known to have markets, festivals, and gatherings throughout the year to celebrate music, art, film, and holidays. We went for the Christmas markets, my favorite being the one held in the picturesque Gendarmenmarkt, one of the prettiest squares in Berlin. But there are more than 50 Christmas markets that pop up throughout the city during the winter season, so you'll have plenty of options to choose from to celebrate—and shop—the holiday spirit. **Rent a bike:** Berlin is a huge cycling city, and it's very easy to get around. Most rental companies offer bikes with baby and toddler seats for kids who can't peddle on their own yet. Biking is one of my favorite ways to explore a city!

• Service: **A Christmas giving tree:** Both Ritz-Carlton hotels we stayed at (in Berlin and Wolfsburg) had Christmas giving trees for Syrian refugees. There were ornament notes with kids' names, ages, and needs and wants. Guests could pick an ornament to sponsor a specific child for the holidays! The Ritz staff then delivered the gifts in person. We were fortunate that they allowed us to go to a nearby refugee center with them to help deliver the gifts. It was a truly special way to honor the holiday season.

WHEN TO VISIT

If you're going to Germany for the Christmas markets, obviously visit during the Advent season. Double-check online for the exact dates the markets start and end. FYI, some smaller markets are open only on weekends.

Germany is also beautiful in the spring, summer, and fall! Spring is nice and not too crowded; summer has beautiful weather, and Berlin has a great bike culture; and then fall is beautiful in the countryside. You can also visit Munich during Oktoberfest!

We found a fun ice-skating rink in the center of one of the Christmas markets.

Berlin is an outdoorsy
city, with many parks that
are open year-round.

WHERE TO STAY

We stayed at the Ritz-Carlton in Potsdamer Platz. This property is super accommodating for families, with their Ritz Kids program and a fun tent set up in your room. Since we were there in the holiday season, they had Santa visits and gingerbread making during our stay.

• **Comfort:** Situated in Berlin's trendy Friedrichshain-Kreuzberg district, Hotel the YARD is a sleek, modern boutique with lovely gardens, a spa, and a bistro.

• **Budget:** Abba Berlin has all the amenities you need and is in a central location, right off Kurfürstendamm Avenue, one of the city's main shopping arteries.

WHAT TO EAT

German food is good home cookin' and extremely hearty. Think stews, sausages, schnitzels, and lots of potatoes. One of Berlin's iconic dishes is currywurst: a bratwurst covered in curry sauce and usually served with a side of french fries. It's not for me, since I don't like hot dogs. But my daughter, Dorothy, who was four years old at the time, loved it, and she ate two while we were being filmed for a national news segment!

At the Christmas markets, you've got to try the crepes, pretzels, cookies, chocolates, mulled wine, brats … Okay, just try everything! It's what you do!

Flatow Tower in Babelsberg overlooks the banks of the Havel River.

Treats galore! Manilla loved
the sweets at a Berlin
Christmas market.

GALÁPAGOS ISLANDS, ECUADOR

Visit the Tortoises at the Darwin Research Station

The volcanic Galápagos Islands boast a unique landscape and some of the most diverse and untouched wildlife in the world.

The Galápagos Islands appear on many people's bucket lists, and rightfully so. You can experience nature in such a raw, untouched way here. Count yourself lucky if you're among the limited number of tourists who get to visit the Galápagos each year!

When we landed on Baltra Island, our group hopped onto a shuttle bus to the marina to board the boat we'd be living on for the week. We immediately noticed a handful of birds called blue-footed boobies dive-bombing into the water. We saw two manta rays mating. We saw dozens of shore crabs combing the rocks and sea lions basking in

the sun. We felt like we had been thrown into a National Geographic video! The animals in the Galápagos looked and acted differently from other wild animals we had seen before. Due to their isolation—and conservation efforts in this part of the world—they are bigger and not afraid of humans. Many animals in the Galápagos are *only* found there.

Most visitors stop at the Charles Darwin Research Station to learn about the Galápagos giant tortoise. They are some of the oldest creatures in the world—and they look like it! They can live up to 175 years!

This was a great experience for our whole family. We've visited twice: First when Dorothy was four and Manilla two, and then again when they were five and three, respectively, and Cali was five months old. The kids love seeing the wildlife and being out in the ocean.

HOW TO GET THERE

You can fly to the Galápagos Islands from Quito or Guayaquil, Ecuador. It's about a two-hour flight from either airport on TAME, LAN-Ecuador, or Avianca, the only airlines that fly to the Galápagos. Take a day or two in Quito or Guayaquil to adjust to the higher altitude.

On leaving the Guayaquil or Quito airport for the Galápagos, all travelers are required to pay for a $20 INGALA transit control card. Upon arrival in the Galápagos, you must pay a national park entrance fee of $100 per person. Have that $100 with you *in cash!*

Look Up

Check out the stars! Some of the best stargazing we've ever done was in the Galápagos, thanks to its low level of light pollution in the area. At the end of each day, we'd go on the top deck of our boat, turn off all the lights, and marvel at the sky!

WHAT TO DO

• Adventure: **Snorkel:** Don't miss an opportunity to see what's below the water's surface! We found the reef fish to be so much bigger and brighter in the Galápagos than in any other place we've visited. We also saw rays, turtles, and penguins, and we even swam with sea lions! Ships provide your equipment and take you to the best spots. Kids are allowed to snorkel if they're able. **Dive:** We are planning our next visit to the Galápagos in the northern islands, which are home to some of the best diving in the

LEFT: Manilla and I roam one of the beaches while Cali takes a mid-hike nap. RIGHT: Sea lions freely roam the beaches and towns of the Galápagos.

We spent some time off the boat exploring the Charles Darwin Research Station and Santa Cruz Island.

At the Charles Darwin Research Station, you can see tortoises that are more than 100 years old.

world. We plan to dive with manta rays, hammerhead sharks, and, hopefully, whale sharks!

• Service: **Visit an orphanage:** On both of our visits, we worked with an orphanage in Guayaquil called the Hogar Inés Chambers Home. We asked in advance how we could be of the most help. One year we helped the orphanage get a new security system. Another year we painted art on the walls and played with the children for a few hours.

WHEN TO VISIT

The best months to visit the Galápagos are between December and May. The weather is pleasant throughout most of the year, but these months will make for the warmest, clearest water for snorkeling and diving.

WHERE TO STAY

While there are land tours, most visits to the Galápagos are on boats to allow for easy access from one island to another.

For both of our visits, we took private boat charters, and I definitely think that's the way to go if you can afford it. You get to sail around to various islands, and you'll wake up in a new place each day!

We worked with Galapagos Luxury Charters on our most recent visit and loved that they had an onboard naturalist to guide you. The boat was lovely, and the staff was so helpful, especially with our young kids.

Small boat cruises with tour companies like National Geographic and Lindblad are another great option, because the smaller boats limit the number of people you're with.

WHAT TO EAT

The boat we stayed on while touring the Galápagos included meals, and we got to dine on all sorts of international food while still eating local Ecuadorian cuisine, like rice and beans, superfresh seafood, and empanadas. Most ships cater to any food requirements on board.

GREEK ISLANDS

Set Sail on the Mediterranean

There is something absolutely magical about a sunset over the white-and-blue towns of Greece.

wasn't expecting to love Greece as much as I do. I mean, it tops travelers' lists year over year, so I figured I'd like it. But, as it turns out, I *love* it!

There's something so special about Greece. Maybe it's the country's gorgeous, iconic ancient architecture, like the Parthenon. Or maybe it's the incredibly generous and family-oriented Greek people. Or maybe it's the 6,000 breathtaking and unique islands with crystal clear water. But really, for me, I think it's the food!

We've been to Greece twice—once with our little kids and once for a couples' trip with some friends. It is the perfect place for both, with loads of family-friendly opportunities but also quintessential romance for couples. I'd go again tomorrow if I could; I love it that much.

HOW TO GET THERE

For both of our visits, we flew into Athens International Airport, but you can also choose from several other international airports, such as in Thessaloniki (the second largest city in Greece), Heraklion on Crete, or Corfu. There are also some smaller island airports, such as those on Santorini or Mykonos.

WHAT TO DO

• Culture: **Take a Greek cooking class:** There are plenty of cooking classes in Greece where a sweet old grandma teaches you to make some authentic dishes! We took one through our hotel in Costa Navarino and learned how to make a proper Greek salad, *melomakarona* (honey biscuits), and the perfect tzatziki. **Learn about Greek mythology:** You can visit places like Mycenae or Mount Olympus to learn the mythological origin stories of the Greek gods. We watched the animated movie *Hercules* before our trip so we could easily reference Zeus, Hades, and Hercules with our kids.

• Service: **Visit a refugee camp:** Greece is known for accepting refugees from war-torn countries. You can connect with many organizations to donate your time and/or money. Look online

Think Small

Consider visiting and staying at some of the smaller, lesser known islands. Mykonos and Santorini are beautiful but quite crowded. We visited Póros and Ídra (Hydra), both of which felt more authentic.

before you go, or ask your hotel or tour service if they partner with any refugee groups that can use your time or resources.

WHEN TO VISIT

The ideal travel time is from late spring through early fall to enjoy the nice weather. If you want to miss the bigger crowds, stick to the shoulder seasons (April to June and September to October). Avoid winter travel to Greece, as

Our home rental in Mykonos was built around the native exposed rock.

it can be cold, hotels often shut down, the number of domestic flights decreases, and some ferries stop running.

WHERE TO STAY

It was a bucket list dream come true for us when we chartered a catamaran with some of our closest friends through the Greek islands with Moorings, a luxury yacht company. Our boat included a hostess, chef, and captain. We were able to relax while they took care of all the hard work. They were flexible with our itinerary too, so we could go where we wanted. We chose to stay north and visited islands like Póros, Ídra (Hydra), and Kéa on our seven-day sail. We wanted to find dolphins to swim with, so we did! We wanted to find cliffs to jump off of, so we did!

We started our trip in Athens and stayed at the historic Hotel Grand Bretagne, which opened in 1874 and has amazing views overlooking the Acropolis, the Parliament, and Syntagma Square.

• **Luxury:** On Santorini, the Grace Hotel offers a cliff-top retreat where each room, suite, or villa comes with expansive indoor-outdoor space and views of the caldera. Some rooms have heated plunge pools.

• **Comfort:** The Elia Ermou Hotel Athens is sleek, modern, and located on one of the city's main drags. On Santorini, Maregio Suites is a boutique hotel in Oia, situated away from the noise of the capital. This property also offers yachting cruises.

• **Budget:** Niki Athens Hotel is a family-owned boutique hotel know for its eco-friendliness and its vegan restaurant. On the black sand beach of Perissa, on Santorini, you'll find the Aqua Blue Hotel, which has three pools and a private beach space with sun beds.

WHAT TO EAT

Greek food is my favorite cuisine. If you visit and there is no feta cheese, it's because I ate it all. The food is so fresh! I love the flavorful grilled meats, Greek salads, and fresh pita bread!

We took a trip to the Greek islands with friends and did some rock running for our workout.

Pro tip: For uncrowded photos, wake up extra early. Mykonos is quite the party town, so evenings and days are busy but mornings are quiet.

BANFF, CANADA

Ski the Canadian Rockies

In the summer, take a paddle under the mountains in Lake Louise.

The only hard part about visiting Banff in Alberta, Canada, is deciding when to go. It's gorgeous year-round. We ended up visiting for Christmas in 2018, and it was an absolute holiday wonderland. Downtown Banff is an incredibly charming area with wonderful little shops and restaurants.

I grew up skiing in the Rocky Mountains in Colorado, but I never knew how much more impressive the Canadian Rockies are. We went to Lake Louise Ski Resort for the day. The resort helped us gear up our kids for a morning in ski school. There was even a small kids' club for Calihan, who

was 11 months old at the time. That gave Garrett and me a few hours to ourselves to get some runs in—and I was so impressed! The trails here are incredibly long. Each felt three times longer than any run down a mountain I'd done before. Sometimes when you ski, it feels like you spend more time in the chairlift lines waiting to get up the mountain than on the actual run, but not here! My quads were burning so bad at the end of the day. That's a good feeling for any skier!

If you are interested in skiing at all, no matter your level, the Canadian Rockies should be on your bucket list! We hardly scratched the surface of things to do in Banff on our first visit. The outdoors are vast and endless in this part of Canada. There are so many small towns and rocky, snowcapped mountains to explore. Do some research, but know you really can't go wrong wherever you end up in Banff!

HOW TO GET THERE

We flew into Calgary International Airport. Since we landed late at night, car rental options were closed, so we took a shuttle the 90 minutes to Banff. The next day, we rented a car to drive around town.

WHAT TO DO

• Adventure: **Banff Gondola:** Year-round, a trip up the Banff Gondola is worth it for the views of the mountain ranges. It's a thrill for all ages that requires nothing more than sitting and enjoying the views. During Christmastime, it's extra special: Santa will meet you at the summit for a photo, and there are Christmas crafts and cookie-decorating opportunities. **Tubing:** Snow tubing was a highlight for our kids in Banff. There are multiple tubing sites around the area, but we spent the second half of our ski day at Lake Louise Ski Resort's Sunny Tube Park, at the base of the mountain. There, we could ride as a whole family (they even offer family passes) on the tubing lanes! You can buy a pass just for tubing, or a combo pass that also gets you on the gondola. **Dogsledding:** We missed out on this activity because there wasn't enough snow, but dogsledding in Banff is definitely a bucket list activity. Book a wonderful tour with some beautiful dogs and learn about the world of mushers and dogsledding. The kids will love meeting the pups! **Go skiing:** There are three ski resorts in Banff: Lake Louise, Sunshine Village, and Mount Norquay. We skied

Get Snow Tires
....

If you're renting a car (which I recommend), make sure it has snow tires. Practice your snow driving. Drive slowly, controlled, and with plenty of space between you and the vehicle in front of you. Accelerate and decelerate slowly to avoid spinning out. And pick up a windshield ice scraper!

at Lake Louise, which offers 164 runs across four mountain faces. Sunshine Village has 120 runs, almost half of which are suitable for advanced and expert skiers. Mount Norquay is the smallest, with 60 runs available.

• Culture: **Playing hockey:** I put this under culture instead of adventure because hockey *is* culture in Canada. There are many places to rent skates and ice-skate or play hockey. We found a lot of locals playing pickup games on icy Lake Louise.

During a winter visit to Banff, Dorothy and I faced off in a friendly game of ice hockey.

The main street in Banff is beyond picturesque— and full of great stores and restaurants.

WHEN TO VISIT

Banff is known for Lake Louise, with its turquoise water surrounded by majestic mountains. Summer is popular for hiking, swimming, kayaking, or stand-up paddleboarding. Fall is stunning with the changing leaves, and you can still get in a lot of outdoor activities. Winter brings all the snow and fun winter sports. And spring often allows for some late-season skiing with much smaller crowds.

WHERE TO STAY

Fairmont Banff Springs looks like a castle. We were so excited to stay there, especially during Christmastime. They went above and beyond with festive holiday cheer, including a massive gingerbread house that filled up the lobby, bedtime stories with Mrs. Claus, and even a special holiday dinner with Santa Claus.

• **Comfort:** Baker Creek, a short drive from Banff, is where we spent our actual Christmas holiday. It is an incredibly charming log cabin–style resort with communal firepits, snowshoe rentals, and an ice hockey rink in the winter.

• **Budget:** Elk + Avenue is a nice, modern boutique hotel very close to downtown Banff. The contemporary hotel is within walking distance of many shops and restaurants. The hotel's own Farm & Fire restaurant specializes in wood-fired cuisine and locally grown ingredients.

WHAT TO EAT

You have to try the world-famous beaver tails. It's not what it sounds like! A beaver tail is basically fried pastry dough in the *shape* of a beaver tail. Then you choose your toppings: cinnamon sugar, whipped cream, bananas, caramel, Nutella, peanut butter, or even candy. It's a delicious sugar rush!

Don't forget to try Canada's famous beaver tails, a sweet treat loaded with toppings of your choice.

CANNON BEACH, OREGON, U.S.A.

Go Crabbing on the Oregon Coast

Cannon Beach is a place I'd visit again and again!

've always had an obsession with Oregon. I don't really know why! I had never even been there until about eight months into our world travels. But in my mind, I thought that I could live there. In fact, in 2016, we spent six weeks living in Portland to see if it was a place where we could settle down. We even enrolled Dorothy in a supercute, hippie-dippie preschool! And my love for Oregon grew throughout our stay. I love all the green space and how, even in its biggest city, there aren't national franchises on every corner. There are mom-and-pop restaurants and lots of farmers markets. You'll find

your fair share of "weird" in Portland. I love that uniqueness. I'd move to Oregon in a heartbeat, but ultimately, we didn't stay because Garrett had uncontrollable pollen allergies during our time there.

Drive about an hour and a half from Portland, and you get to Cannon Beach. It's an adorable little town right on the coast. It's known for the iconic Haystack Rock and never ending sandy beaches. Since our first visit in 2016, we've been back to Cannon Beach multiple times as a family. I've also gone back for a girls' weekend. It's such a charming little town and area.

HOW TO GET THERE

Rent a car at Portland International Airport and take a scenic 90-minute drive through the hills to the Oregon coast.

WHAT TO DO

• Adventure: **Crabbing:** On multiple trips, we've gone crabbing at Kelly's Brighton Marina, and it's always a highlight. Kelly's has a charming little shop where you can rent a dinghy and all the gear you need for your outing: three crab pots and bait. I recommend you also bring gardening gloves. Purchase a crabbing license for $10 per person, and then take off. You're practically guaranteed to catch crabs! You get to keep the ones that are male and legal size. Kelly's will even cook up what you catch! It makes for an absolute blast of a day. **Hiking:** Ecola State Park, just north of Cannon Beach, has countless trails and gorgeous cliffside overlooks along with some secluded

Get to the Beach Early

Parking can be an issue, so if you're not staying within walking distance of the beach, get there early to find a spot. Make sure you're parked legally so you don't get ticketed. Feel free to bring your pup—Cannon Beach is dog friendly!

coves that stretch along the coastline. If it's not rainy, make sure you take advantage of the gorgeous hikes! **Surfing:** We rented some boards and wet suits (the water is cold!) right in Cannon Beach and took them down to Oswald West State Park to a break called Short Sand. It has pretty consistent surf year-round (summer is better for beginners), and it's a nice beach to picnic on. **Beach bonfires:** As you walk down Cannon Beach, you'll see remnants of many bonfires. Grab the family and make your own one night! Get everything you need

Let the kids roam near the tide pools to see all the sea life they can discover.

from the local grocery store, including s'mores ingredients, then set up for sunset.

WHEN TO VISIT

Cannon Beach is best from July through early October. That's when you'll have the nicest weather. We visited in April and May and were lucky with the spring weather—lots of sunny days. I've also visited in early October, and it had exactly the gorgeous fall vibes that I was searching for!

WHERE TO STAY

All of our stays in Oregon have been at vacation rentals. There are so many great properties listed on Vrbo and Airbnb. If you can't find something directly in Cannon Beach, there are a whole bunch of delightful towns along the coast. Check out Astoria (where *The Goonies* was filmed!), Newport, Bandon, and Seaside.

• **Luxury:** The Lodges at Cannon Beach are a collection of townhomes for rent. They are great for large family vacations and are within walking distance of Tolovana Beach State Recreation Site, a great spot for running on the beach, building sandcastles, or flying kites.

• **Comfort:** The Ocean Lodge is a beachfront hotel right near Haystack Rock. The lodge offers a lot of family-friendly activities, including sandcastle building and bocce.

• **Budget:** Surfsand Resort, right in Cannon Beach, is pet and kid friendly; they host daily activities for kids (such as tide pool exploring) and nightly bonfires.

WHAT TO EAT

The Oregon coast is all about seafood. Think fish-and-chips, shrimp cocktails, and crab legs. There are so many great seafood restaurants to choose from in the area, but my favorite is Mo's, which is famous for its clam chowder. You can also drive to Tillamook Creamery for the absolute best ice cream—try my favorite flavors, mudslide or mountain huckleberry.

Dorothy tries to catch a rainbow over the beach.

We chartered a small crabbing boat in Oregon. The guides teach you everything you need to know.

DESTINATIONS FOR TODDLERS

. . . .

Toddlers (18 months to three years) are busy, but they are amazing explorers. Here are a few safe and family-friendly destinations where you can let your toddler roam.

Scotland: Just picture a cute little toddler waddling around the green hills of Scotland. Visit one of the many castles or stroll through old cities like Edinburgh. Scotland is also a great place to introduce some easy hiking at West Highland Way. (See more on page 198.)

Balboa Island, California, U.S.A.: Garrett and I lived on Balboa Island when we moved to California for him to grow the Scan app. It's a great spot for family walks, with tasty restaurants, cute shops, and an adorable Ferris wheel. You can rent bikes with a baby seat and spend a nice day at Newport Beach.

Yellowstone National Park, Wyoming, U.S.A.: America's first national park is a great place to introduce young travelers to the natural world. There are a lot of stroller-friendly walkways, and the little ones will have a blast looking for wildlife such as bears, moose, and bald eagles. The kids love watching the geysers, waterfalls, and hot springs too!

Berlin, Germany: We visited Berlin with our two- and four-year-olds. We were there for the Christmas markets, but I know summer would be lovely too. Berlin is known to have many innovative playgrounds that are perfect for kids under five. (See more on page 240.)

London, United Kingdom: So many of the sites in London are great for little kids, particularly the Natural History Museum, the Diana Memorial Playground in Kensington Gardens, and the London Eye. (See more on page 202.)

Maldives: What could be better for young families than warm, sandy beaches and clear water? The Maldives is my son Manilla's favorite country, and we've been back three times! Most resorts in the Maldives offer kid-friendly amenities such as kids' clubs, childcare, and playgrounds. Our absolute favorite resort is Soneva Fushi in the Maldives.

San Francisco, California, U.S.A.: We lived in San Francisco while I was pregnant with Dorothy. I had planned on raising her in this city until we unexpectedly moved back to Utah. There are so many great activities for toddlers, including Golden Gate Park, the Children's Creativity Museum, and the San Francisco Zoo. There's also a supercharming carousel on Pier 39 that any toddler will love.

Costa Rica: For dynamic beauty and very welcoming locals, head to Costa Rica. There's no absence of family-friendly outdoor activities, including hiking to waterfalls, swimming, playing on the beach, taking canopy tours, and visiting butterfly gardens and animal sanctuaries. (See more on page 164.)

Niagara Falls, New York, U.S.A.: We visited upstate New York with our kids when Dorothy was three and Manilla was one. Most of the views of the falls are accessible with a toddler, but consider sticking to tamer Maid of the Mist tours with littles. Our whole family put on the blue ponchos, and we loved getting misted. And don't miss the Niagara SkyWheel.

Malta: We visited Malta when Manilla had just turned two and have many fond memories from our stay. The highlight was visiting the *Popeye* (1980) movie set, now called Popeye Village, which has a small beach, play area, and interactive characters. Malta also has a great aquarium and water park.

Four-year-old Dorothy and two-year-old Manilla take on the San Francisco hills by trolley car.

ZION NATIONAL PARK, UTAH, U.S.A.

Canyoneer in the Red Rocks

Zion National Park is stunning with fall foliage dotting the river and rock formations.

Zion National Park in southern Utah is unlike any other place on Earth. If you have watched Disney's *Cars,* then you know what I mean when I say that Zion looks like the area surrounding Radiator Springs. Zion National Park is known for its incredible red rock vistas and unique slot canyons (long, narrow channels with cliff walls on either side).

I went to Brigham Young University in Provo, Utah, which is only a few hours from Zion. The park was one of the few places I traveled to during my college days. My friends and I would round up our gear and go camping.

Zion has also been an incredible family destination for us. We've returned multiple times with extended family and even our Bucket List Studio team for a company retreat. We love that it has many adventurous activities like camping, hiking, biking, canyoneering, rock climbing, rappelling, ATV touring, and rafting. Just keep in mind, some trails and hikes are not for the faint of heart (or the young ones), and some routes require reservations and advance planning. Some trails may also close due to weather or rockslides. Whatever you choose to do, endless fun and adventure can be had here.

HOW TO GET THERE

Zion is about an hour drive from St. George, Utah, which has a small airport. Or you can drive two and a half hours from Las Vegas or four and a half hours from Salt Lake City. However you choose to get there, make sure you have a car to get around.

WHAT TO DO

• Adventure: **Navigating the slot canyons:** Zion is known for its spectacular slot canyons, the most famous of which is called The Narrows. When you hike The Narrows, you're often walking through water—pay attention to the time of year, because The Narrows can close due to flooding. Some of the other slots in the park have rappelling or swimming. I highly recommend slot hiking for big adventurers like my husband! **Hiking:** Take your pick from one of the 100-plus named trails in Zion. Our favorites with young kids are the Emerald Pools Trail and the Canyon Overlook Trail. The Lower Emerald Pool is a 1.2-mile (1.9 km) loop to a beautiful waterfall and pool set in a stunning red rock amphitheater. The Canyon Overlook Trail is a one-mile (1.6 km) out-and-back trail with the most stunning views of Zion Canyon. There are tons of hikes to choose from, but be mindful of what level of hikers you have in your family. Some of the more famous hikes, like Angels Landing and The Narrows, aren't suitable for young kids. So do your research before arriving at the park so you don't go off the appropriate trail. **Shopping for geodes and rocks:** Our kids always love going to the geode and rock stores just outside the national park. They can be a little gimmicky, but our kids are always so excited to pick out a cool gem to bring home as a souvenir.

WHEN TO VISIT

Summer can be hot and crowded. Spring and fall are ideal: The weather is nice, and the crowds will be more manageable. In the winter, you have snow to deal with, and some trails may not be open.

WHERE TO STAY

Zion Red Rock Oasis is a private estate set on 15 acres (6 ha). This property is awesome for a family reunion

because it includes a playground, a pool with a waterslide, an indoor soccer field, and a private lake with a trampoline and paddleboards. Along with seven bedrooms, there's also a massive bunkhouse that can sleep up to 29 people!

• **Luxury:** The Zion Hummingbird Villa is a big ol' rental home that borders Zion National Park. With four bedrooms, this would be a really nice space for a big family or large group of friends looking for easy access to the park and a great place to gather after a day of adventuring.

• **Comfort:** Open Sky Zion is a series of nicely appointed safari-style tents. You could call this glamping on the cusp of Zion.

Bighorn sheep roam throughout southern Utah.

A sunset kiss from Daddy
after a day exploring
Zion's red rocks

• **Budget:** Flanigan's Inn is close to the park and offers a pool and spa. A massage might be in order after a day of hiking. Or consider glamping at AutoCamp Zion. Located just outside the park, this area allows for camping in modernized Airstream trailers or canvas tents. There's also a main lodge area with a kitchen and hangout space. You can order a grill kit to make your own dinner at your campsite.

WHAT TO EAT

There are two restaurants in the park, Red Rock Grill Dining Room and Castle Dome Cafe—both located at Zion Lodge, the only in-park hotel option. Red Rock Grill is open for breakfast, lunch, and dinner (try the authentic Navajo tacos!), while Castle Dome Cafe (more like a snack bar with some heavier options like burgers and dogs) is only open for breakfast and lunch. We shop at nearby markets and cook at camp or at our rental. If you are staying for an extended period of time, swing by Costco or a bigger grocery store in St. George on your way in.

Pro tip: Have reusable water bottles that you can refill at stations, or bring water from your guesthouse. Don't drink the water from lakes or rivers in the park. At the time of writing, officials have identified dangerous bacteria in the Virgin River and the waterways that flow through the park. Keep dogs and children away from the water.

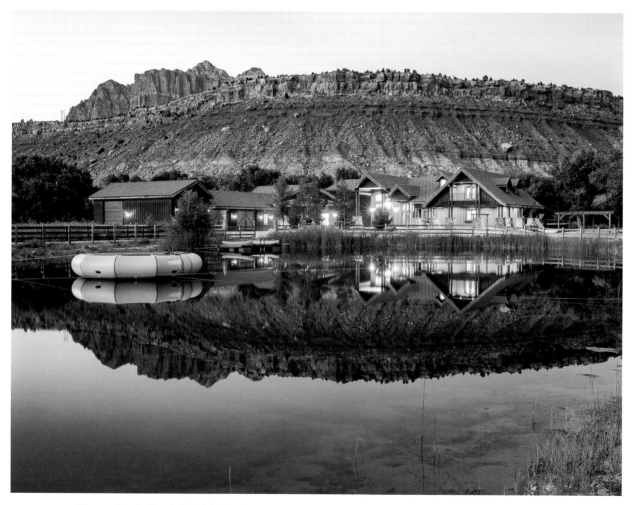

We stayed at the Zion Red Rock Oasis—it's the perfect spot for a large family reunion right outside the national park.

HILTON HEAD ISLAND, SOUTH CAROLINA, U.S.A.

Have a Low Country Boil

Hilton Head Island has incredibly soft sand beaches on the Atlantic Ocean.

As soon as I visited Hilton Head Island, I knew I had to make space for it in this book. I was immediately thrilled by the charm of the South. Hilton Head is green and lush, with Spanish moss growing on the trees. There are no billboards or flashy signs like at some other popular beach destinations. It all just feels very homey. I felt like I had stepped into a Nicholas Sparks novel.

Hilton Head is one of those places where you can just tell that families have been going again and again for years. After a day or two, I was ready to plan a return trip with my whole extended family.

Our trip to Hilton Head Island was my first true "southern hospitality" experience, and it was everything I wanted it to be and more. Southern hospitality isn't just something you experience once or twice, it's a whole way of living. People in Hilton Head were extra kind and inviting, and all the locals seemed to know each other.

Of course, southern cooking is very much a part of this culture. We had the most charming Low Country boil on the beach during our stay. If you've never had a Low Country boil, make it part of your Hilton Head itinerary. Recipes may differ a bit, but typically you boil shrimp, sausage, crab, potatoes, corn, and whatever else the cook wants to add in one large pot. Then you lay down some newspaper, pour out the contents of the pot, and eat straight off the table. It's as much a fun dining experience as it is absolutely delicious!

HOW TO GET THERE

We flew into the quaint airport in Savannah, Georgia, then rented a car and drove about an hour from the airport to Hilton Head. You can also fly into Hilton Head Island Airport, though flight options are more limited.

WHAT TO DO

• Adventure: **Rent bikes:** Most people cruise around on bikes through the Sea Pines resort community. You can also ride your bike for miles on the long sandy beaches during low tide. Calihan was only four during our visit, and we easily rented a bike with a toddler seat on the back. **Go shrimping:** We took a Vagabond Cruise for a superfun afternoon of shrimping. The crew taught us how local fishers cast their nets into the ocean

Lights Out!

Oceanfront rooms and homes are required to turn out the lights by 10 p.m. from May through October. This ensures turtles won't get confused by the lights and can safely return to the ocean.

and bring in their hauls. It was so much fun to catch some shrimp—the kids especially loved hauling up the nets to see what we'd caught—and we got to take our spoils home to cook for dinner. **Be brave at a zip line and ropes course:** If you're looking for some thrilling family fun, check out Adventure Hilton Head's Aerial Adventure and zip line course. We brought our kids for the ropes course—kid-friendly aerial challenges in the treetops—and it was a blast conquering some fears together as a family. They also have seven zip lines, from which you can take in views of the island, and a go-kart track on the property. **Look for dolphins:** We could see dolphins from the beach almost every day. They swim in the ocean, not far from shore. Seeing them was always a highlight of our day!

All about conservation, Hilton Head makes a big effort to protect its sea turtle population.

We got to enjoy a traditional Low Country boil right on the beach.

Just call me Captain Jess! It was fun to charter a sailboat for a day on the water.

• Service: **Help turtle conservation:** May through October, hundreds of loggerhead sea turtles come to shore at Hilton Head to lay their eggs each year. Sea Turtle Patrol Hilton Head Island is a great organization that works to support the sea turtles. Each morning, they scour the beach for new nests, ensuring their safety and relocating the eggs if necessary. You can donate your time or money, adopt your own nest, or help keep the beach clean and clear of debris. Remember, if you see a nest, keep your distance!

WHEN TO VISIT

Hilton Head is best in the shoulder seasons (March to May or September to November) to avoid extra hot temperatures and crowds. But summer is great too, especially for a quintessential beach weekend and swimming in the warm ocean. Just know: Summer in the South is hot, humid, and crowded.

WHERE TO STAY

We stayed at a beachfront rental home in Sea Pines and absolutely loved it. Sea Pines is a private, 5,000-acre (2,025 ha) community with beautiful family-friendly homes, charming streets, a forest preserve, golf courses, and a marina and town center. Many of the homes are listed on Airbnb and Vrbo. There are also a few hotels within the community as well.

WHAT TO EAT

We ate a ton of fresh seafood, some incredible barbecue, alligator bites, and many dishes with plenty of bacon! We enjoyed Hudson's Seafood House on the Docks for its fried green tomatoes and stuffed shrimp; Skull Creek Boathouse for sushi; One Hot Mama's for wings; and Quarterdeck for rock shrimp and gator bites.

BAJA CALIFORNIA, MEXICO

Hug Gray Whales in Ojo de Liebre Lagoon

Remote and beautiful Ojo de Liebre Lagoon is worth the effort to get to for the views alone.

I imagine Guerrero Negro, Mexico, isn't really on many people's radar. It wasn't on mine until I started to dive into the world of underwater expedition—once you go on one trip to dive with whales or sharks, you learn about the other possibilities out there.

So now you know: There is a place in Baja California, Mexico, where gray whales migrate called Ojo de Liebre Lagoon. The whales have been called the "friendliest whales on the planet" and for good reason: They naturally swim up to the local *pangas* (or skiffs) just to engage with humans! That never happens with wildlife! Usually, we are only spectators to nature. But here, mother whales push their calves to the boats to show them off. It's incredible.

Silver Shark Adventures provided us with a very nice, private experience. We chartered a panga for our family so we could have more flexibility around both the weather and the kids. You can also join a group boat for the day. Some operators offer packages with accommodations.

Make a trip to Ojo de Liebre Lagoon a key part of a road trip up and down the coast of Baja California. This is such a special experience that I'd recommend it to anyone at any age. And you'll have lifelong bragging rights: You've snuggled a whale!

Pro tips: It helps if you can speak some basic Spanish. English is less common in this area. And if you are road-tripping, keep in mind that you will encounter a handful of cash-only toll booths while driving around Baja and not all restaurants accept cards, so come prepared!

HOW TO GET THERE

We flew into San Diego, California, and were picked up and driven across the border and down to the lagoon area. The drive is long—12 hours—and makes for a great road trip. We stayed in a town called Guerrero Negro and drove to the lagoon bright and early each day.

Avoid Driving at Night

The roads are very dark here, which makes it hard to spot the wandering cows and dogs and to navigate the very narrow roads (with no shoulder). Avoid night driving if you can!

WHAT TO DO

• Adventure: **See whale sharks:** June through November, whale sharks migrate to Bahía de Los Ángeles for the warm water temperatures. Whale sharks are gentle giants that eat plankton and small fish. You can get up close to some of these animals on a boat tour and check out the gorgeous markings on their skin. **Surf:** There are some great spots to surf all along the western coast of Baja California. Some of the best surf

LEFT: Colorful religious markers adorn a wall in Todos Santos. RIGHT: A palm tree oasis

breaks are at Rosaria, Ensenada, La Misión, and Scorpion Bay. Bigger swells are consistent from March to November, and the water is a bit warmer then too. Winter also has good conditions, just not as consistently.

• Culture: **Visit Todos Santos:** A small but vibrant town in Baja California Sur, Todos Santos is about 10 hours from Ojo de Liebre Lagoon, if you make this a Baja road trip. It has some great historic buildings and fantastic restaurants that take advantage of local and organic ingredients.

WHEN TO VISIT

Whale season in Ojo de Liebre Lagoon runs during the whales' migration season, from late March through mid-April.

WHERE TO STAY

Accommodation options are very limited in the area. We stayed at Raquel and Larry's Hotel, which was quite basic, but cozy, with solid food and a friendly staff.

• **Comfort:** If you're taking a road trip down to Ojo de Liebre Lagoon, the Halfway Inn is a great option that's close to the U.S.–Mexico border. The hotel also has an authentic Mexican restaurant. Breakfast is included with your stay.

• **Budget:** Hotel Malarrimo by Rotamundos is a vibrant hotel on the main street of Guerrero Negro. It's perfect for an overnight stay when you're traveling through. The hotel has an on-site restaurant that serves breakfast, lunch, and dinner to both staying guests and road-trippers in need of a rest stop.

WHAT TO EAT

The food in Baja California is delicious, and the farther south you go, the more seafood you'll find. Most restaurants serve fish and seafood just caught from the ocean—as fresh as you can get. We enjoyed this superfresh seafood in tacos, tostadas, and more. Lobster with butter is a popular dish throughout the area. Our kids lived for the fresh handmade tortillas that came with almost every meal.

The kids were patient as we spent multiple days on the Silver Shark Adventures boat looking for whales, sharks, and unique sea life native to Baja, Mexico.

Gray whales approach boats to interact with humans in the Ojo de Liebre Lagoon—a wildlife phenomenon that has been going on for many years in this region.

NEW YORK, NEW YORK, U.S.A.

See a Show on Broadway

Kids will be awed by the hustle and bustle—and neon lights—of Times Square.

New York City may not be at the top of your list when you think of family-friendly destinations, but we've been a handful of times with our children and we always enjoy it. First of all, it's a completely different world. It's cool to show your kids how more than eight million people live their daily lives in a huge city.

Our first family visit to Manhattan was when Dorothy and Manilla were quite young (two and four years old). Just riding the subway was exciting enough for our kids at the time. My son Manilla loved trains, so a huge highlight for him was just getting around.

My kids have watched so many movies that feature New York: *Enchanted, Annie, The Secret Life of Pets, Elf, Home Alone 2.* Rewatching these ahead of our visits makes it extra fun for them to see their favorite movies brought to life.

In New York City, some of the most touristy sites are still worth all the hype. We love visiting Central Park, the American Museum of Natural History, and the High Line. Some lesser known gems are actually outside Manhattan: In Brooklyn, there's Brooklyn Bridge Park to walk through and play in; we loved seeing the huge soccer field against the Manhattan skyline.

Recently, I took Dorothy to her first Broadway shows. We saw both *Wicked* and *Harry Potter and the Cursed Child*. I hadn't made a big effort to introduce my children to much live theater or music for a handful of reasons (their age, lack of opportunity while on the road), but once I stepped foot in the impressive Gershwin Theatre, I felt ashamed of that. I was inspired to bring more music, art, and dance into my family's life.

HOW TO GET THERE

Multiple international airports make flying into New York City super easy. Take your pick from LaGuardia, John F. Kennedy International (JFK), and Newark Liberty International. You can easily get a cab or hop on the subway or commuter train (grab a weekly subway pass if you're staying more than a few days!) from any of these. If you're on the East Coast, take a train into Moynihan Train Hall (an extension of Penn Station).

WHAT TO DO

• Adventure: **Governors Island:** A quick ferry ride from downtown Manhattan takes you to Governors Island, a sweet, family-friendly place where you can rent bikes, ride down slides, and swing in hammocks, all while viewing the iconic skyline of Manhattan and the Statue of Liberty in New York Harbor. There are a ton of great food trucks there too. **Sporting events:** Whether it's seeing the Yankees in the Bronx, the Mets in Queens, the Nets or Liberty in Brooklyn, or the Knicks or Rangers at Madison Square Garden in Manhattan, catching a game in New York is an unforgettable experience. The fans are so passionate! Use the subway to get to and from all of these stadiums; if you're worried you'll get lost, have no fear: Just follow all the people in jerseys and gear! **Playgrounds:** Central Park is just one of many amazing places in the city for kids to run around. All the way downtown in Battery Park, there's a great playground with views of New York Harbor. Union Square has a nice little playground (and an incredible farmers

market), as does Madison Square Park. Also check out Brooklyn's Prospect Park (designed by the same architects as Central Park). At the north end of Brooklyn Bridge Park is the cool Jane's Carousel; grab some famous hot chocolate nearby at Jacques Torres.

• Culture: **Broadway:** You can book tickets for a Broadway show way ahead of time, or, if you can be flexible with the show you want to see, show up to the TKTS booth in Times Square for cheap same-day tickets. The TodayTix app is another great resource for discounted tickets. **Statue of Liberty and Ellis Island:** It's worth braving the lines of tourists to see Lady Liberty up close. Even more powerful is a visit to Ellis Island, where you get all that immigration history and a great conversation starter for kids: Talk about America's melting pot or your own family history! **The museums:** Across Central Park from the Museum of Natural History is Museum Mile, where you'll find the Metropolitan Museum of Art, aka The Met (kids love the mummies in the Egyptian section), the Guggenheim

The iconic Lady Liberty

Manilla uses Garrett for
a better view of the
Manhattan skyline.

(such a cool, circular, winding space), and some lesser known institutions like the Neue Galerie (don't miss the apple strudel in the fancy café).

WHEN TO VISIT

New York has its pros and cons during any season. April/May and September/October will have nice weather and fewer crowds. We visited in December—it is so special to be there during the holiday season, but it's crowded!

WHERE TO STAY

I definitely prefer to stay in a rental apartment in New York and live more like a local. There's a learning curve to grocery shopping and finding the easiest subway routes, but once you get the hang of it, there's a lot of joy in living like a true New Yorker.

We were lucky enough to spend a few days in December at the Ritz-Carlton, Central Park. It's right on the edge of the park, and it was so special to be very close to the ice-skating rink and sledding hills.

• **Comfort:** The Refinery Hotel is housed in a former hat factory and Prohibition-era tearoom. It has a funky, fun feel to it, and it's just a couple blocks from Bryant Park, which has movies on the lawn in the summer and ice-skating in the winter.
• **Budget:** The Moderne is a boutique hotel in Manhattan's Theater District, so it's a solid choice if your trip will be focused on attending Broadway shows.

WHAT TO EAT

The good food in New York is endless and, frankly, overwhelming! You can literally find any type of cuisine from any country around the world. Head to Chinatown for dim sum, a fun experience for kids (and adults); Nom Wah is a great choice. John's of Bleecker Street offers a classic New York pizza slice right by Washington Square Park. From there you can walk down Bleecker Street and find great ice cream shops and the famous Murray's Cheese Shop. If you go to the American Museum of Natural History, try to make time for bagels and lox at the nearby Barney Greengrass.

Take the kids on a fabulous culinary adventure with authentic dim sum in Chinatown.

NORTH SHORE, OAHU, HAWAII, U.S.A.

Surf the Best Waves

We visited the North Shore of Oahu during our college days. Who knew we'd eventually return to the islands?

The thing we love most about Hawaii is the rich culture. When you step foot off the plane in Honolulu, you can hear the island music, and people are immediately happy to share their culture and history with you.

I fell in love with North Shore, Oahu, in college. I visited every summer break and spent my time eating my way around the North Shore and pretending to know how to surf. The vibe there is so chill and laid back—exactly what you want when you picture paradise.

My husband and I visited Hawaii for our honeymoon and went back multiple times in our early years of marriage. We've visited every Hawaiian island and have now put down roots in Hawaii ourselves. Each island has a different personality and reason to visit. Oahu is big, beautiful, and busy. Kauai is a more rural and stunning jungle paradise. The Big Island feels like a different planet, with huge lava rocks and really great ocean wildlife (you can snorkel or dive at night with manta rays!). Maui is gorgeous and a little more fun and playful.

The North Shore offers a ton of Hawaiian culture plus those paradise vibes. It's a bit out of the way, but that usually makes things more special.

HOW TO GET THERE

It's going to be a minimum five-hour flight from the U.S. mainland, but Daniel K. Inouye International Airport is easy to fly in to and out of. On Oahu, you'll want to rent a car. The North Shore is on the opposite side of the island from the airport and takes about an hour to drive to.

WHAT TO DO

• Adventure: **Shark diving:** Set up a tour with One Ocean Diving on the North Shore of Oahu to get in the water with brilliant marine biologists and researchers who will teach you all about sharks. You're safe under the watch of professionals to get in and swim cage free with Galapagos and sandbar sharks. **Military training:** Started by retired Navy SEALs, Trident Adventures spends the day taking you through the really fun parts of being a Navy SEAL. They offer an array of

Read the Signs

Most beaches have warning signs about strong rip currents, heavy shore breaks, slippery rocks, and where swimming is prohibited. Take these warnings seriously.

activities, including scuba diving, skin diving, helicopter jumping, free-range shooting, hunting, night vision training, and more. They'll help curate the most adventurous day for you and your family. **Surfing:** Oahu has great beginner surf spots, like White Plains on the southwest shore, Canoes in Waikiki, and Haleiwa on the North Shore. You can find surf instructors around the island who will provide boards, teach you and your kids how to paddle and pop up, and help push you into waves. Just know that weather and time of year make a huge difference on where and when to surf.

Always the daredevil, Garrett hangs out of a helicopter with Trident Adventures in Oahu.

Dorothy and Manilla
at a luau at Aulani,
A Disney Resort & Spa

The North Shore offers waves for all levels of surfers.

- Culture: **Polynesian Cultural Center:** If you want to experience Polynesian history, spend a day here learning about the different island nations, such as Fiji, Tahiti, Hawaii, Rarotonga, and Samoa, and their cultural intersections. You'll find out how the communities lived, cooked, foraged, and battled—and how their culture is being preserved and celebrated today. Make sure you stick around for the luau and night show. It's worth it!

WHEN TO VISIT

Hawaii is lovely year-round. It's paradise, after all! Just try to avoid summer and big holidays, because it's busy then. December through March is typically the best time to visit, especially for surfing. Plus, the humpback whales are around, and you're bound to see some from the shore!

WHERE TO STAY

I prefer to find a rental home on the North Shore. Pro tip: Book a home through the Turtle Bay Resort, an iconic hotel on the North Shore, and for good reason—it's beautiful. The experiences they offer are never ending—from surf lessons to turtle-watching to helicopter tours—and their restaurants are great.

- **Budget:** Courtyard Oahu North Shore has a family activity center and resort-style pool, all in a great location on the water.

WHAT TO EAT

Oahu has some incredible food options. There's a decent list of foods you have to make time for, including fresh poke, Spam *musubi* (grilled Spam with rice and seaweed), kalua pork, shave ice, acai bowls, and *malasadas* (a Portuguese take on a donut), to name just a few!

Some of our favorite restaurants on the North Shore are Ted's Bakery for chocolate *haupia* pie, Matsumoto Shave Ice (the kids love the Rainbow flavor), Seven Brothers for the teriyaki burger, Banzai Sushi Bar, the Elephant Shack for Thai food, and Waialua Bakery and Juice Bar for sandwiches (make sure to also order a cookie or two!).

CHILEAN PATAGONIA

Hike in Torres del Paine

There's possibly no better mountain view in the world than the famous Torres del Paine.

There are a few places where the views have literally taken my breath away. Torres del Paine has got to be in the top three. On the south end of Patagonia, in Chile, this region is known as a hiker's paradise. I won't pretend that we are avid hikers, but it is worth the trek (no pun intended) just for the sights.

We arrived at our hotel in Torres del Paine National Park in the evening and purposely closed the blinds in our room so that we could have a proper "reveal" of where we were in the morning. At daybreak, we went outside and saw perhaps the most stunning landscape I had ever seen. The

iconic towering mountains sit above a gorgeous blue lake. If you catch it at the right time of day when the water is still, the lake reflects the mountains.

The landscape seems to morph throughout the day from various angles and weather patterns. You find yourself frequently turning your head or peeking outside just to catch a glimpse of the current postcard-worthy view.

In Torres del Paine, there are trails for every level of hiker. We had six- and four-year-olds and a six-month-old, so we knew we weren't in for anything extreme. But we loved the one- to two-hour hikes that our guides took us on every day. It was a special experience going horseback riding through this vast landscape. The kids joined too!

I think Chile, as a country, is underrated. The landscapes alone are so unique and cover so many different types of geography—arid deserts, volcanoes, huge mountain ranges, lakes, forests, and glaciers. It was an added bonus that all of the people we met in Chile were very down-to-earth, family oriented, and extremely welcoming.

HOW TO GET THERE

Getting to Torres del Paine isn't easy. We flew to Santiago, Chile, and spent one night in the city. It was modern and had great restaurants. We then flew to Punta Arenas: LATAM Airlines flies there with a quick stop in Puerto Montt; it takes nearly five hours altogether. You then get in a car and drive four hours to the national park. Our lodge arranged our transfer. You can also rent a car and drive yourself, but when

Watch for Wildlife

·······························

Keep an eye out for guanacos and pumas. A guanaco is similar to a llama, and you have a high chance of seeing one. Keep your eyes peeled to see a puma; those are rare, but they're around!

booking this type of trip it's common to go through an agency that arranges all transportation.

WHAT TO DO

• Adventure: **Trekking:** The most famous trek is the Torres del Paine Circuito W. It's a 50-mile (80 km) hike that takes five days. You can either go with a group and a guide, who'll lead you to prepitched tents and food prepared for you on your trek, or you can do it yourselves and backpack all your gear. You can also do day hikes that are portions of the W. Overall, the hike is not an extremely rigorous or technical trek. Keep

Beautiful guanacos roam the steppes of Patagonia.

in mind that reservations for treks are required in advance for *refugios* (campsites) and lodges have a limited number of spots that fill up quickly. There are three organizations that manage different parts of the park, so you have to go through multiple systems for reservations. Go through a service like Booking Patagonia if the process seems overwhelming.

Kayaking: In Torres del Paine you can do a kayak trip down the Grey River, where you'll take in the stunning mountain backdrops among fjords, glaciers, and icebergs.

• Culture: **Horseback riding:** We did a guided tour through the park with a proper gaucho, or South American cowboy. There's much history and culture behind the modern-day cowboys in Patagonia. They are experts on the terrain and wildlife, and we learned so much from them.

WHEN TO VISIT

Chile's summertime (December to February) is warm and beautiful and, of course, very busy with tourists. It also happens to be the windiest time of the year. Spring (think wildflowers in bloom) and fall (for incredible colorful foliage) are some of the best times to visit. No matter the time of year, the region is known for unpredictable weather, so pack layers!

WHERE TO STAY

We stayed at the Explora Lodge in Torres del Paine National Park. It's an incredible luxury property right in the heart of the national park. It arguably has one of the most stunning views I've ever experienced.

• **Comfort:** Hotel Remota is indeed remote, with a beautiful hangout room, spa, and restaurant, all with those incredible views of the Gulf of Almirante Montt.

• **Budget:** Simple Patagonia is a boutique hotel with a cool design—the bamboo-like exterior mimics the look of the surrounding farmland.

WHAT TO EAT

There aren't many food options or grocery stores within the national park, so we mostly ate at our lodge. The most popular local food is lamb spit-roasted over an open fire. The meat options in Patagonia were plentiful, and everything came with a tomato and cucumber salad.

We took a horseback-riding tour through the mountains, and our guides kindly rode with the older kids. We even saw a wild puma!

This pic of baby Cali is framed in our house. I snapped it on my iPhone from our hotel room at the Explora Lodge in Torres del Paine National Park.

There is a full array of
hiking options of various
difficulties in Patagonia.
Many kid-friendly hikes
have magnificent views!

IGUAZÚ FALLS, BRAZIL

See the Iconic Falls From the Sea or Air

Iguazú Falls sits on the border of Argentina and Brazil.

guazú Falls is one of those bucket list places that is out of the way but worth the effort. It's an extra flight from pretty much anywhere, but again, totally worth it. We've been to Niagara Falls and Victoria Falls, and I can soundly say that I enjoyed Iguazú Falls the most!

Made up of more than 250 separate cascades, Iguazú Falls is the world's largest broken waterfall. The waterfalls are fed by the Iguazú River, which cuts through the border of Argentina and Brazil. About 20 percent of the falls cascade down the Brazil side of the border, with the rest in Argentina. So from the Brazil side, you can see a larger array of falls across the border. The cascades converge at what is called Devil's Throat. Surrounding the waterfall is a subtropical rainforest that you can explore; you can spot tons of wildlife there, including howler monkeys and tapirs.

We stayed at an incredible Belmond hotel on the Brazil side called Hotel das Cataratas. It has a magnificent view of the falls. There are gorgeous walkways just outside the hotel that give you a nice panoramic view.

There are a few other ways to experience the falls. The first way is by helicopter. A few minutes down the road from our hotel was a helicopter port where flights come in and out every few minutes. They fly you on a quick 15-minute jaunt around the falls. It was beautiful, but not my favorite way to see Iguazú.

The second option is by boat. This was the most fun way to experience Iguazú Falls. We joined a jet boat filled with people. The boat wound up and down the river, even taking us right under the falls. Warning: You will get wet! Thankfully, each participant gets a rain poncho. It was thrilling to weave through the rapids and feel the power of Mother Nature.

You can also see the falls on foot. Bring your passport and book a car (or take a bus!) to ride across the border to Argentina to enter the park from that side. There are multiple hiking routes to the falls, or you can jump on the Jungle Train to either of two stations, a good option if you are traveling with young kids. The full 25-minute train ride will drop you off near a shorter, paved trail leading up to an incredible lookout point right above the falls. The closer you get, the mistier it becomes. Grab a poncho, unless you want to get drenched. And put away your nice cameras! Pull out a GoPro or something water-proof instead!

HOW TO GET THERE

From Argentina, fly into Puerto Iguazu Airport, also known as Cataratas del Iguazú International Airport; from Brazil, fly into Foz do Iguaçu International Airport. The falls are about a five-minute drive from the Brazilian airport. Keep in mind when you plan: There's a park entrance fee on both the Brazil side and the Argentina side of the falls.

WHAT TO DO

• Adventure: **Enjoy Parque das Aves:** This park, filled with native jungle birds, actually turned out to be such a highlight of our entire trip to South America. We had the opportunity to throw little pellets of food to the resident toucans and learned that they are skilled catchers! Most of the birds in this park are rescued victims of trafficking or mistreatment. Their safe space is a beautiful park with large, comfortable aviaries. **Visit three countries at once:**

Visit Both Countries
....
"Choosing a side" is difficult. Try to do both if you can. If you must choose one: For the views, go with Brazil. To get up close, go with Argentina. You only need two to three days in the area.

The Triple Frontier is where Paraguay, Brazil, and Argentina meet. Standing on the Marco das Três Fronteiras platform, you can see the fork in the Iguazú and Paraná Rivers where all three countries come together.

• Culture: **Visit the Guaraní community:** You can take a tour of the rainforest and an Indigenous settlement called La Comunidad Mbya Guaraní Yriapú, which are both easily accessible from the Argentina side. On the visit, you'll learn about the customs of the ancient Guaraní people and their lifestyle, history, and culture. You can also purchase handicrafts from the community members.

Jungle flowers grow in the falls' surroundings.

We loved walking to the falls from the Hotel das Cataratas on the Brazil side—the closest place you can stay to the falls.

WHEN TO VISIT

It is very hot and rainy most of the year here, and very jungly. Shoulder seasons (March/April/September) are better times to visit Iguazú Falls, as the water levels will still be high, but temps are a bit milder. December to February is rainy season; water flows less during dry season (June to August). No matter when you visit, pack the right gear. You'll want a hat, waterproof jacket, sunscreen, insect repellent, and comfy walking shoes. Make sure everything is waterproof—you're going to get wet!

WHERE TO STAY

Belmond's Hotel das Cataratas is the only hotel *in* Iguazú National Park. You have direct walking access to view the falls from the Brazil side. It's a gorgeous pink structure with all the luxury amenities.

- **Luxury:** The Grand Meliá Iguazú, the only hotel in the national park on the Argentina side, offers views of the falls.
- **Budget:** El Pueblito Iguazú is an eco-sustainable hotel built around the historic cultural monuments of Puerto Iguazú, which is a gateway city to the falls.

WHAT TO EAT

Being in the rainforest, you'll find no shortage of fresh papayas, mangoes, pineapples, avocados, and bananas. We had a lot of fresh juices and fruit plates each morning. The most traditional food is barbecue made with quality grass-fed Argentine beef. The fresh-caught river fish is tasty too.

Keep an eye out for toucans! Growing up, these birds seemed to exist only in the pages of *National Geographic* and on cereal boxes. What a treat to see them in the wild!

EXUMA, THE BAHAMAS

Go Swimming in Crystal Clear Caribbean Water

As your island-hopper plane prepares to land in Exuma, look out the window to see the white sandbars and the swirls of turquoise water.

From day one of traveling, we've been on a quest to find the clearest water in the world. We believe we found it in Exuma, the Bahamas.

If you ask me to name my favorite color, I'll say it's "Bahamas blue." Well, more of a turquoise. If you're in the Exuma district and looking at the water, that's the blue I'm talking about. It's my favorite!

In 2016, on our first visit as a family to Exuma (a chain of 365 little islands), we had a boat take us to a place that the locals call Windex, because the water is exactly the color of the cleaning product!

Adventuring around Exuma affords endless opportunities. Most of the islands are uninhabited, which means untouched, footprint-free beaches. We found one beach where sand dollars were super easy to find, another area with hundreds of large bright orange sea stars, and an island filled with iguanas. The tides and currents are in constant motion, so the feel of the beaches is also constantly changing, and it is seriously so fun to explore.

We based ourselves on Great Exuma for most of our stay, which was a wonderful spot for the kids to play on the beach and in the water. Garrett even taught Dorothy how to dive underwater here!

HOW TO GET THERE

Exuma International Airport is just north of George Town and receives a few flights a day from Miami and Fort Lauderdale, Florida, and Montreal, Canada, as well as from Nassau, the Bahamas. There are a handful of smaller airports throughout Exuma, including Staniel Cay, Black Point, and the private airstrip on Farmer's Cay, where you can charter a plane.

Once you've arrived on the islands, most hotels will arrange to pick you up, though taxis are also easy to secure. There are also many boats available for hire so you can explore surrounding islands.

Key Fact

"Cay" is pronounced KEY, not KAY.

WHAT TO DO

• Adventure: **Swimming with pigs:** It's gimmicky and a bit odd, but it's something special that pigs in Exuma do, in fact, swim. For years now, tour boats have come with food scraps, and the pigs will gladly swim out to eat while you wade in the water. Be mindful: The pigs can be aggressive and do have a strong bite. Mommy pigs are very protective of their piglets, so make sure to give them plenty of space. **Boating to Thunderball Grotto:** Thunderball Grotto near Staniel Cay is

LEFT: This might look like a swimming pool, but it's the clear water of Exuma. RIGHT: The Bahamas are known for their conch fritters.

We introduced baby Cali—
and the other kids—to a
giant red sea star.

Uniquely Exuma: swimming with pigs!

a great spot for swimming and snorkeling. Depending on the tide, it may require a short swim underwater to reach. Once there, you enter into a glowing dome with an incredible reef and fish below. Currents can be strong, so make sure your boat is properly anchored. **Exploring Compass Cay:** Compass Cay has a protected harbor and marina where there's a cute little restaurant and nurse sharks that like to lounge near the shallow dock. Help kids (and adults!) overcome any shark fears by swimming with these nice creatures in the clear water. There is a daily docking fee (about $10 to $15 per person), so have cash on you. **Snorkeling a plane wreck:** Another short boat ride from Staniel Cay is an old drug smugglers' plane that crashed back in the '70s. It's a great little spot to snorkel for an hour and sits in such shallow water that you can see it from the surface!

WHEN TO VISIT

The Bahamas is a great year-round destination, with temperatures that rarely go below 60°F (16°C). Just a heads-up, if you travel June through November, you are in Atlantic hurricane season.

WHERE TO STAY

Our favorite place in Exuma is called Fowl Cay Resort. The private island resort has only six villas, and each comes with a golf cart to get around Fowl Cay. The best part: Every villa also comes with its own personal powerboat and chef-prepared picnic meals, so you can go out and explore the surrounding water on your own!

Exuma is also an incredible place to travel by sailboat, catamaran, or yacht. The Staniel Cay Yacht Club has a really cool community for boaters.

• **Comfort:** We've also visited the wonderful Grand Isle Resort. The hotel has a great fitness center, a restaurant, and kayaks to take out. You can also join tours to play in the water with the famous swimming pigs or help tag sharks with scientists.

WHAT TO EAT

The Bahamas are best known for their conch. Bahamian food is flavorful and has a southern flair. You'll see things like fried conch fritters, cracked conch, conch salad, johnnycakes, peas and rice, and grits.

DOMINICA

See Leatherback Turtles

The colorful seaside town of Roseau: In our opinion, this is one of the most underrated places on Earth.

Before we planned our trip, I had never heard of Dominica. My husband saw an underwater photographer post a photo with sperm whales in Dominica and was instantly intrigued. Turns out, Dominica is the only country in the world where sperm whales reside all year long. And they didn't disappoint. But Dominica quickly turned into our favorite Caribbean island for a number of reasons beyond its whale population.

First of all, Dominica is stunning. It's largely covered by rainforest, with incredible waterfalls and natural hot springs, and it is known to have lots and lots of rainbows.

It didn't feel touristy like other islands in the Caribbean often can; most people who visit are more into nature and wildlife than tours and spring break spots.

The highlight of our trip was a special place called Rosalie Bay, a black sand beach where dozens of leatherback sea turtles return every spring to lay their eggs. A small and cozy hotel, the Rosalie Bay Eco-Resort and Spa, has a great turtle research and protection program. When you stay there, the resort offers wake-up calls throughout the night so you can watch the leatherbacks come ashore to do their thing.

On the first night we visited, we got the call! Around midnight we were told there were two leatherback females about to lay their eggs. Using low light so as not to disturb them, we watched the turtles dig their holes and then lay their eggs (about 100 of them!), bury the nest, and return to sea. I had no idea how *huge* leatherbacks are. Like, one is equivalent to the size of a monster truck tire. They can reach seven feet (2.1 m) long and weigh up to 1,500 pounds (680 kg)! On another morning we got a call closer to 5 a.m. and were lucky enough to see a mother lay her eggs during the sunrise. It was so special.

Unfortunately, Hurricane Maria really did a number on Dominica in 2017, and it's still recovering. We hope to be back again someday soon—and tourism dollars to the island can help it rebuild!

HOW TO GET THERE

You can fly directly into Dominica from Miami, Florida, or San Juan, Puerto Rico. You can also fly in on smaller airlines

Be Patient

Dominica is not a place for fast, convenient, Americanized tourism. Roads are not super well kept. It's rugged and wild, and that's part of why it's so amazing!

from nearby islands, including Antigua, Barbados, Martinique, St. Maarten, Guadeloupe, St. Lucia, and Trinidad.

Most people stay in Roseau, the capital city. Since we stayed for 10 days, we rented a car so we could explore the island.

WHAT TO DO

• Adventure: **Hike to Trafalgar Falls:** The twin cascades of Trafalgar Falls are just a short drive from Roseau and easy to get to for kids of all ages. There is a paved path that takes just 10 to 15 minutes to walk, and you'll wind up on a wooden platform overlooking the beautiful falls. Younger kids can splash in the spring that crosses the trail, and older kids can

Dorothy was just three years old when we visited Dominica. She had no problem diving in.

swim in the pool from the smaller waterfall. There's also a hot spring by the taller falls. **See sperm whales:** Dominica is home to nearly 200 resident sperm whales. You can join one of the multiple boats that go out daily to see them. If you want to get in the water to snorkel, you'll need to be in a permitted boat. **Visit Morne Trois Pitons National Park:** There are some incredible spots inside this national park, including the Emerald Pool (a great natural swimming hole with a small waterfall), the famous three- to four-hour hike to Boiling Lake, and a few zip-lining courses.

• Service: **Adopt a turtle:** You can adopt a leatherback turtle at Rosalie Bay. The money goes toward research and conservation of leatherbacks.

WHEN TO VISIT

The island is driest February to April; the rainy season (and hurricane season) starts in June and goes through October. Turtles lay eggs in the spring, and eggs hatch in the summer. Sperm whales are there year-round.

WHERE TO STAY

We stayed at a few different places during our visit. Fort Young Hotel and Dive Resort in Roseau made for very easy daily departures to see the sperm whales. The all-inclusive hotel is affordable and has a kids' club.

The Rosalie Bay Eco-Resort and Spa is in the jungle and has such a lovely, homey vibe. The kids loved the pool, and we all enjoyed learning so much about the leatherbacks.

Our final spot was a luxury cliffside property called Secret Bay, which has only a couple of private villas. The whole resort is based around green and clean practices, nutrition, and healing biodiversity.

WHAT TO EAT

Dominica supplies the majority of the produce to other nearby Caribbean islands, so of course the food was very fresh. The markets were stocked with amazing tropical produce, including pineapples, plantains, sweet potatoes, and bananas.

This is a giant mother sperm whale, its calf, and, if you look closely, Garrett!

Photographer in train-
ing! Garrett shows
Dorothy the ropes
at Trafalgar Falls.

Baby Manilla gets a very rare experience: seeing a massive leatherback turtle head back to sea after making a nest on shore during sunrise.

DESTINATIONS FOR YOUNG KIDS

....

Young kids (ages four to seven) are sponges. My absolute favorite thing to do is connect my kids to friends that may not look, talk, or live like they do. It reminds all of us to celebrate and embrace our beautiful differences. Here are a few destinations where your kids can really start to experience this beautiful world.

Bali, Indonesia: We love the perfect mix of adventure, culture, and service that comes with traveling to Bali. For a deep cultural experience, check out Ubud. Our family loved the Monkey Forest and seeing so much of the Balinese Hindu culture. (See more on page 226.)

Cape Town, South Africa: South Africa was the first country we visited in Africa, and it was a great place to start. Aside from the easy access to safaris outside the city, there are great beaches, Table Mountain (take the cableway up with kiddos), Two Oceans Aquarium, and Boulders Beach to hang with penguins! (See more on page 216.)

New York, New York, U.S.A.: New York City is awesome with kids. Eat your way through the city: pizza, cookies, dumplings, you name it! Our family's favorite spot is the American Museum of Natural History. (See more on page 276.)

Whistler, Canada: We spent a magical Christmas in Whistler, a perfect spot for our kids to learn to ski. Whistler Village is super family friendly and has great restaurants, escape rooms, a skating rink, and lots of live music. Tubing was also a highlight for the whole family.

Florida Keys, Florida, U.S.A.: The Florida Keys are where my family vacationed when I was a kid. We'd spend a few days visiting beaches; going to John Pennekamp Coral Reef State Park, where you can take kayaks out or do glass-bottom boat rides; and, as we got older, scuba diving. Make sure you find some local key lime pie. Don't miss Everglades National Park. It's one of my favorite places in the whole world!

San Diego, California, U.S.A.: You could easily have a multi-week vacation in San Diego. Check out Coronado Beach, Legoland, the U.S.S. *Midway* Museum, and, of course, the famous San Diego Zoo! My favorite spot is Torrey Pines State Natural Reserve for ocean views and hiking trails.

Brussels, Belgium: Dorothy celebrated her fifth birthday in Brussels in 2017. We rented an apartment and spent our time living like locals, including getting a temporary pass to the David Lloyd gym and putting our kids in dance and gymnastics classes. The absolute highlight of the trip was the Belgian waffle–making class that Dorothy and I took.

Bermuda, U.K.: We've visited Bermuda twice now, and it's such a unique and underrated country. There are great beaches (pink sand!), underground caves, an incredible aquarium, and, in the summer, Harbour Nights with live performances, local food, and musicians. (See more on page 352.)

Exuma, the Bahamas: We've visited Exuma with babies, toddlers, and kids. Honestly, it's great at any stage! The kids especially love snorkeling, seeing the swimming pigs, petting sharks at Compass Cay, and looking for sand dollars. (See more on page 294.)

Seoul, South Korea: We love the food and culture of South Korea. We spent our week there eating Korean barbecue and *bingsu* (shaved ice) and enjoying Korean spas, one of which also had an indoor water park! (See more on page 338.)

Bermuda is the perfect destination for families with kids of all ages. Here, Dorothy is 10, Manilla eight, and Cali five.

FALKLAND ISLANDS, UNITED KINGDOM

Walk With Penguins

The Falkland Islands are so remote that we doubled the population on one of the islands we visited.

This is not the first international destination I would recommend you visit with your family. (That would be Costa Rica! See page 164.) In fact, I was not a huge fan of the idea of traveling to the Falkland Islands (known in Spanish as the Islas Malvinas) because they are so far away. Having young kids in such a remote destination felt scary. But our trip to the Falklands ended up being one of the coolest family adventures we've ever had. And I'd recommend you try it for yourself!

I had actually never even heard of the Falkland Islands until our whale guide in Tonga mentioned them. He thought it would be a great place for our family and helped us arrange our trip. Reluctantly, I agreed.

The Falklands are so remote that some places have zero (and I mean zero!) connection—no cell service, no internet, and, in some cases, no people! At one point, we stayed on a large island with only five other people on it—and those five people were about 45 minutes away!

There's one big reason to go to the Falkland Islands: wildlife. More specifically, penguins. Five different types of penguins inhabit the Falklands—king, gentoo, rockhopper,

Magellanic (aka jackass, seriously), and macaroni. Despite my hesitation, I wound up loving exploring this area entirely on our own, teaching our kids about the wildlife, and completely (I mean completely!) disconnecting from the world.

HOW TO GET THERE

There is only one daily flight in and one daily flight out of the Falkland Islands. The other way to visit is on a cruise to Antarctica, which often stops at the Falklands.

We tacked our visit on to our trip to Chilean Patagonia. About 15 minutes before touchdown, the captain announced it was too windy to land and we would be turning around. We ended up spending the next two nights in Punta Arenas, Chile, until the flight could be rescheduled. This is an important reminder to make room for flexibility in any trip!

Once you do arrive, little private hopper planes depart from Port Stanley (the local airport) to take you around the more

than 700 different islands in the Falklands. Register for flights in advance; schedules are only drawn up the day prior to departure.

WHAT TO DO

• Adventure: **Volunteer Point:** Our visit to Volunteer Point was one of the crowning moments on our trip. Here, we got to witness a king penguin colony. It was about a three-hour, bumpy off-road drive from Stanley to get to the colony, but these penguins were a beautiful sight. Needless to say, the kids loved watching them waddle around. This spot was also special because it's where Cali took his first steps. He wobbled

Albatrosses, seen here in a colony, can go years at a time without setting foot on land.

around just like a penguin and couldn't be stopped (even when he fell in some penguin droppings)!

• Culture: **Falkland Islands Museum:** This museum is located right at the dockyard in Stanley. Exhibits cover the history of the islands, geography, wildlife, and the 1982 war—a brief dispute between Argentina and the United Kingdom—over the islands.

WHEN TO VISIT

The best time to visit the Falkland Islands is between October and April, summer in the Southern Hemisphere, when the Falklands have the longest daylight hours and the most wildlife.

WHERE TO STAY

You need to book a trip to the Falkland Islands through a tour company. There are limited options for accommodations, and travel between islands is complicated. We were very pleased with everything that International Tours and Travel arranged for our family.

We stayed on three different islands. The first was East Falkand, in the Falkands' capital city, Stanley, where we stayed at the Malvina House Hotel. Stanley is a supercute (and crazy windy) town with a charming post office, gift shop, and the hotel. That's pretty much it.

The Sea Lion Lodge on Sea Lion Island was a highlight of our stay. It's a very cozy lodge where all meals are provided. The lodge is situated right next to a giant colony of penguins and, down the beach, hundreds of elephant seals.

On Saunders Island, we doubled the population! The five residents of the island dropped us off at the Rookery Inn, a basic but cozy home, leaving us with a box of food and a radio. We spent the next two days enjoying the wildlife and the complete isolation.

WHAT TO EAT

The Falkland Islands are a self-governing British overseas territory, and the food reflects that British heritage. There was fresh seafood, including scallops and snow crab. Our kids ate a lot of fish-and-chips. Sea Lion Island even had a formal teatime.

We loved being completely disconnected from the outside world and letting the kids roam the wide expanses.

What an amazing milestone moment: Cali took his first step among the penguins!

ALASKA, U.S.A.

Go Fishing in the Last Frontier

Alaska is truly America's last frontier—and must be explored by land and water.

Alaska had been on my bucket list for years before we visited in 2020. And it absolutely did not disappoint. I feel like everyone who visits says the same thing: Alaska is wild and raw, yet comfortable and homey at the same time. We stayed for one week and saw two different parts—Homer and the mountains outside Anchorage. I can't speak highly enough about both of our experiences.

Alaskans seem so rugged and hard-core. I guess you have to be to put up with that winter six months out of the year! I loved how the Alaskans we met all had a deep love for the outdoors and nature and were so proud of their state.

While hiking and skiing draw a lot of people to Alaska, fishing has got to be the biggest reason to visit. We tried to plan our trip perfectly for the salmon in August. In Anchorage, we simply walked down to Ship Creek, right in town, and got our fishing licenses and gear. We joined a bunch of locals on the river to fish for salmon. Almost every three minutes we'd see someone hauling in a good-size pink fish. Everyone was cheering one another on, and it was a great spot for kids.

In Homer, 200-plus miles (320 km) south, we had big plans to do some fun halibut fishing. It's hard work to reel these fighters in, but catching them is easy if you go to the right spot at the right time of year.

HOW TO GET THERE

Flights to Anchorage are quite easy from the lower 48. We really enjoyed flying Alaska Airlines, which has a hub in Seattle, just a three-hour flight away. You can also fly into Fairbanks or Juneau.

Once we arrived, we took a seaplane to our mountain lodge in Skwentna, just north of Anchorage. To get to Homer, we rented a car in Anchorage and drove about four and a half hours south. We loved driving around Alaska; it's incredibly scenic.

WHAT TO DO

• Adventure: **Bear-viewing tours:** The most popular way to see bears in Alaska is on a day tour to one of the parks, such as Katmai National Park and Preserve or Lake Clark National Park and Preserve. Most tours fly guests into the parks via helicopter or small plane. We did two different tours—one in Katmai National Park with Alaska Bear Safaris and one on a boat at Lake Clark, where we saw bears come to the water to eat. Watching these big bears in their natural environment, with my kids beside me, brought me so much joy. There's nothing better than showing your children the incredibleness of this Earth, and its creatures. **Girdwood:** On our drive to Homer, we stopped in Girdwood for a nice meal and a ride up the Alyeska Aerial Tram. Check out Alyeska Resort—Alaska's only year-round resort; it has great hiking, biking, and skiing. We also came across the Alaska Wildlife Conservation Center, where we took a great 90ish-minute stop to learn about bears, moose, bison, foxes, lynx, and porcupines. **Bore tide surfing:** A bore tide is a rush of seawater through a shallow inlet like Turnagain Arm outside Anchorage. The rush

Plan for Long Commutes
....

Alaska is huge. It takes a long time to get from place to place. There's either a long drive or a plane ride involved, so when you're planning, pull out a map.

of water is basically a long flowing wave. Surfers can ride the bore tide twice a day for miles on a fast-moving wave with a five- to ten-foot (1.5 to 3 m) face. **Homer Spit:** Homer Spit is a narrow strip of land jutting into Kachemak Bay. There are cute little shops, seafood restaurants, and a marina. There's also the "Fishing Hole"—you can rent a rod from across the street and have some fun fishing with the whole family. Tell the kids to look to the skies: You'll probably catch a glimpse of a bald eagle or two. When you get hungry, grab a bite from the iconic Salty Dawg Saloon. **Kenai Fjords National Park:** This incredible national park boasts more than 600,000 acres (240,000 ha) and is only accessible by boat from the coastal town of

We caught—then cooked up—our own salmon.

On our trip around Alaska, we spent some time exploring Homer Spit.

Seward. Visitors can see wildlife such as whales, sea otters, and puffins. More than 60 percent of the park is blanketed in ice and snow year-round, with stunning glaciers and fjords. You can rent kayaks or spend the day hiking.

WHEN TO VISIT

The best time of year to visit Alaska for fishing is mid-June through mid-September. It will be quite busy, but that's when you'll get the best fishing. In the winter, you can see the aurora borealis, ski, ice-fish, and go dogsledding.

WHERE TO STAY

We spent the first part of our trip at Tordrillo Mountain Lodge, northwest of Anchorage. Fishing lodges are popular in Alaska, and this particular one sits right on its own private lake in the Tordrillo Mountains.

In Homer, we stayed at the incredible Second Star Mansion. This property is made for a family reunion, wedding, or other special occasion. We fit much of my extended family in this home, and it was the absolute best. The whole estate is themed around Peter Pan, and the top floor has the most breathtaking Neverland-themed kids' playroom.

WHAT TO EAT

I hope you enjoy salmon, crab, scallops, and, well, all the seafood. We learned how to make "poor man's lobster" with the halibut that we caught: Boil in water with sugar and salt, poach the fish until done, and then eat it with butter. Delicious!

Alaska had some tasty game too, with local sheep, moose, deer, and caribou. The local produce was very fresh, and we even had a bunch of raspberry bushes to pick from in the yard in Homer.

Look closely: Can you see the grizzly in the field behind us?

"Merman" Garrett always finds his way to the water—here in the cold at sunrise in Judd Lake at the Tordrillo Mountain Lodge.

GOLDEN CIRCLE, ICELAND

Drive From Natural Wonder to Natural Wonder

Iceland's Golden Circle is a route that connects many of the country's most beautiful natural wonders.

The 2013 movie *The Secret Life of Walter Mitty* is ultimately what put Iceland on our map. But it took us until July 2018 to visit. At that time in the summer, the sun started to go down at 11 p.m. but never quite finished setting. Even if you woke up in the middle of the night, there was still light. It was an absolute trip to be somewhere that never got dark.

We met up with some friends and rented a home in Reykholt, with easy access to the Golden Circle route. While the home we stayed in was lovely and cozy, there is so much to see and so much driving to do that I'd

definitely go the camper van route next time. It'd make for the ultimate Golden Circle road trip!

If your family is good at road-tripping, this is the place for you! The Golden Circle is a popular, must-do route that hits three of Iceland's top sights—Thingvellir National Park, the Geysir geothermal area, and Gullfoss waterfall. The full circle can be driven in about three hours, but with all the stops, you should plan for about an eight-hour day. Or break it up across a couple of days so you can spend more time in each place. There's also more to explore beyond the Golden Circle if you do your research.

HOW TO GET THERE

More than 80 airports have flights directly to Reykjavík's Keflavík International Airport. And Icelandair offers a free layover in Reykjavík for up to seven days on routes between the U.S. and Europe. That would be a great extension to a European vacation and save you a bunch on airfare.

If you rent a car for a self-guided tour, make sure to fill the tank often and avoid speeding. There are speed cameras throughout the country—we learned that the hard way!

WHAT TO DO

• Adventure: **Snorkeling or diving a continental rift:** The Silfra fissure is where the North American and Eurasian tectonic plates divide. There is an incredible opportunity for adults and older kids to snorkel or dive the continental rift in stunningly crystal clear water within Thingvellir National Park. Your tour will provide all the snorkel gear as well as a dry suit to keep

Budget Right
....

Food and gas are expensive in Iceland. Prepare to pay $25 to $30 per person for a dinner entrée, and sometimes more. It's expensive, but the food is high quality.

you warm in the Silfra fissure's chilly water (temps are typically 35 to 39°F [2 to 4°C] year-round). **Blue Lagoon:** The Blue Lagoon is one of Iceland's most touristy destinations, but it's still worth the stop. A geothermal spa with milky blue water like you've never seen before, it's full of minerals and good bacteria that are beneficial for your skin. This was such a great spot for the whole family—the water is shallow, and in some spots even little kids can stand! There are also private spa treatments available for the adults—we'll have to check those out next time! **Skógafoss:** This waterfall was the setting for an iconic scene in *The Secret Life of Walter Mitty,* so we had to

LEFT: You're sure to see lots of puffins out in the wild in Iceland. RIGHT: There's a lot of meat on the menu here.

We reenacted our favorite scene from *The Secret Life of Walter Mitty* at Skógafoss.

All of us enjoyed a healthy soak and mud mask in the Blue Lagoon's mineral waters.

make time for it. Because it's not far off from the Golden Circle, we tacked it on to our driving adventures. Skógafoss is one of the biggest waterfalls in Iceland at 197 feet (60 m). Just walking up to it, you'll feel the power of the falls and get quite wet. A campsite by the falls would make for a gorgeous place to wake up in the morning.

WHEN TO VISIT

July and August are Iceland's warmest months, but also the most crowded. These months have 24 hours of sunlight, so you can literally explore at all times of the day. Most accommodations have blackout curtains to help you get some sleep. If you're going to chase the northern lights, peak season is September through March. Stay up late and be patient!

WHERE TO STAY

We found a really great home rental in Reykholt that was big enough for four adults and four children. It was nice to have a cozy home to return to after adventuring.

• **Luxury:** A lot of hotels claim to be eco-resorts, but Torfhús Retreat walks the walk: It runs entirely on geothermal and hydroelectric energy. They also reuse local materials in beautiful ways: The interiors are made of reclaimed oak and pine, and a sofa in the lounge is made out of a fishing boat.

• **Comfort:** ION Adventure Hotel has a distinct, otherworldly look amid mountainous lava fields. People might come for the design, but the real sell is the variety of tours on offer, including horseback riding, snowmobiling, and volcano exploring.

• **Budget:** Hótel Kría, on Iceland's southern coast, has lovely mountain views and a complimentary breakfast. Bonus: If you travel in the winter, the staff will call you in the middle of the night when the northern lights are visible.

WHAT TO EAT

Iceland has a ton of sheep farms, so delicious lamb roasts are common on menus. There's a lot of great dairy as well, including ice cream and a thick, yogurtlike cheese called skyr.

BHUTAN

Hike to the Tiger's Nest

The Tiger's Nest monastery is built into a cliffside. It takes a long hike to reach, but it's worth the effort.

Bhutan is for elite travelers. It's expensive, hard to get to, and requires a completely unique style of travel. Even so, I'd recommend you get to Bhutan at some point in your life, if you can. The country is extraordinary in every sense of the word. It literally feels like you're stepping into a fairy tale. While much of Asia feels incredibly modern, Bhutan does not, in the most beautiful way.

When you land in Bhutan, you can immediately see how unique this place is. Everyone wears the customary dress, called a *gho* for men and a *kira* for women. Our guide took us to town to purchase these on our arrival. I really appreci-

ated this and loved seeing how the people of Bhutan were proud of their history and culture, and they were thrilled to share it with us.

When planning a trip to Bhutan, you have to go through a registered tour operator (we used Breathe Bhutan). The government of Bhutan has instituted a "high value, low impact" tourism policy, which is part of what makes this country so special. Only a limited number of visas are offered, and they're quite pricey—currently $200 per day, per person. That doesn't include food, tour guides, or accommodations. Bhutan uses this money to promote carbon-neutral tourism and build more sustainable tourism and industry sectors.

The biggest bucket list attraction in Bhutan is Paro Taktsang monastery (aka the Tiger's Nest monastery). Built by monks in the 1600s, the impressive, still-in-use monastery clings to the side of a mountain cliff. Guru Rinpoché, the "Second Buddha," meditated at a nearby cave and taught students there. It's a rigorous hike to the monastery—about four hours round-trip; our guides carried our kids almost the whole way!—but the views both of it and from it are stunning and absolutely worth the effort.

HOW TO GET THERE

Paro International Airport is nestled between two mountain peaks. It's known as the most dangerous airport in the world, and fewer than two dozen pilots are even allowed to land in this narrow valley. Book a window seat on the left side of the plane! The view while landing between the two mountain peaks is absolutely incredible.

GHI > GDP

....

Bhutan's government makes decisions based on the happiness of the Bhutanese people according to a Gross National Happiness Index. This is factored by looking at nine different categories—psychological well-being, health, time use, education, culture, good governance, community vitality, ecology, and living standards. How cool is that?!

Once you're there, you'll want to stick with a tour guide and driver to take you around the country. They'll provide helpful knowledge and navigate the hair-raising roads; I can't imagine driving them myself!

WHAT TO DO

• Culture: **Monasteries:** About 85 percent of Bhutanese people are Buddhist, and you'll have plenty of opportunity to visit multiple monasteries and learn all about the religion. It was such an honor to see these monasteries and learn

We joined young monks at a monastery for some butter tea. (It tastes like it sounds—like butter!)

about the lives of monks. Some of the monks even invited Garrett and Manilla to shave their heads, which monks do as *pabbajjā,* a symbol of ridding the self of worldly ego. **Buddha Dordenma:** This 167-foot (51 m) statue of Buddha is easier to reach than the Tiger's Nest: It was a fun, short hike up the stairs to see the Buddha and a great first site for us all to learn about Buddhism. *Dzongs:* The most famous of these fortified monasteries is Punakha Dzong in Punakha. Once built as strategic fortresses for gaining Buddhist influence, nowadays dzongs house administrative offices and monks' accommodations.

WHEN TO VISIT

Spring and fall are the best seasons to visit Bhutan. The fall has crisp, clean air and beautiful foliage. Spring brings some gorgeous blooms. Punakha Drubchen and Punakha Tshechu, two of Bhutan's most popular festivals, are held in February or March.

WHERE TO STAY

Our most unique stay was at the Bhutan Spirit Sanctuary. It's a spa-inclusive resort focused on traditional Bhutanese medicine. An Eastern medicine doctor recommended natural supplements and a diet that we followed during our visit.

Gangtey Lodge is a gorgeous property in the rural hills of Bhutan. I'll never forget waking up to the mist running through those hills. The lodge arranged incredible hikes for our whole family as well as tours through traditional villages.

WHAT TO EAT

Two words for you: butter tea. You'll undoubtedly be offered black tea with butter in it. It literally tastes like butter.

Two more words: red chilies. We visited in the fall when most roofs were covered in red chilies that had been laid out to dry. They are spicy and used in pretty much every meal. The national dish is called *ema datshi*—chilies, onions, and a generous amount of cheese served with rice.

Monks offered to shave Manilla and Garrett's heads, a symbol of leaving behind outside vanities.
The special moment was a spiritual experience for our family.

Our guide in Bhutan helped outfit our family in customary clothes: *ghos* for the boys and *kiras* for me and Dorothy.

SINGAPORE

Enjoy the Incredible City of Gardens

Singapore is a spectacular city that combines technology, glass-and-steel high-rises, and green space so beautifully.

Singapore wasn't on our itinerary. We ended up there when ash from a volcanic eruption rerouted us on our way from Australia to Bali. And it was such a pleasant surprise. (See, flexibility *is* key!)

Singapore is a huge, bustling city with big, skyscraping buildings, large hotel chains, and lots of malls. It's modern and fast paced. And it's also a melting pot of cultures. We visited in early December, and everything was decked out in Christmas decorations, even though the majority of the population isn't Christian. Our taxi driver explained that the country celebrates all holidays and

all nations. I was impressed with how open-minded and accepting that was.

Within this busy city you'll also enjoy some of the most incredible gardens, parks, and manicured landscaping. One such spot, Gardens by the Bay, is hands down the world's most impressive garden. It's a nature lover's paradise and horticulturalist's dream. There are more than 1.5 million plants in total, including species from every continent except Antarctica. Plus, you'll find 250 acres (100 ha) of waterfront gardens that you can stroll through.

My favorite parts were the Cloud Forest (boasting one of

the world's tallest indoor waterfalls) and the Flower Dome, the largest greenhouse in the world! I promise, the architecture, art, and sheer grandeur of this place are worth the visit. Keep your cameras handy; around every turn is an Instagram-worthy shot!

HOW TO GET THERE

Singapore Changi Airport is a huge hub in Southeast Asia. And it's a destination in and of itself. You can eat a good meal, chill in an airport lounge, enjoy a rooftop pool and Jacuzzi, go shopping, take in some impressive art, watch a (free) movie, ride down the world's biggest airport slide, or relax in some incredible gardens. It isn't a bad place at all for a long layover! If you're staying in Singapore, you don't need to rent a car; taxis are super easy and convenient to use.

WHAT TO DO

• Adventure: **Night Safari:** Most animals in zoos rest in the shade or sleep during the hot day. At night, it's a different story! The Night Safari is an open-air zoo set in a tropical forest. You can get on a tram to check out the active nocturnal wildlife. The animals are separated by natural barriers rather than cages, so they feel comfortable roaming. **Kids' parks:** Singapore has a large assortment of amusement parks, water parks, kids' museums, and other spots for family fun. Visit Universal Studios Singapore, the aquarium at Resorts World Sentosa, Adventure Cove Waterpark, Wild Wild Wet, and more. There's plenty to do with little kids here, and a lot of it is either indoors or involves water to keep you cool.

• Culture: **Wet markets:** Wet markets are marketplaces where vendors sell fresh meat, fish, and produce. There are different wet markets throughout Singapore, including in its Little India and Chinatown neighborhoods. One of the city's biggest wet markets is Geylang Serai, which is a Malay emporium. The market is open daily from 10 a.m. to

midnight. Also be sure to check out a hawker center: These open-air complexes, which you can find throughout Singapore, have lots of different street food vendors offering delicious bites.

WHEN TO VISIT

There is so much to do indoors that Singapore is a good place to visit year-round, even during the crazy hot and humid summers. The nicest months to visit are February to April,

One of our favorite spots to eat in Singapore was Din Tai Fung.

It's safe to say we stood out roaming the (very clean) sidewalks in Singapore.

during the country's dry season, when there is the least humidity and the most sunshine.

WHERE TO STAY

The most unique property in Singapore is the bucket list–worthy Marina Bay Sands. Enjoy a rooftop infinity pool on the 57th floor and the incredible views of Marina Bay and the cityscape. If you don't want to spend the money to stay there, you can get a $20 day pass to the observation deck.

• **Comfort:** The Warehouse Hotel, on the Singapore River, was originally built in 1895. It has since been renovated into a sleek modern boutique hotel.

• **Budget:** You'll find yourself enjoying the views at the ST Signature Tanjong Pagar, in the Central Business District, whether at a morning yoga class in the rooftop studio or having an evening nightcap at the rooftop bar.

WHAT TO EAT

One of the great things about Singapore is the delicious food. You can find the best-of-the-best Chinese, Indian, and Malay restaurants. Singaporean food is a yummy fusion of all three. Signature dishes include chicken rice, chili crab (Singapore's national dish), and *laksa,* a spicy and creamy noodle soup.

Din Tai Fung, a Taiwanese restaurant where they make dumplings fresh in front of you, was so delicious! We ended up eating there every single day. The chain has now spread to the U.S., and you can try it in L.A., Seattle, and Las Vegas, among other locations.

Something to note for restaurants, hotels, and taxis: You don't need to tip in Singapore. Tipping is not part of the culture, and workers don't expect it. Most restaurants already include a 10 percent service charge on your bill. However, if you would like to tip, I'm sure it'd be appreciated!

A scarlet macaw takes flight.

DESTINATIONS FOR OLDER KIDS

. . . .

I'm more and more at the stage when my children are *so much fun* to travel with! We're learning more, able to do more, and really experiencing more together. Here are a few spots for older kids (ages eight to 12).

Iceland: Once your kids are good hikers and road-trippers, Iceland is epic. On our next visit, I'd really love to get an RV and cruise around the country. Don't miss the Blue Lagoon, snorkeling the continental rift, and Skógafoss Falls. (See more on page 316.)

Lake Tahoe, Nevada, U.S.A.: Tahoe is incredible with kids of all ages. We've loved skiing in winter at Diamond Peak. In the summer, the water is perfect for kayaking, boating, and swimming. (See more on page 362.)

Sayulita, Mexico: Sayulita is such a fun little surf town, less than an hour's drive from Puerto Vallarta International Airport. We love to visit with my husband's extended family. The cousins all rent surfboards and spend hours on the easy, sandy shore break. There's great food, fun music, and a vibrant town that kids will love!

Nairobi, Kenya: For a mix of culture and wildlife, Nairobi can't be beat. You can visit the Giraffe Centre or, if you can swing it, go to Giraffe Manor for a real bucket list experience. Both offer chances to interact with and learn about giraffes. On our trip, we took cooking lessons so the kids could learn how to make traditional dishes like *ugali,* a dense corn meal porridge.

Galápagos Islands, Ecuador: I think the Galápagos are perfect for kids in the 8-to-12 age range! We loved the incredible wildlife in and out of the water. The Charles Darwin Research Station on Santa Cruz Island offers the chance to see baby tortoises and also admire the adults, some of which are more than 100 years old. (See more page 246.)

Moorea, Tahiti: Tahiti is one of our favorite places to visit as a couple and as a family. Specifically, we love the superplayful island of Moorea. On our most recent visit, we spent the week snorkeling, surfing, fishing, and playing at beaches. Tahiti is also one of the few places in the world where you can swim with humpback whales.

Athens, Greece: Once kids get a little older, they can really start to understand and enjoy Greek history and mythology. Take a hike up to the Acropolis to visit the ancient ruins. And make sure to walk through the Plaka District, a picturesque neighborhood with great shopping, street entertainers, and restaurants.

Hana, Hawaii, U.S.A.: The Road to Hana is a famous bucket list experience on the east side of Maui. It's a great day adventure, but if you have extra time, you should stay! Hana is quite remote and is known for its natural, unspoiled beauty. Be sure to check out the black sand beach at Wai'ānapanapa State Park, Wailua Falls, and the Seven Sacred Pools. Don't miss the yummy food trucks!

Chilean Patagonia: Torres de Paine offers perhaps one of the most bucket list–worthy views on Earth. If your kids are good hikers, this is paradise! Our family loved horseback riding through the park. If your family is the active, outdoorsy type, this place is a must! (See more on page 284.)

Istanbul, Turkey: The food, culture, history, and people combine to make Turkey one of my favorite countries! Even if you just have a long layover at Istanbul Airport, book a day tour through the city. Be sure to visit the Blue Mosque, Grand Bazaar, Basilica Cistern, and Hagia Sophia.

"Good morning, Mr. Giraffe! Care to join us for breakfast?" We had a one-of-a-kind experience at Giraffe Manor in Nairobi, Kenya.

ESPERANCE, AUSTRALIA

See Kangaroos on the Beach in Lucky Bay

Yachts and sailboats dot the turquoise water off the coast of Esperance.

We visited Sydney, Brisbane, and the Gold Coast of Australia back in 2015 when we first took off traveling. I loved them all, and I'd highly recommend the trip. But a little more off the beaten track is Western Australia, and it's well worth the trek. It's way more raw and remote, and we love it!

Western Australia came on our radar after years of traveling and getting really into wildlife. Boy, is Western Australia *wild*.

Our first stop was Perth, where there are quokkas and sea lions. Our last stop was Ningaloo Reef, on the north-

west coast, where we swam with whale sharks!

In between, we visited Esperance and nearby Lucky Bay. The area reminded us of what Southern California might have been like 100 years ago. Empty beaches, a gorgeous coastline, and beautiful ocean views of incredibly turquoise water. I don't know if the people there realize how special the area is.

The coolest part is that wallabies and kangaroos frequent these beaches! We spent multiple days driving from Esperance to Lucky Bay, just enjoying the beach, boogie boarding, and hanging with wallabies.

Esperance is a slow-paced destination, with sluggish Wi-Fi and only a handful of restaurants and parks. We enjoyed chilling out and living a slower life. We visited in early March 2020, right before the world shut down. I'll never forget this peaceful life right before the pandemic.

HOW TO GET THERE

The state of Western Australia takes up almost half the Australian continent. We flew into Perth, then took a domestic flight south to Esperance. From Esperance, we flew to Learmonth Airport, an hour from Coral Bay. There are daily Qantas flights to these airports. In each place, we rented a car. Western Australia would be a great spot to RV.

WHAT TO DO

• Adventure: **Visiting Rottnest Island:** Rottnest is the only place in the world where you'll find the quokka, a cat-size marsupial

There is so much wildlife in Western Australia. You can see— and oftentimes get in the water with—sea lions, orcas, dolphins, manta rays, whale sharks, and so much more. We'll definitely be back to visit again to experience more wildlife!

related to kangaroos and wallabies. They are super cute from the front, but their long tails caused early Dutch settlers to mistake them for rats, hence the island's name. You take a ferry from Perth to the island. We rented bikes for the whole family, had a nice meal at a restaurant, and spent our time looking at quokkas. What's fun is that quokkas will sometimes take selfies with you. (Be sure not to touch them.) And when they do, it looks like they are smiling. **Swimming with sea lions in Jurien Bay:** We drove early in the morning from Perth (which wasn't a problem because we were so jet-lagged) for about two and

These friendly sea lions were playing tag and catch with Dorothy's yellow Bucket List adventure band!

a half hours to board a boat with Jurien Bay Oceanic Experience. The sea lions in Jurien Bay are like puppy dogs and love to play and be engaged. They are really curious, and our whole family even played a game of "catch" with them! **Sandboarding:** Our favorite activity in Esperance was sandboarding. A few shops in town rent sandboards or sleds. We took them out to the nearby dunes and spent the day completely alone playing and sandboarding. Our little Manilla (five years old at the time) couldn't get enough of it.

WHEN TO VISIT

Esperance is a four-season destination, but the best time to go is October and November (late spring in the Southern Hemisphere), when the weather is mild and the flowers are in bloom.

WHERE TO STAY

We stayed in home rentals throughout our trip. It was a great opportunity to get a more local experience.

Fill Up the Tank

Make sure you fill up on gas when you can. Gas stations are few and far between in this area. And be careful driving in the dark—there is a lot of wildlife and it's not uncommon to hit a kangaroo!

WHAT TO EAT

Western Australia is known for some incredible seafood, like fresh, local rock lobster. (Prawns and Pacific and Sydney rock oysters are also popular.) Definitely try the Australian fave, meat pie, filled with chicken or beef, mashed potatoes, mushrooms or cheese, and sometimes bacon. There are also unique and delicious Australian staples—and some have some really adorable names too: Vegemite (a spread of brewer's yeast, vegetables, and spices), Tim Tams (a chocolate cookie), fairy bread (sliced white bread with butter and sprinkles), and pavlova (a meringue dessert).

All of us (especially Manilla!) loved sledding down the sand dunes of Esperance. We did it daily, for hours!

Curious kangaroos may come right up to you on the beaches.

GOLDEN TRIANGLE, INDIA

Visit the Sites on a Tour of New Delhi, Agra, and Jaipur

There's no question why the Taj Mahal is one of the New Seven Wonders of the World.

f it's not already, the Taj Mahal should be on your bucket list. Actually, you definitely need to make it to India once in your life.

In India, all of your senses are heightened. The colors are extra bright, the smells are extra strong, the tastes are extra intense, and the sounds … let's just say there's a lot of honking. But that's all part of the appeal.

Back in 2016, toward the beginning of our travels, our family visited Kathmandu, Nepal. We spent a week there working with a nonprofit called Effect.org that works to fight human trafficking in the region. After an emotional

week learning about the girls being trafficked in bordering Nepal—most from low-income families who had no government record or photo of their daughters—we partnered with the nonprofit to build a school in India. Along with our online community, we raised more than $75,000 to build and support the school, named Kalpana (which means "imagine"), in a high-risk area outside New Delhi. It wasn't until 2018 that we were finally able to visit the school in person.

We were so excited to spend a day with the 75 students at Kalpana. We joined in on their morning prayers and yoga. We witnessed how phenomenal the teachers and staff were, and it was an honor to be a small part of their lives.

After our visit to the school, we set off to tour the famous Golden Triangle—the iconic three cities of New Delhi, Agra, and Jaipur. The pinnacle was the Taj Mahal in Agra.

The Taj was built in the 17th century to honor a Mughal emperor's wife after losing her during childbirth. The monument, an absolutely stunning testament to love and loss, is one of the New Seven Wonders of the World.

HOW TO GET THERE

Delhi Airport is a huge international hub. Since India is vast (and can be overwhelming), I highly recommend using a tour group or a guide. We worked with Cox and Kings and were so happy with our experience. They especially helped curate our trip around the kids. For example, we really wanted to explore the souks (marketplaces) in New Delhi. Our guide felt that might be a little too intense for young kids, so he took us to a smaller, more curated one just outside New Delhi that was still really special.

WHAT TO DO

• Culture: **New Delhi:** In New Delhi, we visited the Akshardham Temple, Jama Masjid, India Gate, Qutb Minar, and Red Fort. Each spot had incredible architecture and a remarkable history. Our guide also took us to an Indian wrestling gym about an hour from the city. Wrestling has been popular in India since ancient times, and we even got to work out with some of the young trainees. Chandni Chowk is one of the largest, busiest, and most chaotic markets in India. It's a fascinating place where you will get an immersive Indian experience! There are plenty of persistent sellers, so it's a good place to work on your haggling. **Agra:** The crown jewel of Agra is the Taj Mahal. We visited early in the morning to try to avoid the heat and the crowds. We still found both! It's hard to avoid crowds at the Taj. But there's a reason: This is one of the most beautiful cultural treasures in the world. Not far from the Taj is the impressive Agra Fort, encompassing palaces and halls. **Jaipur:** We visited Fatehpur Sikri on the way

from Agra to Jaipur, our final stop. The highlight of Jaipur is the Amber Fort. It sits at the top of a bluff and is famous for its large gates, ramparts, and cobblestone streets built out of red sandstone and marble. Please skip the popular elephant ride to the top—the animals are often treated inhumanely. In Jaipur, we spent an evening in Chokhi Dhani Village and had a lovely, authentic Rajasthani meal. Finish your visit to Jaipur with stops at the Jal Mahal, Hawa Mahal, and Jaipur City Palace.

WHEN TO VISIT

We traveled to India in July, right in the middle of rainy season (June to September). It was incredibly hot and humid with monsoon rains. I wouldn't recommend that! The best time of year to visit is October through March, when the weather is pleasant and the flowers are in bloom.

We loved strolling India's markets and seeing the colorful spices.

A view of Agra from the
walls of the Red Fort

WHERE TO STAY

It's difficult to stay in such nice places when you see so much poverty on the streets in India. But the hotels provide safety and sanitation for Western travelers. We stayed at the luxury ITC properties in New Delhi, Agra, and Jaipur.

• **New Delhi:** The Lodhi is a quiet seven-acre (3 ha) oasis 10 minutes from the city center. Another spot, Haveli Dharampura, earned a UNESCO Heritage award for preserving Indian culture; you'll see intricate woodwork, sculptures, and Hindu goddesses engraved in the stone throughout the hotel.

• **Agra:** The Oberoi Amarvilas, with its impressive fountains and terraced lawns, is an easy walk to the Taj Mahal. The PL Palace has a rooftop pool and is in a great location, with nice restaurants right down the block.

• **Jaipur:** Devi Ratn was inspired by an 18th-century astro-nomical observatory, or Jantar Mantar; the influence is seen throughout the hotel.

WHAT TO EAT

The food might just be the number one reason to visit India. It's amazing. Our guides took us to some fantastic local restaurants. Garrett doesn't do particularly well with spicy foods, but he couldn't stop eating, because it just tasted so good!

Suffice it to say, we loved everything we ate. We actually asked our tour guide to order for us, and we were never disappointed. We loved the curries, dals, unique sauces, and, of course, the naan. My favorite thing about Indian food is that it all tastes good together. You can put six completely different dishes on your plate, and somehow it all still tastes amazing!

Our guides gave us bright and unique headwear for our special visit to the Amber Fort in Jaipur.

SEOUL, SOUTH KOREA

Go to a Jimjilbang

Seoul is a city I've visited a number of times—and could go back to again and again.

When I was 20 years old, I traveled with a missionary group through eastern Russia. Every few months, we had to go to South Korea to renew our visas. I loved visiting Seoul then, and I still do now. Seoul is one of the coolest cities—unique, modern, and sophisticated. I love the style, the music, the food. And most of all, I love the people!

We were lucky to get an insider's tour of Seoul when we visited in 2016. My best friend since childhood was living there, teaching English. She knew the ins and outs of the city and showed us a great time.

My husband's best friend introduced us to the Korean *jimjilbang,* or bathhouse. When you arrive at a jimjilbang, you're given special clothes to wear in a coed area, where people can relax, nap on the heated floor, eat delicious food, watch Korean dramas on TV, and go into various small rooms dedicated to traditional medicine. Then you enter a gender-separated area, where you have access to hot and cold pools, dry heated rooms, and services like body scrubs, massages, and acupressure.

Americans tend to think of spas as a fancy day of R&R. In South Korea, however, the jimjilbang is a part of the culture and seen as a necessary part of South Koreans' lives. When you get a scrub at a Korean spa, it's not meant to feel good. The attendants are there to get down to business and clean your body. You'll see entire families spend full days at the jimjilbang together.

When you're in the bathhouse, you are completely naked. It's empowering and a good reminder that a body is just a body—and we need to take good care of it!

HOW TO GET THERE

Incheon International Airport is easy to get in to and out of, and it's quite nice, with many options for food and shopping. It's a great layover airport if Seoul isn't your final destination.

From the airport, we taxied to our hotel. But the easiest way to get around is by subway. It's clean and easy to navigate, and you can hop on right at the airport!

Visit the App Store

Google Maps doesn't work in South Korea. Download another maps app, like Naver. A subway app and a translating app wouldn't hurt either!

WHAT TO DO

• Adventure: **Namsan Tower:** We went to the Namsan Tower (officially known as the N Seoul Tower) late one afternoon so we could catch a nice sunset view of the city. You can take the Namsan Cable Car up to the top, and there are hiking paths as well. Bring a lock with you to add to the famous Love Lock Bridge.

• Culture: **Gwangjang Market:** This market was one of the highlights of our visit. It's such a cool atmosphere seeing all of the different types of local foods, like *bindaetteok* (mung

Street vendors whipped up a delicious dinner on the spot, including our new favorite: stone bowl bibimbap.

Dorothy bravely raises her hand while attending a school with kids her age in Seoul.

Korean barbecue—grilled tableside—is one of our favorite cuisines around the world.

bean pancakes). We walked through the market looking at the fresh, live seafood. We parked at an older woman's stall. With no menu available, she asked us what we wanted to eat and whipped up a meal right in front of us.

WHEN TO VISIT

Seoul has a great four-season climate. The best times to visit are the spring and fall. It'll be less crowded, and you won't have the crazy heat. We visited in July, and it was hot! The last week of March/first week of April is when the cherry trees bloom and would be a great time to visit.

WHERE TO STAY

• **Luxury:** The Shilla Seoul looks traditional and peaceful from the outside, but it has all the modern amenities inside. It houses the world's first Korean restaurant to be awarded a Michelin three-star rating.

• **Comfort:** Nine Tree Premier Hotel Myeongdong II is downtown, nicely located in the bustling Myeongdong district, which is home to a lot of great restaurants and shops.

• **Budget:** Hotel Gracery has great urban views of the surrounding cityscape, and it is located close to the rail station, allowing for easy day trips outside the city.

WHAT TO EAT

Korean food is really delicious. It's my husband's favorite food in the whole world. We especially love Korean barbecue, where you order marinated meats and veggies and then you grill your own food right in front of you. It comes with sides of kimchi, rice, and sauces.

Our next favorite thing to eat in South Korea (especially since we were there in the summer!) is called *bingsu,* a shaved ice dessert topped with fruit, condensed milk, syrups, or red beans.

TONGA

Swim With Humpback Whales

The whales bring us to Tonga almost every year, but the culture has made us truly fall in love with this country.

Years ago, my husband saw a photo taken by Scott Portelli of a person in the water with a humpback whale. It blew his mind that it was even possible to get in the water with these creatures. He quickly did some research and found out the photo was taken in the waters of Vava'u, Tonga. No surprise, the very first thing on our family's bucket list was to swim with whales in Tonga! We made it there in September 2015.

The waters surrounding the Tongan islands are the birthing and breeding grounds for southern humpback whales. And Tonga is one of the very few countries in the world where it is legal to get in the water with these magnificent mammals. The government allows this interaction with caution geared toward conservation: Only a limited number of permits are issued, and only a few operators are licensed to go out with the whales. On top of that, only four people are allowed in the water with a group of whales at a time. I am so impressed by the level of respect the Tongans have for the whales and the care they take in teaching visitors how to interact with the whales too.

There are not enough words to adequately describe what it feels like to be in the water with a humpback whale. It's an experience I truly wish everyone could have in life. I'll never forget holding my daughter's hand while looking at a mother whale swimming with her calf.

HOW TO GET THERE

Getting to Vava'u isn't easy. You can only get there by flying through Fiji or New Zealand. There's a direct flight from Nadi, Fiji, to Vava'u two days a week. Otherwise, you need to fly through the Tongan capital, Nuku'alofa.

Book your humpback whale excursion through one of a few permitted operators. These operators follow strict guidelines to ensure the safety of the whales and to protect and preserve their natural environment. Each boat has a maximum of eight guests. Spots fill up quickly, so plan and book far in advance. We have been back to Vava'u four times and worked with

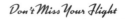

Don't Miss Your Flight
....

If you're flying through Nuku'alofa, be aware that the international and domestic terminals at Fua'amotu International Airport are about a three-minute taxi drive apart.

Whales in the Wild for each visit. Your whale tour operator can help you arrange lodging and airport transfers as well.

WHAT TO DO

• Adventure: **Swallows Cave:** This is an incredible cave for divers and snorkelers. The mouth of the cave is quite large to swim through, and once inside, the sunlight coming through gives off some incredible blue silhouettes. Thousands of small fish form a kaleidoscope to swim through. It's a magical

LEFT: Tonga pelargonium RIGHT: Did a rainbow really lead us to whales in Tonga?

place! You can ask your whale boat to stop at Swallows at the end of your day for a quick snorkel.

• Culture: **Sunday services:** Everything shuts down in Tonga on Sundays, including the whale boats. If you walk around on a Sunday morning, you'll hear beautiful a cappella singing coming from different churches. It's one of my favorite things to do in Tonga. Tongans have beautiful singing voices, and we go out of our way to make sure to attend church in Tonga. **Utaka-longalu Market:** This is a small market with local fish, fruits, vegetables, jewelry, art, and wooden crafts.

WHEN TO VISIT

Whale season runs from July through October, when mothers are there to give birth. You'll have different types of encounters throughout the course of the season. Early on, the mothers are protective of their babies. As they grow older, the calves become more curious and playful. In mid-season, you'll see more heat runs, when male whales pursue a female whale.

WHERE TO STAY

• **Luxury:** Fafa Island Resort is guarded by a coral reef, allowing for great snorkeling in the crystal clear water. This island feels like a private hideaway, with only 13 rooms. The resort was destroyed in a tsunami but is rebuilding.

• **Comfort:** Mystic Sands is located on a private beach with its own pier for taking boats out to dive or go whale-watching.

• **Budget:** Reef Resort has five bungalows situated across from the Japanese Coral Garden—a popular snorkeling spot.

WHAT TO EAT

If I'm being honest, the food in Tonga is not the best. Grocery stores are equivalent to 7/11s, with mostly processed foods, since so much of the food here has to be imported from far away. I highly recommend bringing some staples from home. Lunch is provided on whale boats. Given the lack of grocery options, it's better to eat out for dinner, and there are a handful of good restaurants to choose from.

Stroll the streets of Tonga on Sundays and listen to the congregations sing hymns.

Garrett soaks in the moment at this special spot.

Swimming with humpback whales will fill your heart with joy—and your dive mask with tears.

TANZANIA

Go on Safari in the Serengeti

We don't visit places more than once too often, but Tanzania is a place we visit every other year.

'm at my happiest on an African safari. There's nothing like it in the whole world: waking up with the sunrise, having a quick sip of warm tea, and bundling up in your safari vehicle as you go out on a game drive. Each day is so different, and you never know what you're going to see. Over the last few years, we've probably spent more than 60 days on safari. It never gets old for me. We've gone on safari in South Africa, Zimbabwe, Zambia, and Kenya, and while each has amazing aspects, I have to say, safari in Tanzania is my favorite!

The Serengeti is famous for having a ton of wildlife.

We've gone multiple times during the summer months to catch the Great Migration. This is the time of year when millions of zebras, wildebeests, and other herd animals migrate from the southern parts of the Serengeti to the Masai Mara National Reserve in Kenya. It's an absolute sight to see!

Safari is a classic bucket list experience. If you're only going to go once in your lifetime, go when your kids are old enough to appreciate it. That being said, we took our kids as young as eight months old on safari, and they did great! Important note: Not all—or many!—lodges will allow young children on game drives. So make sure you find a lodge that not only allows their participation but also caters to families. It will make such a difference if the lodge has activities for the kiddos.

HOW TO GET THERE

The best way to get to the Serengeti is to fly into Kilimanjaro International Airport. There are direct flights from Amsterdam and Doha. (If you're coming from the U.S., it might be worth taking a long layover in one of these cities to help adjust to the time difference.) Flights usually arrive late in the day, so spend a night in a lodge or hotel near Kilimanjaro or in nearby Arusha. In the morning, little hopper "bush planes" get you to your lodge. Beware: These little bush planes often allow only soft luggage and have weight restrictions—so pack light! The good news: Almost all lodges offer daily laundry!

WHAT TO DO

• Adventure: **Go on a night drive:** Find a lodge that offers night drives, because a whole lot more action happens in the animal world after the sun goes down! We love going out after dinner when you can hear the lions and hyenas on the prowl.

• Culture: **Visit the Maasai:** Most lodges in Tanzania have a close relationship with the local Maasai, a seminomadic pastoral tribe, recognizable by their red clothing. The Maasai culture, in my opinion, is one of the most unique in the world. Village visits often include watching how they milk and draw blood from cows, as well as an overview of daily life. Talk to your lodge in advance about what you might bring to the village—such as little toys like Matchbox cars or treats for the kids. Visiting the Maasai has been eye-opening, humbling, and, for me, life-changing. **Play soccer:** Soccer is the world's most beloved sport and is played even in the Serengeti. We like to play soccer and volleyball with

Extend Your Trip

If you have time, add a night or two in Arusha or Kilimanjaro to the front of your trip to help adjust to the time zone before heading off on safari. On the back end of your trip, add a beach stay in Zanzibar after your safari adventure.

the lodge staff, even if that means we need to shoo away the wildebeests and zebras!

• Service: **Bring supplies:** Ask your lodge or your travel agent what their local outreach programs include. There are often opportunities with schools, clean-water initiatives, or health clinics that are grateful for helpful visitors. Before arriving, we message the program and ask, "What do you need right now?" Then we pack these supplies to donate.

Visit in the summer during the Great Migration when you can see a massive dazzle of zebras.

No visit to Tanzania is complete without a day at a local Maasai village. This is our guide, Sekato, who proudly showed us his home.

WHEN TO VISIT

The wildlife in the Serengeti changes year-round. In January and February, you can catch lots of babies being born. Late June through September are the best months for the Great Migration. You can't really go too wrong with the Serengeti, though!

WHERE TO STAY

• **Luxury:** TAASA Lodge is our favorite place to safari. It's a home away from home, and the staff here is family to us! We don't go back to many places more than once, but we've been here five times now and continue to host group expeditions every other year at TAASA. The lodge is right outside Serengeti National Park in a concession that allows safari jeeps to go off-roading and take night drives in the area. And they really cater to kids.

• **Comfort:** Siringit Serengeti Camp is an intimate lodge with just 10 tents. Located in Serengeti National Park, it is right along the Great Migration path. The camp also offers a hot-air balloon experience for a different view of the Serengeti.

• **Budget:** Each tent at Kubu Kubu Tented Lodge has its own private terrace in the center of the Serengeti. That means you can sometimes see the Great Migration right from your tent!

WHAT TO EAT

The safari lodges all do a nice job with food, which is usually included in the cost of your stay. Every day starts with a nice spread, perhaps eggs and pancakes. Lunch and dinner are often multiple courses. While on safari, the jeep will stop in the afternoon for tea and cookies. Some lodges also offer a sundowner experience with drinks and snacks at sunset (usually deep in the bush).

Most safaris include a two- or three-night stay at three different lodges, and each property is very different.

BERMUDA, UNITED KINGDOM

Explore Caves and Shipwrecks

You can see Bermuda's colonial British history while roaming downtown.

Bermuda is an underrated gem. If you, like me, thought Bermuda was part of the Caribbean, well, you're wrong! Bermuda is actually about 900 miles (1,450 km) north of the Caribbean—on the same latitude as North Carolina—but its crystal clear, turquoise water will have you fooled. The archipelago is also the world's northernmost tropical reef, and boy, does it have some incredible ocean wildlife.

The main island is actually quite small (just 20 miles [32 km] from tip to tip), and as soon as you land, you can feel the tropical-yet-classy vibe. Most buildings are painted a fun, vibrant pink, blue, green, or yellow, and they all have matching white limestone roofs. These brightly colored buildings, paired with pink sandy beaches and turquoise water, add up to some absolutely beautiful surroundings. And as it is a U.K. territory, you'll see the British influence, like old British phone booths, around the island.

If your family is new to international travel, Bermuda is an easy place to start. It's incredibly clean, they accept the U.S. dollar, and English is the predominant language. Plus, Bermudans are especially wonderful and welcoming people—and super proud of where they are from.

You don't necessarily need a ton of time to "do" Bermuda. A lot of the beauty of the island comes with the beaches. So pack your sunscreen and towel and just go relax. Did I mention the south shore's *pink* sand!?! It's beautiful!

HOW TO GET THERE

The flight to Bermuda is an easy two hours or so from cities in the eastern United States, including New York; Washington, D.C.; Boston; Charlotte, North Carolina; and Atlanta. L.F. Wade International Airport will be your arrival point no matter where you're flying in from.

Taxis, scooters, ferries, and water taxis are the main means of transportation on the island. Tourists are not allowed to rent cars in Bermuda! And getting a driver's license on the island is a rigorous process.

WHAT TO DO

• Adventure: **Crystal Caves:** Bermuda has an impressive cave system formed over millions of years and filled with stalagmite and stalactite formations. Our family loved our day spent underground. The caves are huge and quite open (which is great for claustrophobes like me!), and there are beautiful, clear blue pools. **Wreck diving:** The Bermuda Triangle may be a myth, but there sure are a lot of wreck dives in Bermuda! There's a reason it's often called the "shipwreck capital of the world." Garrett and I enjoyed a great dive with three wrecks, one from the U.S. Civil War called the *Mary Celestia,* and two in Thunder Bay, the *Montana* and the *Constellation.* The reefs around these ships are stunning, and the history is fascinating! **Bermuda Aquarium, Museum, and Zoo:** This is a family favorite, and we visited on both of our trips. The aquarium showcases ocean wildlife from local waters. Go early to catch the morning feedings!

The Bermuda Aquarium, Museum, and Zoo is worth a visit with the family.

We always tried to end our days in Bermuda with a sunset pool session at the Hamilton Princess.

Bermuda has an incredible cave system where you can stroll through the stalactite formations.

• Service: **Accessible resources:** WindReach Bermuda, a non-profit focused on accessibility, is a beautiful, four-acre (1.6 ha) facility that includes an activity center, animal zone, therapeutic riding center, and fully accessible playground. WindReach accepts volunteers and donations.

WHEN TO VISIT

The busiest season is between May and September. The island can be windy, so pack a jacket. Winters are slower, less crowded, and a bit chilly (average temps in the 60s Fahrenheit [high teens Celsius]). Diving is nice in the winter, with great visibility, but bring a wet suit since the water gets cold. Many restaurants and tours shut down in the winter. But visitors still come for the year-round golf or the many running, sailing, and boating races.

WHERE TO STAY

• **Luxury:** On both of our visits, we stayed at the Hamilton Princess, an iconic pink luxury hotel. Throughout the property, there's incredible art, adorable shops, delicious restaurants, and all the amenities you could want, including a kids' club. It's right on Hamilton Harbour, within walking distance of all the happenings on Front Street.

• **Comfort:** Newstead Belmont Hills is 20 minutes from everything you want to see, and there's complimentary transportation to both downtown Hamilton and the beach. The infinity pool overlooking Hamilton Harbour is a draw, as is the world-class golf course.

• **Budget:** We *love* having our own kitchen, and the ones at Rosemont Guest Suites come fully equipped. The gardens are lovely as well.

WHAT TO EAT

Most of the meals in Bermuda focus on superfresh seafood, and that's great by me. The traditional dish is codfish and potatoes, which is eaten as a standard Sunday breakfast in Bermuda. We also like the fish chowder, fish cakes, and fish sandwiches. Peas and rice is another must-have.

SEYCHELLES

Explore a Tropical Paradise in the Indian Ocean

The giant rocks and pristine sandy beaches of Seychelles are truly special.

This archipelago of 115 islands in the Indian Ocean is an absolute bucket list destination. If you've seen photos of an untouched coastline with sandy shores, bright blue water, and giant granite boulders, that very well might have been Seychelles!

Flying into Seychelles, I was reminded of Oahu, Hawaii. The main island, Mahé, holds 90 percent of the population and is centered around a lush mountain. But unlike many other islands, this one isn't volcanic; it's made of granite.

We tacked Seychelles on to a trip to Africa in the summer of 2021. It was a luxurious and relaxing way to end our time bouncing around five countries on the continent. Besides having some of the most beautiful beaches in the world, Seychelles is also home to Desroches Island, known for its great surfing and deep-sea fishing and an incredible tortoise sanctuary.

HOW TO GET THERE

There are direct flights from London or Middle Eastern hubs like Doha or Dubai. Plus, there are a handful of flights within Africa via Nairobi, Johannesburg, or Cape Town. The small Seychelles International Airport is easy to get to via domestic hopper flights, or you can arrive by ferry from the nearby islands of Praslin or La Digue. Many of the smaller islands in Seychelles are owned by private resorts. Once you reach your destination, you can explore by foot or bike.

We spent a few days in Mahé, then flew to Desroches on a private charter, which flies a few times a week.

WHAT TO DO

• Adventure: **Island-hop:** Visit the incredible beaches of Praslin or La Digue on a short (1 hour to Praslin, 1 hour 45 minutes to La Digue) ferry ride from Mahé. One of the prettiest beaches, the Vallée de Mai on Praslin, is a UNESCO World Heritage site famous for its unique flora and fauna. **Scuba:** Diving is great year-round, with visibility at its absolute best (100-foot [30 m] visibility) in the shoulder months. Whale shark diving season runs from September through November. **Surf:** We visited in the summer and were excited to be there during big-wave surf season, which runs from April to October. We used Tropicsurf to book full-family surf lessons.

They helped each of us at our varying skill levels—Dorothy was eight, Manilla six, and Cali four—and we *all* got so much better! **See the giant tortoises:** Visit the Aldabra Atoll, the second largest coral atoll in the world and home to giant Aldabra tortoises. (We saw them on Desroches.) These incredible reptiles can live more than 100 years and weigh over 750 pounds (340 kg). This is the only place in the world where you can see this species!

• Culture: **Visit Sir Selwyn Selwyn-Clarke Market:** At this market, widely known as the Victoria Market, you'll find local handicrafts as well as bright and bold textiles. You'll see (and smell!) all the local fresh fish, fruits, and incredible spices like cinnamon, saffron, cloves, anise, and nutmeg. It's a great

Flavorful Creole food

place to learn about local food and culture, as this is where locals go to shop. The market is open 4 a.m. to 5 p.m., Monday through Saturday.

WHEN TO VISIT

Temperatures in Seychelles are usually around a balmy 85°F (29°C) year-round. The best months to visit are April/May or October/November, when the trade winds are calmer. You'll also see fewer crowds if you avoid the summer months.

Because of their location, the islands generally stay out of the path of major cyclones that occur in the Indian Ocean. A huge bonus!

WHERE TO STAY

• **Luxury:** We stayed at the Four Seasons properties on both Mahé and Desroches. As a family with young kids, we loved having a spacious villa and our own pool. Our kids especially loved the kids' club. On Desroches, each guest is given a bike to get around the island.

• **Comfort:** The Carana Beach Hotel is located in a picturesque bay on Mahé and has only 40 chalets, so it's a pretty intimate experience. The spa treatments are nice too.

• **Budget:** Le Nautique on La Digue is fringed by a reef and the granitic boulders that define Seychelles. Each apartment has ocean views.

WHAT TO EAT

Seychellois food has a lot of Creole influences. Traditional dishes include freshly caught grilled fish, coconut curries (that do tend to be *hot*), lentils, breadfruit cooked every which way, and sweet fried bananas. We especially enjoyed the fresh tropical fruit and juices.

Tortoises roam throughout Desroches Island. Our kids loved offering them tasty leaves.

The markets in Seychelles are full of fresh produce and spices.

Garrett, Cali, and Manilla catch a party wave on Desroches Island.

LAKE TAHOE, NEVADA, U.S.A.

Try Wakesurfing

I can't decide which season is best in Lake Tahoe! We've experienced each and have never been disappointed.

hesitate to share Lake Tahoe, because it's so awesome I almost want to keep it as our little secret.

Frankly, I'd take a lake over an ocean (don't tell my husband!). I have fond memories of spending time on my family's boat as a child, waterskiing and tubing in a reservoir near our home.

Recently, our family has fallen in love with wakesurfing. We visited Lake Tahoe in early August, when the lake is just warm enough that you don't need a wet suit. We rented a wakesurfing boat for some afternoon sessions with a great company called Tahoe Surf Company. They had patient and knowledgeable instructors who helped each of us get way better in such a short time!

Lake Tahoe's water … words just can't do it justice! You truly have to see it for yourself!

HOW TO GET THERE

We get to Lake Tahoe from Reno, Nevada, which has a small yet convenient airport (Reno-Tahoe International) just a 50-minute scenic drive from the lake. Rent a car while you're there. Agencies are conveniently located right at baggage claim.

If you're looking for a great road trip, you can also drive to Lake Tahoe from California and either stay on that side of the lake or cross to the Nevada side. It's about a two-hour drive from the Sacramento airport and about five hours from San Francisco.

WHAT TO DO

• **Adventure:** **Tahoe *via ferrata*:** We had tried via ferrata—a climbing route with cables—in Alaska and gave it another shot at Palisades Tahoe. I thought it was the perfect amount of challenge and overcoming fears while staying perfectly safe. **Rafting in Truckee:** The Truckee River is filled with people of all ages rafting, tubing, and floating by. You can go at any speed you like on a perfect summer afternoon. **Kayaking in Sand Harbor State Park:** Rent kayaks to explore the shoreline of Sand Harbor. We loved our time swimming in the crystal clear, brisk water! **Wakesurfing:** This might be something for families with older kids. If that's you, and you love water sports, Lake Tahoe is a great place to give wakesurfing a try. You can rent a wakesurfing boat or charter one with a crew who will teach you the ropes. **Skiing/snowboarding:** If you're visiting Lake Tahoe in the winter, enjoy the slopes at Diamond Peak Ski Resort. The resort is known for its stunning panoramic views of Lake Tahoe. **Snow tubing/sledding:** There are a few ski resorts in Tahoe that offer snow tubing, which is a really fun activity for the whole family. Palisades Tahoe and Boreal Mountain have good hills. Or just grab a sled and find a good hill nearby. We loved sledding at Tahoe Meadows and at the Incline Village snow play area. It wouldn't hurt to have a friendly snowball fight while you're there, either!

WHEN TO VISIT

Tahoe is a great four-season destination. We've been during Christmastime and actually experienced the "storm of the century" when Tahoe got 17 feet (5 m) of snow! We had to dig our-

Don't Miss
....

Check out South Lake Tahoe too! Each side of the lake has its own vibe. While North Lake Tahoe is a bit more relaxed, with small-town charm, the South Shore has more restaurants and activities along with a buzzier nightlife.

selves out of our rental home and sled down the hill just to get to the car. Still, it was charming around the holidays!

Our second visit was during the summer. Lake Tahoe is quite busy in the summer, but a warm lake is just perfection—offering ample opportunity to kayak, boat, and participate in water sports.

Garrett pretends he's not terrified of heights on a *via ferrata*.

Someone should buy
Dad some winter shoes!

For time in or on the lake, September is the best month for warm water *and* stunning foliage.

Pack for all weather conditions. The lake weather can change quickly, so make sure you have layers, waterproof gear, and good walking shoes.

WHERE TO STAY

We loved staying in the cute town of Incline Village, which has a great Hyatt Regency that is very family friendly. The resort has a pool, beach access, a casino, and fantastic restaurants.

We've also stayed in a cute condo right in town and in a rental mountain home. I really enjoy cooking for my family when we have the opportunity while traveling, and there's a great grocery store in Incline Village that made that easy for us!

WHAT TO EAT

There are excellent restaurant options for fresh seafood, barbecue, craft beer, pizza, and comfort foods in downtown Tahoe. For a nicer night out, try Chart House, which overlooks the lake and is known for its legendary seafood dishes (but you'll also find steak and vegetarian alternatives on the menu). If you can find childcare, Edgewood Restaurant, in a lodge-like setting, is a terrific date night spot. The American fare is delicious and the lake views are gorgeous! In South Lake Tahoe, on the California side, Driftwood Cafe and Base Camp Pizza Co. are great family-friendly options near the resorts.

The highlight of our summer visit was rafting the Truckee River.

ANTIGUA, GUATEMALA

Explore the Brightly Colored Streets

There is so much color throughout the city in Antigua.

Guatemala will always have a special place in my heart. When I think of Guatemala, I picture the beautiful smiles on the locals' faces.

We first visited the country in 2018 for a project with an NGO called Healing Waters International, which works to end the global water crisis. Our goal was to introduce systems for clean, filtered water to more rural areas.

We went back to Guatemala in 2019. Let me tell you, it has so much to offer. Guatemala has the trifecta in our book—adventure, culture, and service. There's a whole lot of history in places like Tikal, a ton of adventure with great jungles and beaches on the coast, and some really special opportunities for acts of service.

Our hub for both our visits was Antigua, which was once the capital city and is now a UNESCO World Heritage site. It's an incredibly charming and vibrant city with adorable cobblestone walkways, brightly colored buildings, artsy shops, boutique hotels, and lots of delicious food.

HOW TO GET THERE

Guatemala is very easy to get in to and out of through its capital, Guatemala City. Avianca airlines has direct flights from the U.S., as well as Central and South America. You can also find direct flights on United, American, and Delta from international hubs in the U.S., including Atlanta, Miami, Dallas, Houston, and New York. Guatemala City itself isn't the safest area for tourists, so once you arrive, head directly to your hotel or final destination.

Antigua is about 30 miles (50 km) from the airport, but plan for traffic. It should take around an hour. The roads can be difficult to drive; ideally book a guide or driver to help you navigate. On both of our visits, we had a driver with a van. If you're moving around a bunch, I suggest you do the same. If you're only visiting Antigua, you can grab a taxi from the airport. It's easy to get around Antigua by bus or on foot.

WHAT TO DO

• Adventure: **Lake Atitlán:** Central America's deepest lake, Atitlán, sits just 50 miles (80 km) outside Antigua. It's one of the most stunning and unique lakes in the world, as it is surrounded by three volcanoes. The handful of quaint villages scattered around the area are only accessible by boat. Spend

Plane Hop
....

Tikal National Park in Guatemala is a must-visit, but it's a plane ride away from Antigua. If you can tack it on to a trip, please do! There is so much incredible Maya history throughout Guatemala that shouldn't be missed.

the day walking its perimeter or rent a boat to go out on the water. **Cerro de la Cruz (Hill of the Cross):** The Hill of the Cross is a great hike that ends with a stunning overlook of the Antigua Valley and Volcán de Agua. The short hike, just a half mile (0.8 km), seems easy, but you can get in a good workout climbing the 333 concrete steps to the overlook. If that's not in the cards for you or the kiddos, there are *tuk-tuks* (motorized three-wheelers) and taxis for hire that will take you up to the summit. Make sure you go on a clear, cloudless day for the best views of the volcano. **Iglesia de San Francisco:** If you stay in Antigua, you have to stop by Iglesia de San Francisco. This church was built more than four centuries ago and experienced

LEFT: A northern emerald toucanet perches on a branch. RIGHT: Manilla, Cali, and Dorothy share a sweet moment.

Garrett delivered clean water to a rural community as part of our service trip with Healing Waters.

Guatemala has a ton of fresh, flavorful, and locally sourced foods.

significant damage in an earthquake back in the 1700s. The church was rebuilt and is still an active place of worship, but many of the ruins of the original 16th-century building can still be seen.

• Culture: **Explore:** Antigua is a World Heritage site that dates back to the 1500s. You can see Renaissance and baroque architecture, and the streets, shops, restaurants, and markets are easy to get lost in. Snag your Instagram picture at the iconic Santa Catalina Arch with the glorious Volcán de Agua in the background. Get there early for fewer crowds and nice light.

WHEN TO VISIT

Guatemala's temperatures are quite nice year-round. Dry season, with cooler, less humid weather, runs from November to April.

WHERE TO STAY

Part of Antigua's charm rests in its many adorable boutique hotels. On both of our visits, we stayed at the Casa Santa

Rosa Hotel. The hotel was cute and comfortable, and it had a lovely staff, plus a big open courtyard for kids to play around in. It was the perfect home base for our service expedition.

• **Comfort:** Posada de Don Rodrigo is a boutique hotel with quaint rooms that have mahogany furniture and handwoven blankets on the bed.

WHAT TO EAT

One of my favorite things about Guatemala is the food. Because of the mineral-rich volcanic soil here, they have incredible produce. We stopped at multiple farm-to-table restaurants, many of which also offer farm stays. One of my favorites was Saberico, where we ate breakfast—and returned for dinner!

As for local cuisine, it's a delicious blend of Spanish and Maya cuisines. A typical Guatemalan breakfast consists of eggs, black beans, corn tortillas, avocado, cheese, and fried plantains. Yum!

DESTINATIONS FOR PARENTS

....

Garrett and I have always made our marriage and time together (apart from kids) a priority. At least once a year we try to get away, just the two of us. There are some things that are just more fun and enjoyable without the littles (although we miss them deeply!). Here are a few of our favorite spots we've visited over the years.

Bora Bora, Tahiti: Garrett and I have visited Tahiti nine times since we've been married. One of the most stunning, iconic, bucket list–worthy views in the world is looking onto the island of Bora Bora from one of the motus (reef islands). We've stayed in overwater bungalows at both the Four Seasons and the InterContinental. I don't know if there's a more romantic place on Earth!

Raja Ampat, Indonesia: Garrett and I share a love of scuba diving, and Indonesia is one of the best places to dive in the world, thanks to its healthy fish and coral reefs. Along with some friends, we chartered a boat called *Tiger Blue* to take us to Raja Ampat. We did some hiking and swimming, but, most important, we went scuba diving.

Greek islands: If you can't tell by now, Garrett and I love traveling by boat. Perhaps my favorite vacation together was on a catamaran through the Greek islands. There are a bunch of different islands to stop at, each unique in its own way. There's a lot of history, culture, and incredible food in Greece, and I'm here for it! (You can also do this with kids; see more on page 250.)

Northern California, U.S.A.: We celebrated our 10-year anniversary in Northern California revisiting our old stomping grounds in Silicon Valley; relaxing at the Ritz-Carlton, Half Moon Bay; playing tennis; and taking nice long walks on the beach. Then we had a vow-renewal ceremony at a property in Carmel-by-the-Sea, a small beach town on the Monterey Peninsula. If you visit Carmel, there's some great surfing near Carmel Beach and a few state parks to hike.

Panama: If you are looking for a remote, unique, and luxurious getaway, check out Islas Secas in Panama. Garrett and I spent a week here scuba diving, learning how to ride eFoils (a combination of a hoverboard and surfboard), and relaxing at their spa.

Queenstown, New Zealand: I've already expressed my deep love for New Zealand as a great family destination (see page 182), but it's also a great couples' retreat, because there are so many "grown-up" activities. We loved our experience bungee jumping, white water rafting, and sleeping over at Milford Sound.

Venice, Italy: It's no secret that Venice is a romantic hot spot. It's a great place to roam cute streets while holding hands, eat at romantic canalside restaurants, and take a gondola ride, of course! We stayed at the Westin Europa & Regina, now the St. Regis.

Kauai, Hawaii, U.S.A.: I love all of the islands of Hawaii, but the most beautiful, green, and lush by far is Kauai. There are great waterfall hikes, beaches, snorkeling spots, and the famous Nāpali Coast. Plus, there are tons of romantic resorts and hotels to choose from.

Kigali, Rwanda: Kids under the age of 16 are not allowed on gorilla treks; otherwise I'd bring them along. But I highly recommend a volcano safari with your partner. Trekking for wild gorillas in the mountains with Garrett is something I'll never forget. You hike a few hours a day and are rewarded with the sight of families of gorillas—it's magical!

We fell in love every day in Islas Secas, Panama, on a kidless getaway.

ZIMBABWE

Witness a Buzzing Water Hole on Safari

Whether you zip across it or just stand above it, you *must* make a visit to Victoria Falls.

If visiting a country in Africa is on your bucket list, Zimbabwe is a great place to start! "Zim," as Zimbabweans call it, not only has incredible landscapes and wildlife but also some of the most down-to-earth people we've met. And it's one of the more modern countries in Africa, which makes it a good introduction to the continent.

We spent all of May 2021 in Zimbabwe. We started our visit at the mystical and magical Victoria Falls. The famous Zambezi River flows through the country, with its pinnacle at the falls. You can visit the gushing cascade from both Zambia and Zimbabwe—bring your passport if you want to cross the bridge between the two sides. There is so much for thrill seekers to do at the falls, including white water rafting, bungee jumping, rope swinging, zip-lining, rappelling, and hiking the beautiful trails surrounding the falls. You can also stand right on the edge of the falls in Devil's Pool, a thrill in itself!

But our Zimbabwe highlight was at Somalisa Camp in Hwange National Park, where we were told that elephants frequent a nearby water hole. On our first night, we were eating dinner under the stars when we heard some splashing and slurping sounds. We slowly got up and walked over to the water hole, where we were mere feet away from a group of elephants drinking! We learned that these elephants come through every few hours, along with such other animals as zebras, giraffes, warthogs, and lions.

HOW TO GET THERE

We flew into Victoria Falls Airport. Our trip included six different stops in Zimbabwe; some required ground transfers and others small chartered bush plane transfers. We ended our trip in Harare, the capital of the country.

WHAT TO DO

• Adventure: **Zip-lining at Victoria Falls:** We split up to ride tandem for this one—Mom with Dorothy, and Dad with Manilla. (Cali was too young to do this at the time so hung back with one of us while the other had their turn.) The kids loved it so much that Dorothy and Manilla asked to ride again together—without Mom and Dad! These brave kiddos zipped 1,394 feet (425 m) across the gorge by themselves! We booked our

Use an Agent
....
In Zimbabwe, we used Mavros Safaris, a local family-owned travel agency. They are absolute experts on Zimbabwe and southern African travel.

experience with Wild Horizons, and their staff made us feel very safe. **Fishing in the Zambezi River:** The prize fish in the Zambezi is the tigerfish. We spent one afternoon catching multiple fish in an hour. Our chef back at camp made fish nuggets with our catch for our dinner. Careful, though—if you catch a catfish, you have to give it a kiss. It's a local tradition!

• Culture: **Cave art:** Throughout Zimbabwe, there are caves full of art painted by the San people. This art dates back 5,000 to 10,000 years! You can see some of the incredibly preserved art at Matobo National Park, which is also known for its healthy populations of black and white rhinos.

• Service: **Amalinda:** During our stay at the Amalinda Lodge, we spent an afternoon playing soccer and doing activities with

We looked for hippos and crocs on a water safari at Singita Pamushana Lodge.

the kids at a nearby orphanage. In Gonarezhou National Park, there are opportunities to sponsor newly introduced black rhinos or the preservation of a baobab tree. **Malilangwe Trust:** At the Singita Pamushana Lodge, we learned all about the Malilangwe Trust program, in which local scouts are hired and trained to guard the Malilangwe Wildlife Reserve against poaching. We were so impressed with their work that we ran a social media campaign to raise $5,000 toward their junior ranger program.

WHEN TO VISIT

The ideal time to visit is July through October, and the best months for good weather and lots of wildlife are August and September. Game-viewing is at its peak in these months, when the natural water holes have dried up, pushing large herds to congregate at lakes and human-made water holes and rivers.

WHERE TO STAY

We stayed at four different lodges on our monthlong visit: Matetsi Victoria Falls (a luxury lodge that offers family suites and private villas); Somalisa Camp in Hwange, where we saw animals congregate around nearby water holes; Amalinda Lodge (a safari lodge in the Matobo Hills, a UNESCO World Heritage site and the oldest national park in Zimbabwe); and Singita Pamushana Lodge (set on the 123,500-acre [50,000 ha] Malilangwe Wildlife Reserve). We also camped in the bush under the stars in Gonarezhou National Park. I can't recommend each of these places and experiences enough. They were each so different and worthwhile!

WHAT TO EAT

The most popular local meal is *sadza,* a dough made from finely ground cornmeal and water. Locals eat sadza with almost everything, especially meat stew. It's often compared to polenta because of its denseness and texture.

The most popular local products in Zim are Mazoe Orange Crush, a soda, and Dr. Troubles chili sauce. You gotta try them both!

You can see herds of wild African elephants while on safari in Zimbabwe.

Dorothy was in awe of the painted rock art.

Family swim in Zimbabwe! If any of us look a little nervous, it's because we know that crocs aren't far away (but our guides told us they don't go into water this shallow).

COOK ISLANDS, NEW ZEALAND

Get Your Passport Stamped at the World's Smallest Post Office

Verdant mountains tower over the coast of the stunning Cook Islands.

The Cook Islands were the perfect spot for our family. This self-governing collection of islands in the South Pacific had both my and my husband's favorite things: For me, it was the New Zealand influence. I love all things Kiwi, and a lot of Kiwis vacation in the Cook Islands. For Garrett, it was that cool Polynesian vibe.

We arrived in the Cook Islands directly after a visit to French Polynesia, via a direct flight from Papeete to Rarotonga. When New Zealanders travel, they like to have a kitchen, so we were thrilled that all of the places we stayed in the Cook Islands had that homey atmosphere.

As much as we loved Rarotonga, the real jewel of the Cook Islands for us was an even smaller island called Aitutaki, which has a quintessential tropical vibe and is usually sunnier than Rarotonga. If you're gonna go this far around the globe, make the time to check out Aitutaki!

HOW TO GET THERE

It's about a four-hour flight from Auckland to Rarotonga. Keep in mind, the flight crosses the international date line, so plan on losing or gaining a day on either end. You can also fly to Rarotonga from Honolulu, Papeete, Tahiti, or Sydney.

It's easy to rent a car at the airport terminal. The island of Rarotonga has one road with two roundabouts and no stoplights. It takes about 50 minutes to circumnavigate the whole island. It's a hopper flight to Aitutaki.

WHAT TO DO

• Adventure: **The S.S. *Matai* wreck:** This is the most famous shipwreck to snorkel or dive near Rarotonga. The passenger and cargo ship was en route from San Francisco to Wellington in 1916 when it sank 2,625 feet (800 m) offshore. After more than 100 years on the ocean's floor, it has a nice reef around it. You can even see the ship's boiler from above. **The lagoon on Aitutaki:** Aitutaki's Coral Lagoon has the most gorgeous crystal clear water and sandy bottom. You can explore on your own and walk out at low tide, or you can hire a boat for the day. The boats take you to get your passport stamped at the world's smallest post office, on One Foot Island, where you can also stop for lunch. (The stamp is in the shape of a foot!) You can enjoy the day island-hopping and snorkeling around beautiful ocean reefs.

• Culture: **Muri night market:** Every Tuesday, Wednesday, Thursday, and Sunday, the night market in Muri Beach on Rarotonga boasts a ton of good food and music and a few vendors. It attracts plenty of locals and tourists alike. **Island night:** On both Rarotonga and Aitutaki, multiple resorts offer an Island Night show. Similar to what people think of as a Hawaiian luau, these shows include a massive buffet with traditional foods and Polynesian fire dancers. **Church:** Plan to spend part of your Sunday like the locals. You'll be welcomed with smiles at one of the many churches and treated to beautiful singing!

WHEN TO VISIT

The shoulder months of April/May and September/October are great times to visit, as the weather is warm and there's less rain.

When we return, we plan to go during humpback whale season, July to October.

WHERE TO STAY

On Rarotonga, we stayed at Moana Sands Villas. We loved having a small kitchen and an extra room for the kiddos. The villas are right on the beach with full access to kayaks that you can paddle around the offshore reef. We were also within walking distance of a grocery store and a short drive to a handful of restaurants.

We love watching Dorothy and Manilla explore together.

While roaming the sandy shoreline, we stumbled upon a beached boat. These small islands have such big history!

- **Luxury:** Crystal Blue Lagoon Villas is in the heart of Rarotonga's Muri Beach, so you can access everything from a lagoon cruise to cultural village tours to local cafés. The Muri lagoon is great for kitesurfing, paddleboarding, and swimming.
- **Comfort:** Nautilus Resort Rarotonga is an eco-friendly spot with ocean views. Guests can spend their days snorkeling, visiting local markets, or swimming with sea turtles.
- **Budget:** The Islander Hotel on Rarotonga has a great pool scene, breakfast with your stay, and a spa. It's also near the Punanga Nui Market, where vendors sell handicrafts and snacks accompanied by live music.

WHAT TO EAT

Cuisine on the Cook Islands incorporates a lot of fresh fish, coconuts, and taro (a root vegetable). One of the most popular dishes is *ika mata*, raw fish marinated in lemon juice (like ceviche) then mixed with coconut cream and aromatics like onions and chilies.

Be prepared to stop at an ATM when you arrive, and bring cash to restaurants. Most hotels and rental car places accept credit cards, but other places, especially local food vendors, typically expect cash, in the form of the New Zealand dollar. (By the way, Cook Island coins are some of the favorite foreign currency we've collected. They have unique, quirky shapes!)

You have a chance to visit the Muri night market every Tuesday, Wednesday, Thursday, and Sunday evening starting at 5 p.m.

LISBON, PORTUGAL

Sample Delicious Pastel de Nata

The National Palace of Pena stands tall in Sintra.

Portugal is the hidden gem of Europe. Especially Lisbon! I was so pleasantly surprised by the beautiful, historic city. The people there seemed young, vibrant, and like they were just all-around go-getters. There was a love and respect for history in Lisbon, and a deep sense of pride in the country. And there was so much to do there!

Lisbon is one of Europe's oldest cities, due to its ideal trading location. The city reminds me of a European-style San Francisco, because there are a lot of hills and it's right on the water. Lisbon is known to get 300 days of sunshine a year, and its citizens are active and enjoy being outdoors.

HOW TO GET THERE

Lisbon is incredibly easy to get to from most places in Europe, the U.S., Australia, and Dubai. There are lots of direct flights into Lisbon from international hubs, or routes with short layovers in major European cities. If you're already in Europe, taking a train is a great option too. If you're in Spain, there's a 10-hour night train from Madrid that costs about $70. We rented a car for one of our days in Lisbon to get out of the city, and it was pretty easy to drive around. We left Lisbon to check out the famous surf spot Nazaré on our way to a football (aka soccer) match between Portugal and the United States.

WHAT TO DO

• Adventure: **Enjoy date night:** We left the kiddos behind with some sitters from the kid-friendly Martinhal Lisbon and went out on a private sidecar tour though Lisbon's hills. We cruised around with a guide to see the unique neighborhoods and finished the night at Belcanto, a Michelin two-star restaurant.

• Culture: **Eat at Time Out Market:** Portugal's best chefs, food, and cultural events are all here under one roof. Time Out is not just for tourists; you'll also see young tech and business workers out for lunch here. The indoor market offers dozens of different kiosks for food and shopping. There's also a park and grassy area, so grab your food and have a picnic outside where the kids can run around. **Visit Sintra:** This is a must-do in Portugal. Sintra is about 20 miles (32 km) northwest of Lisbon and is known to be one of the most stunning, luxurious, and historic areas in all of Europe. You'll see majestic palaces, extravagant villas, and mansions. **Find some fado music:** Book

Get Cash

For a European country, Portugal is surprisingly not that credit card friendly. There are way more ATMs than exchange kiosks, so have a reliable debit card to pull out some euros for your trip.

a reservation at a fado house in Lisbon. Fado dates back to the early 1800s and is a large part of Portuguese culture. The music is characterized by its mournful and melancholy melodies and lyrics.

WHEN TO VISIT

Lisbon has decent weather year-round. Even in the winter months, the temperature hovers around 50°F (10°C) during the day. Crowds are large in the summer, so stick to the spring or fall for fewer tourists.

A moment with my two oldest at the Praça do Comércio, a large plaza near Lisbon's harbor, while seven months pregnant

Lisbon is full of beautiful
architecture, including
the Arco da Rua Augusta.

VIRTVTIBVS
MAIORVM

VT. SIT. OMNIBVS. DOCVMENTO. P. P. D.

Head to Time Out Market for an array of food stalls and local crafts. There's something for everyone in the fam!

WHERE TO STAY

On our visit to Portugal, we worked with a really special company called Martinhal for our stay. They manage multiple properties in Portugal, and we stayed at their Lisbon and Sagres locations. Each property offers hotel and resort rooms as well as residences. Martinhal might be the most family-friendly accommodations we've ever stayed in. They've literally thought of everything, from diaper bins to high chairs to kids' clubs and family-centered activities. I wish this chain would expand globally; they have nailed family-friendly travel!

• **Luxury:** The Lumiares Hotel and Spa is in the heart of lively Bairro Alto. The hotel was once an 18th-century palace and now offers stylish rooms and family suites.

• **Comfort:** AlmaLusa Baixa/Chiado is in a great location right in Lisbon's city center. It's a small hotel with only 28 rooms and is within walking distance of a lot of monuments and worthwhile sights.

• **Budget:** My Story Hotel Ouro has a superfriendly staff, offers an inclusive breakfast, and is within walking distance of many attractions.

WHAT TO EAT

The most popular food to try in Portugal is *pastel de nata,* an absolutely delicious custard tart. Monks first made this pastry years ago, and it's now a must-try for any visitor. *Bacalhau* (salted and dried cod) is also popular in Portugal. It was introduced in the late 15th century after Portuguese fishermen sailed through Newfoundland. The *francesinha,* a sandwich made with meat such as ham or steak and sliced cheese, and topped with a tomato-and-beer gravy, has its roots in Porto.

Lisbon is a dreamy city,
especially at sunset.

WALT DISNEY WORLD, ORLANDO, FLORIDA, U.S.A.

Be a Kid Again at the Happiest Place on Earth

I spent my childhood visiting Walt Disney World and couldn't wait to bring my own kids one day.

Back in 2017, we were asked to take part in a project called 30 Stays in 30 Days at Walt Disney World in Orlando, Florida. The premise was to stay at *every single* Walt Disney World hotel and resort over the course of 30 days. And we did!

It wasn't until that project that I learned what a real Disney fan is. There are people who know the detailed history of every park and where every Hidden Mickey is. I won't claim to be as knowledgeable as these Disney aficionados, but over a lifetime of annual visits—plus 30 days straight at Disney—I've learned a thing or two.

WHERE TO STAY

Growing up, my family never stayed on property. My parents found a nearby resort called Caribe Cove that had pretty nice three-bedroom villas. We ate breakfast at the villa and also cooked dinner there two nights a week. It was a 15-minute drive to get to the parks, and we had to pay the additional parking fee. If you are on a budget, Disney can be expensive, so staying off property can be a good way to go.

But there are perks to staying on property. As of today, we've stayed at every single hotel and resort, and these are our top choices:

• **Beach Club:** My favorite park is EPCOT, so I love all of the resorts that are right next door (actually in walking distance!), including the BoardWalk and the Yacht Club. The Beach Club has a really unique pool with a sandy bottom and a cool waterslide. Be sure to check out Beaches & Cream Soda Shop, where you can get what's called the Kitchen Sink—a giant sink-shaped bowl filled with ice cream and all the fixins.

• **Art of Animation:** I always suggest Art of Animation for a budget property. I thought the food was better than at every other property in the same price range. Plus, you can take animation classes and learn how to draw Mickey Mouse. There are multiple different sections to the property: *Cars, The Little Mermaid, The Lion King,* and *Finding Nemo* each have themed buildings and pools. We stayed in the *Cars* section when Manilla was obsessed with Lighting McQueen. It was magical!

• **Polynesian Village Resort:** My husband loves Disney's Poly- nesian, which is on the luxury side of things. It's directly across from Magic Kingdom and has a great view of the castle and the fireworks at night. It has a fun pool, character dining with Lilo and Stitch, and Dole Whips. If you're a Disney Vacation Club member, you can book the overwater bungalows, which are reminiscent of bungalows in the Maldives or Bora Bora.

• **Honorable mentions:** Check out Disney's Treehouse Villas at Saratoga Springs Resort and Spa or Disney's Fort Wilderness Campground, where you can stay in your own RV or an ador- able log cabin. At Disney's Animal Kingdom Lodge, you can wake up to a scene from the African savanna, with wildebeests, giraffes, warthogs, and crowned cranes right on property.

DISNEY FOOD

Sure, theme park food is plentiful at Walt Disney World, but there are some standout spots for the true foodies as well.

Cali was all smiles meeting Mickey!

• **Sanaa:** Our favorite restaurant is located at Disney's Animal Kingdom Lodge. It's African cuisine fused with Indian flavors. The bread service is a must-do, with multiple types of naan and flatbread and eight dipping sauces. Reservations are strongly recommended for lunch and dinner.

• **Teppan Edo:** If you can, snag a reservation at the teppanyaki restaurant in the Japan section of EPCOT's World Showcase. You get a really special cultural experience watching the chef throw knives and cook with fire (the kids love it!). The food is so fresh and delicious.

• **Satu'li Canteen:** This is hands down our favorite restaurant in the parks. We'll go out of our way to be in Disney's Animal Kingdom Theme Park for lunch or dinner just to eat at Satu'li. We love the superfresh, flavorful, and healthy options here.

• **Docking Bay 7 Food and Cargo:** Located in *Star Wars: Galaxy's Edge,* this is a great option in Hollywood Studios for something fresh and healthy.

• **Disney Springs:** This shopping and dining complex, located outside the parks and resorts area, has some excellent options. We like Frontera Cocina for Mexican food, the Boat-house, and the Polite Pig.

HOW TO DO DISNEY

Disney truly is such a special place. I love seeing parents work so hard and sacrifice so much for their kids to experience a little bit of magic. There are super-early mornings and even later nights—all to just be repeated the next day. You'll be exhausted, but it's worth seeing the wonder through your kids' eyes.

My only tip is to just enjoy your time there. If you stress about the high prices, you'll be worrying and counting dollar signs all day. If you're annoyed with the lines, you'll miss the fun of the experience.

Remember to meet your kids where they are. If you need to stop in the shade for a break, just do it. Don't be afraid to go back to your hotel for a nap.

Try your hardest to enjoy the magic yourself, and everyone will have a better time.

Talk about a Hidden Mickey! Dorothy dove to this one at Castaway Cay on our Disney cruise.

A rare, quiet moment on Main Street, U.S.A.: We had an early morning filming project with Walt Disney World that afforded us this special experience!

FLORENCE, ITALY

Take an Italian Cooking Class

The Ponte Vecchio is just one of the stunning features that make Florence my favorite Italian city.

taly is a country that's likely on everyone's bucket list—and for good reason. It was actually the *only* place on my bucket list when I was young. But where to go?!

Rome is Italy's biggest city and holds incredible history, churches, fountains, and piazzas with 2,000-year-old buildings. It's expensive, touristy, and busy, but definitely worth a visit. Venice is absolutely iconic for its beautiful winding canals and bridges—and it's one of Europe's most romantic cities. Milan is known as Italy's thriving fashion and design center. And then there's Florence.

A trip to Italy should include multiple cities, but if I *had*

to choose one, I'd choose Florence—it's the best city of all. Florence is a mecca for lovers of Renaissance art and history. It is the home of works by Leonardo da Vinci and Michelangelo. It also has incredible architecture. The Arno River flows through the city, with the iconic Ponte Vecchio crossing above. Plus, Florence is in the heart of Tuscany, making a day trip or extended stay to the countryside very easy.

HOW TO GET THERE

Fiumicino Airport (aka Leonardo da Vinci International Airport) is about a 40-minute drive to Rome, oftentimes longer with traffic. On our first visit, we grabbed an Airbnb just outside Rome and explored from there for a few weeks.

On our second visit, we arrived at Venice Marco Polo Airport and traveled by train to Milan and Florence. We really enjoyed seeing the country by train. It felt like a more cultural experience and was a fun adventure trying to get our young kids and all our luggage on and off trains.

To fly into Florence directly, arrive at either Florence Airport (aka Peretola or Amerigo Vespucci Airport) or Pisa International Airport, which is about 60 miles (95 km) west of the Tuscan capital.

WHAT TO DO

• Adventure: **Get out of the city:** My favorite days in Italy were the ones when we got out of the city and explored smaller towns. Each town or village holds so much culture, and the

Postpone Bedtime

....

Florentines eat dinner late! Most locals have dinner between 8 and 10 p.m., and a lot of restaurants don't even open until 7 p.m. Keep that in mind when planning around kids' bedtimes.

small mom-and-pop restaurants are the best! You can easily rent a Vespa scooter to explore more on your own. **Take a cooking class:** I love taking cooking classes when we can—it's a great way to get the real flavor (pun intended) of a new place. As a family, we learned how to make strawberry and chocolate gelato and took a pizzamaking class. Family-friendly classes tend to be more chill and "just for fun." But if you really want to dig into the intricacies of pasta and other Italian specialties, ask your hotel for recommendations on cooking classes.

Live like a local and shop for fresh cheeses and fruits throughout Florence's streetside markets.

WHEN TO VISIT

The best time to visit Florence is April to June or September to October. In the spring, you'll see gorgeous flowers throughout the Tuscan countryside. In the fall, you'll enjoy crisp autumn days. September 7 is the Festa della Rificolona, or the Festival of the Paper Lanterns, which includes a lantern and boat parade and a fair.

WHERE TO STAY

Our tour of Italy included a hotel partnership with Westin. We stayed at the Westin Europa & Regina (now the St. Regis) in Venice, Westin Palace in Milan, and Westin Excelsior in Florence. All three were incredible properties. Our favorite, though, was the Westin Excelsior, which overlooks the Ponte Vecchio.

WHAT TO EAT

I hate to sound arrogant, but you haven't had Italian food until you've had Italian food *in* Italy. Italian food can actually be quite basic, but in Italy, they use the highest quality ingredients, and that makes all the difference! Their fresh tomatoes are more flavorful than any tomato I've ever had in the U.S. Their cheeses and meats are equally fresh and high quality. Nothing compares.

Each region of Italy has its own specialties. Pizza, for example, can differ greatly depending on what part of Italy you're eating it in. Pasta, too, varies from city to city in Italy. Florence, in particular, is known for quality meat and a dish called *bistecca alla fiorentina* (Florentine steak). Gelato (our favorite) is said to have been invented by a man named Bernardo Buontalenti from Florence!

Dorothy and Manilla loved making pizza at a cooking class.

The Duomo stands tall above the beautiful city of Florence.

OSLO, NORWAY

Live in a Fairy Tale

For a chance to see the northern lights, make a trip to Oslo in the winter.

We visited Norway when Dorothy and Manilla were quite little. I think of that trip so fondly because they were at such a fun age. I remember wanting to stop time and bottle up the memories. What made our trip to Norway one for the bucket list was that our stay there was so pure and timeless.

The beauty of our visit to Norway came in the two incredible Airbnbs that we rented. The first was far south, a couple hours from Oslo. We rented a teeny-tiny red cabin on a little island. When we arrived, the host brought us to our home in a dinghy, which was ours to use for the entire stay. The house had a small kitchen and a loft where we all slept together. The bathroom was an outhouse and a two-minute walk away—the kids thought this was so funny. The kitchen table was also outside. And the best part: There was no Wi-Fi!

Our second Airbnb was exactly what you'd picture in a Norwegian fairy tale. It was in the mountains, surrounded by farms, and the home had a grassy roof. Each morning a lovely older couple made us a cute Norwegian breakfast with warm homemade bread and delicious local jam.

The beauty of Norway, for me, is the simplicity of life.

There's no pomp or frills, just a pure embrace of nature. That's how I remember those days exploring Norway with my little family.

HOW TO GET THERE

Oslo is the capital city and a great hub airport to get anywhere in Europe. Norwegian Air is a solid budget airline to get you around. Unfortunately, they ended their U.S. routes a few years back. But Oslo Airport has more than 100 international destinations and will serve as your domestic hub as well as get you to your final destination in Norway.

We rented a car and used it for our entire stay. It was easy driving—nice roads and gorgeous road trip scenery!

WHAT TO DO

• Adventure: **Fjords:** Norway is most famous for its gorgeous fjords. You can explore them on cruises or on hiking, biking, or kayaking trips. Whatever way you choose, you'll also see some incredible wildlife, including whales, eagles, and otters. One of our next bucket list adventures is to swim with orcas in the Norwegian fjords in the winter. **Northern lights:** One of the best places in the world to see the aurora borealis is in Norway. You can see it between late September and early April. Tromsø, in northern Norway, is a great spot to see the lights, as well as take a dogsledding or snowmobile tour. **Camping:** Nature is hugely protected in Norway for all to enjoy. Wild camping allows you to pitch a tent in forests, mountains, and along the coast. There are handful of rules, mostly making sure that you take care and clean up after yourself. But for the most part, you're free to explore and enjoy nature!

• Culture: **Berry picking:** Norway is bursting with wild berries in the late summer and early fall. In Norway, the right to pick berries is protected by law, so you can have your pick in most places.

WHEN TO VISIT

Norway is a four-season destination, each of which is beautiful and unique! The summer months are great for warm temperatures and longer days. Up north, you can experience the famous midnight sun, when the sun never quite goes down in the summer. To avoid the crowds and surging prices, August

Life was like a fairy tale in our little cottage in the hills of Norway.

There is something so
peaceful and majestic
about Norway's fjords.

and September are great, and that's also the perfect time for berry picking. If you're looking for a beautiful, white winter, Norway is a great choice. You might even be able to catch the northern lights!

WHERE TO STAY

I suggest a home rental. There are so many unique and beautiful homes throughout the country. Many Norwegians have summer homes, which are commonly referred to as *hytter.* These hytter are typically in the countryside, by the sea, near lakes, and in other scenic areas. They're often for rent too.

• **Luxury:** Bolder Lodges focuses on immersing oneself in nature while leaving no footprints behind. Hovering above the Lysefjord, it has panoramic views of stunning mountains and trees.

• **Comfort:** Only a short distance from Oslo, WonderInn allows you to take a break from the city and get into nature. Their mirrored, glass cabins are situated in a unique area where two of Norway's longest rivers meet.

WHAT TO EAT

Yummy Norwegian waffles are a family favorite. They're a lot thinner than Belgian waffles and crunchy when fresh. They're served with butter, cream, jam and—the most popular—traditional brown cheese!

Norwegian cuisine is full of fresh, locally sourced ingredients, and the meals are wholesome and hearty. Both lamb and fish are on most menus. A lot of the meat dishes involve preservation methods like smoking, salting, or drying.

Visiting Norway in the summer afforded us lots of time to explore outdoors.

BYRON BAY, AUSTRALIA

Kayak With Dolphins

The coastal town of Byron Bay is the perfect spot for surfing, snorkeling, and diving.

Australia was the third country we traveled to. I was so pumped to be there, to go to Sydney Harbour, cage-dive with great white sharks, swim the Great Barrier Reef, and visit Byron Bay. Little did I realize that's like someone saying they want to go New York City, Disney World, Dallas, and Denver all in one trip! We had to significantly alter our plans so that we could go slow and take it all in. It makes me laugh now thinking what a newbie I was at travel planning back then.

We flew into Sydney and spent the next two weeks driving up Australia's east coast. We spent a week in Port Macquarie and went up to Byron Bay for another week. Byron Bay is everything you'd want in a beach town. It's famous for its chilled-out, hippie, small surf town vibe. Everyone there is incredibly active, healthy, and appreciative of nature. The town is also very artsy, with galleries, live music venues, and festivals throughout the year.

We rented a house and some surfboards and bought a gym pass for the week. After our short stay, we thought Byron Bay would be a great place to settle down one day. It was a huge inspiration for us finding our long-term home in Hawaii.

HOW TO GET THERE

Getting to Byron Bay is easiest by car. It's a two-hour drive from Brisbane (nine hours from Sydney). There's a small regional airport that's about 30 minutes away called Ballina Byron Gateway Airport, or there's Gold Coast Airport, which is about an hour north of Byron Bay. These airports have regular domestic flights from Sydney, Melbourne, and Brisbane.

I suggest getting a rental car for exploring the town and nearby areas. We also rented bikes to cruise around town.

WHAT TO DO

• Adventure: **Kayak in Byron Bay:** Kayaking is a great way to see the water! Multiple kayak companies advertise the opportunity to kayak among dolphins. There are several resident dolphin pods that are known to be playful and curious. We booked a two-hour tour and saw some bottlenose dolphins, my absolute favorite! **Hike to Cape Byron Lighthouse:** Definitely take a hike up to the iconic Cape Byron Lighthouse. I suggest going up for sunset. It's a great spot for whale-watching during migration season (June to November), and you'll have some stunning views of the coast.

• Culture: **Byron Bay farmers market:** It's held every Thursday morning between 7 and 11 a.m. It has tons of local produce, artisan products, and prepared foods, including everything from handmade jewelry to soaps and art. There's live music and a superfriendly community vibe.

WHEN TO VISIT

We visited in October (Australia's spring), which is a great time for mild weather and fewer crowds. Summer (December

Bottlenose dolphins are the real locals of Byron Bay.

The light just hits differently in eastern Australia—I love its golden hue.

Garrett and Dorothy take in the ocean views from the Cape Byron Lighthouse.

to February) is peak season and super busy, with higher prices. Fall (March to May) is probably the best time to visit since the water is still nice and warm for surfing, paddle-boarding, and kayaking, but the crowds have slimmed down.

WHERE TO STAY

We booked a home rental for our visit in Byron Bay. We really wanted to spend more time living like locals, shopping at neighborhood grocery stores, and visiting nearby parks. But there are also plenty of boutique hotels to choose from.

• **Luxury:** Elements of Byron offers a variety of fun for everyone, from horseback riding on the coastline to 20 acres (8 ha) of walking trails to a spa for unwinding afterward.

• **Comfort:** The Bower combines Byron Bay's beachy, low-key lifestyle with New York's boutique hotel scene. With only 14 suites, guests can be sure to have an intimate and relaxed time in paradise.

• **Budget:** The Sunseeker offers guests an authentic and localized experience through its support of the community. With facilities that focus on sustainability, the Sunseeker does its part to preserve the beautiful environment of Byron Bay.

WHAT TO EAT

Byron Bay has an incredibly vibrant food scene, with a great mix of Australian dishes and international cuisine. Popular Australian dishes include fish-and-chips, which you can find at most restaurants. And don't miss the meat pies. Australians love their meat pies, and Byron Bay is no exception.

There are local fresh and healthy eateries throughout Byron Bay. You'll find trendy breakfast dishes like avocado toast, acai bowls, and smoothie bowls throughout the town. It is a great place to visit for vegetarians and vegans too. All the food we had in Australia was so fresh, and we loved it. It's refreshing to be able to eat healthily so easily while traveling!

Leave No Trace

Byron Bay's residents are very focused on sustainability and conservation. Bring reusable bags and water bottles, and choose eco-friendly activities and accommodations. Pack reef-friendly sunscreen too. The people of Byron Bay offer a great example of how we should take care of our home!

We celebrated Dorothy's third birthday on the beach in Byron Bay.

The question we're always asking: Where to next?

WHAT'S STILL ON MY BUCKET LIST?

. . . .

Someday I'd like to bike around Copenhagen, swim with orcas in Norway, take cooking classes in Vietnam, eat beignets in New Orleans, and see panda bears in their natural habitat. The more I travel, the more I want to see and experience!

But you may be surprised to know I actually no longer have a bucket list. I know, I'm a fraud. Truth is, I've never really had one.

The thing about a bucket list, at least the way our family views it, is it's not really a list at all. It's about living every day with purpose and intention, passion and excitement. It's about enjoying this world we share. A bucket list is about experiencing what you love with the ones you love.

If you've followed our family over the past nine years, I hope you have seen beneath the surface of The Bucket List Family. Really, we are two parents trying to teach our children about different cultures and people. We're teaching our children there's no one "right" way to live your life. We're teaching our children to be open-minded and kindhearted. We're teaching our children to get outside their comfort zones and try new things. And we're teaching our children that family is the most important thing.

Bucket list moments can come in all shapes and sizes. They are the special moments you have in your own backyard and brave new journeys around the world.

I hope, more than anything, that this book has inspired you to find and share those bucket list moments, and that you look for adventures big and small. I hope you strive to see what is new, different, and beautiful in the world. I hope you discover that some of the biggest growth and happiness happen just outside your comfort zone. And I hope you realize your own bucket list can start right at home. For me, I signed up for "a little bit of traveling" back in 2015, and it has forever changed my life. I can't wait for many more bucket list moments with my little family. And I wish you and your family safe and happy travels. ≋

For my love, Garrett

♡ ♡ ♡

ACKNOWLEDGMENTS

....

This book is in large part thanks to a super-duper supportive (dance mom status) husband. Garrett, thanks for seeing the potential in me and encouraging me to shine. Thank you for making life so much more meaningful and joyful—and for getting me to step outside my comfort zone. Thank you for letting me run with this opportunity solo and make it my own. And look at you! You're officially a NatGeo photographer, just like you dreamed you'd be as a young child exploring the world through the magazines. This book wouldn't be what it is without your photography skills and painstaking journaling of our family's memories!

Dorothy, Manilla, and Cali: It's an honor to experience this life with you. This book will be a treasure in our family for years to come. Thank you for your patience as I sometimes took time away from you to write it. I hope you are proud of me for all my hard work. Here's to many more memories at home and around the world together. This is for you, and your future kids, and forever onward. I love you all.

To my mom and dad: While traveling wasn't always my game plan, you gave me everything I've needed to thrive at it. You taught me to love learning, to be inquisitive, to hold great conversations with complete strangers, to be positive, to be of service—and that I am, in fact, the one who chooses my attitude. I couldn't have asked for better parents to lead me through this life.

To my siblings, Jim, Parker, and Amanda, for not being on social media whatsoever. I love it. Never change. You never know what part of the planet I'm currently on, you give me a hard time for being all "Hollywood," and you still would rather vacation at Disney. I appreciate our pure interactions and your support. To my sister, Amanda, for being my best friend, cheerleader, and listening ear. Thank you for always answering my calls and asking, "Where in the world is Carmen San Diego?" And for that one time I called at 4 a.m. to invite you to fly to Africa in four hours and you came!

I also couldn't have written this book without two very supportive people: Miristi, you are one of the strongest humans on this earth and we are so blessed to have you in our lives. Thank you, from the bottom of my heart, for your tireless love of me, Garrett, and the kids. And to Kristy, the greatest publishing attorney, business manager, protector, Hawaiian neighbor, eight-year-old-girls' soccer coach, Cali assistant, and pizza chef there ever was. My life is substantially better with you in it.

A very big shout-out and special thank-you to the lovely Gina Bergman. Thank you for being a mentor and guiding light through this book-writing process, seeing the big vision, helping me find my voice, and helping shape this book into what it is. Thank you for listening to every single travel story, experience, and tip, and for taking my jumbled thoughts and memories and bringing them into this format. I'm so proud of the work we did together.

And to my editor, Allyson Johnson, for bringing me this opportunity many years ago. I remember driving my family to Seattle when Garrett, from the passenger seat, said, "Uhhh, we just got an email from an Allyson of National Geographic!" We screamed a little, we danced a lot, and then we pulled over so I could immediately call you. You have allowed me to share my message with the world, and for that I will always be grateful. You are great at your craft and have made this process so enjoyable. I know this is the beginning of an everlasting working adventure and friendship together!

Thank you to Elisa Gibson and Katie Dance, who helped turn our family memories into a beautiful family heirloom. This book is truly a priceless treasure for my family. And to the entire National Geographic family, we're so proud to be a part of it.

To The Bucket List Friends and worldwide Bucket List Community who have been with us from the very beginning: Your support and positive words have empowered me to overcome the stresses, judgment, and intensity of social media so that I can continue sharing our family journey with love. You mean so much to me.

Thank you to the countless tourism boards, airlines, hotels, resorts, destinations, and brands that have supported our family over the years. We pioneered the job title Family Travel Journalists, and thanks to you, our supportive partners, it became a sustainable career.

Last, but definitely not least, to my dear friends and family who have continued to reach out and stay in touch with me over the years while I've been away: thank you. You are true friends. Thank you to the many of you who let us crash in guest rooms and on couches over the years and in between flights. Thank you for accepting our crazy last-minute invitations to join us for adventures like cage-diving with great whites or drinking blood milk with the Maasai. Nothing brings me more joy than sharing these experiences with you, the humans I love dearly.

Here's to many more adventures with all of you!

ILLUSTRATIONS AND MAP CREDITS

· ·

All photographs by Garrett Gee unless otherwise noted below.

Jessica Gee: back cover, 27, 142, 152–3, 170, 179, 206–7, 211, 228, 266, 278, 287, 301.

2–3, Brad Devine; 6, Shelly Hadfield; 12, Abigail Keenan Field; 16–7, illustrations by Brian Clayton; 20, Scotty Portelli; 30, Abigail Keenan Field; 38, Jim Ward, SeeThroughSea; 41, Jessie Matteson; 42–3, rudi1976/Adobe Stock; 54–5, Bree Hanneman; 60–1, illustrations by Brian Clayton; 62, Abigail Keenan Field; 66–7, oneinchpunch/Adobe Stock; 73, Josh Dance; 77, Abigail Keenan Field; 78, Lindsay Daniels; 84, Serenity-H/Adobe Stock; 87, Abigail Keenan Field; 94–5, Bree Hanneman; 98, Marzky Ragsac Jr./Adobe Stock; 109, Scotty Portelli; 110, Abigail Keenan Field; 126 and 127, Abigail Keenan Field; 128, Natalie Madsen; 132, Josh Whalen/TandemStock; 134, Abigail Keenan Field; 138–9, Justin Jansen Van Vuuren; 147, Brooks Laich; 148, Abigail Keenan Field; 150, Joanna Gee; 154, Michele Burgess/Adobe Stock; 156, Chaunte Vaughn; 158–9, Joanna Gee, with illustrations by Brian Clayton; 162, Abigail Keenan Field; 164, Alexey Stiop/Adobe Stock; 166, Kim/Adobe Stock; 168, Jan Wlodarczyk/Alamy Stock Photo; 171, Tomekbudujedomek/Getty Images; 172–3, Kotangens/Adobe Stock; 174, Sean Pavone Photo/Adobe Stock; 175 (RT), J Marshall—Tribaleye Images/Alamy Stock Photo; 177, Jordan Banks/TandemStock; 178, Jim Patterson/TandemStock; 182, Colm Keating/TandemStock; 183 and 184, Bree Hanneman; 185, Grant Ordelheide/TandemStock; 188, Angelo Cavalli/robertharding; 189, Jenny Herz; 190, Egmont Strigl/Alamy Stock Photo; 192, Alexander Spatari/Getty Images; 193, Steve Vidler/mauritius images GmbH/Alamy Stock Photo; 198, Frances Gallogly/TandemStock; 201, Highland Club Scotland; 202, Brendan van Son/TandemStock; 203 (LE), Grant Ordelheide/TandemStock; 204, Ezume Images/Adobe Stock; 208, zgphotography/Adobe Stock; 212, creativenature.nl/Adobe Stock; 214, Wim Wiskerke/Alamy Stock Photo; 215, Ian Dagnall/Alamy Stock Photo; 216, David Keith Jones/Images of Africa Photobank/Alamy Stock Photo; 217, Iván Vieito García/Adobe Stock; 218, Jane Cresswell; 219, Andy Merch; 222, Daniel Holz/TandemStock; 223, Manachai/Getty Images; 226, Andras Jancsik/Getty Images; 227 (RT), trubavink/Adobe Stock; 230, Michael Hanson/TandemStock; 232, Frank Gärtner/Adobe Stock; 233, Small World Production/Adobe Stock; 236, vadim.nefedov/Adobe Stock; 237, Stuart Forster/Alamy Stock Photo; 238, Denys/Adobe Stock; 240, vitleo/Adobe Stock; 242, ingaj/Adobe Stock; 243, Sliver/Adobe Stock; 246, jkraft5/Adobe Stock; 247 (LE), Abigail Keenan Field; 250, Thomas/Adobe Stock; 254, R.M. Nunes/Adobe Stock; 257, Awana JF/Shutterstock; 258, Tracy + David, Tracy Boulian and David Ahntholz; 259, Dene' Miles/Adobe Stock; 264, Jason Hatfield/TandemStock; 265, Michael/Adobe Stock; 267, Zion Red Rock Oasis; 268, Rachid Dahnoun/Cavan Images; 269, John Dreyer/Alamy Stock Photo; 272, Galyna Andrushko/Adobe Stock; 273 (LE), Douglas Peebles/Alamy Stock Photo; 273 (RT), James Forte/National Geographic Image Collection; 276, Frances Gallogly/TandemStock; 277, Francesco/Adobe Stock; 279, Richard Levine/Alamy Stock Photo; 280, Bryan Jolley/TandemStock; 283, Ryan Struck/TandemStock; 284, Kushnirov Avraham/Adobe Stock; 285, Ekaterina Pokrovsky/Adobe Stock; 290, Nick Dale/Design Pics/Alamy Stock Photo; 291, Cavan/Adobe Stock; 293, Lucas/Adobe Stock; 294, Chris Hannant Photography/Cavan Images; 295 (RT), Michael Ventura/Alamy Stock Photo; 297, bearacreative/Adobe Stock; 298, napa74/Adobe Stock; 304, Bermuda Tourism Authority; 306, Michael Nolan/robertharding; 307, Paul Nicklen/National Geographic Image Collection; 308 and 309, Abigail Keenan Field; 310, Steven Miley/Alaska Stock/Alamy Stock Photo; 311, Douglas Peebles/Alamy Stock Photo; 312, Gunter Marx/AR/Alamy Stock Photo; 316, Victor Bordera/Stocksy; 317 (LE), forcdan/Adobe Stock; 317 (RT), hollydc/Adobe Stock; 318, Jesse Howard; 320, Eitan Simanor/Alamy Stock Photo; 324, martinhosmat083/Adobe Stock; 325, ADX Collections/Getty Images; 327, Andrew JK Tan/Getty Images; 330, Sky Perth/Adobe Stock; 333, anekoho/Adobe Stock; 334, Michele Bellomonte/EyeEm; 335, Curioso.Photography/Adobe Stock; 336, Sean Hsu/Adobe Stock; 338, Sean Pavone Photo/Adobe Stock; 339, Valerie Lunsted; 341, dodotone/Adobe Stock; 342, mdurinik/Adobe Stock; 343 (LE), Florapix/Alamy Stock Photo; 345, Jim Ward, SeeThroughSea; 348, Suntichai/Adobe Stock; 349, gudkovandrey/Adobe Stock; 351, Siringit Collection; 352, Eric/Adobe Stock; 355, Solitary Traveler/Alamy Stock Photo; 356, Beboy/Adobe Stock; 357, Fanfo/Adobe Stock; 359, Aurélien Brusini/hemis.fr/Alamy Stock Photo; 360–1, Justin Jansen Van Vuuren; 362, Sandra Foyt/Alamy Stock Photo; 367 (LE), Glenn Bartley/All Canada Photos/Alamy Stock Photo; 368, Jessie Matteson; 369, Aleksandra/Adobe Stock; 372 and 374, Karine Aigner/TandemStock; 378, @ Didier Marti/Getty Images; 381, chameleonseye/Getty Images; 382, Pavel Dudek/Alamy Stock Photo; 384, Matteo Colombo/Getty Images; 385, Alexandre Rotenberg/Alamy Stock Photo; 386–7, Sean Pavone Photo/Adobe Stock; 388, Shawn.ccf/Adobe Stock; 392, Westend61/Studio in the Wild/Getty Images; 393 (LE), Rob Tilley/DanitaDelimont/Alamy Stock Photo; 395, sborisov/Adobe Stock; 396, Tim Graham/robertharding; 398, Voyagerix/Adobe Stock; 400, Peter Harrison/Getty Images; 401, Gary/Adobe Stock; 402, Michael/Adobe Stock.

Map data sources: Shaded relief and bathymetry derived from: ETOPO1/Amante and Eakins, 2009; Polar Geospatial Center (PGC), University of Minnesota: ArcticDEM Porter, Claire; Morin, Paul; Howat, Ian; Noh, Myoung-Jon; Bates, Brian; Peterman, Kenneth; Keesey, Scott; Schlenk, Matthew; Gardiner, Judith; Tomko, Karen; Willis, Michael; Kelleher, Cole; Cloutier, Michael; Husby, Eric; Foga, Steven; Nakamura, Hitomi; Platson, Melisa; Wethington, Michael, Jr.; Williamson, Cathleen; Bauer, Gregory; Enos, Jeremy; Arnold, Galen; Kramer, William; Becker, Peter; Doshi, Abhijit; D'Souza, Cristelle; Cummens, Pat; Laurier, Fabien; Bojesen, Mikkel, 2018, "ArcticDEM" and Reference Elevation Model of Antarctica (REMA); Howat, Ian; Morin, Paul; Porter, Claire; Noh, Myong-Jong, 2018, "The Reference Elevation Model of Antarctica," Harvard Dataverse, V1. data.pgc.umn.edu/elev/dem/setsm/REMA/.

INDEX

Boldface indicates illustrations.

A

Jessica Gee is the ultimate family adventurer and the driving force behind The Bucket List Family. Growing up in Denver, Colorado, she always had a love of travel and learning about other cultures. Her passions only grew stronger after meeting her husband and travel partner, Garrett Gee, while on an LDS mission in Vladivostok, Russia.

Together with their three children, Dorothy, Manilla, and Cali, the family has been exploring the world full-time since 2015. They have visited more than 90 countries and have had countless bucket list adventures along the way: swimming with humpback whales in Tonga, camping in the African bush, trekking in Patagonia, taking cooking classes in Italy, and sleeping in castles (including Cinderella's in Walt Disney World) around the globe.

Jessica is an expert on not just traveling but also experiencing life to its fullest (with kids in tow!). She is the mastermind behind their family travels, ensuring every trip is about more than just vacation; it's also about adventure, culture, and service.

Through their social media accounts, The Bucket List Family has inspired millions to follow in their footsteps. They have been named Family Travel Influencer of the Year in 2021 and 2022 by the American Influencer Awards and were nominated for Best Social Media Family at the 2023 Nickelodeon Kids' Choice Awards.

Despite the globetrotting lifestyle, Jessica keeps herself grounded in the simple pleasures of home and family life. When they aren't on the road, the family is based in Hawaii, where Jessica enjoys sleeping in her own bed, cooking in her own kitchen, and spending quality time with loved ones. She also loves a good dance party and the innermost part of a cinnamon roll.

You can follow Jessica and The Bucket List Family on Instagram @thebucketlistfamily and watch their videos on their YouTube channel. Or join The Bucket List Friends for exclusive content and even opportunities to travel with the Gees.

Scan the QR code
for more from The
Bucket List Family.

Since 1888, the National Geographic Society has funded more than 14,000 research, conservation, education, and storytelling projects around the world. National Geographic Partners distributes a portion of the funds it receives from your purchase to National Geographic Society to support programs including the conservation of animals and their habitats.

Get closer to National Geographic Explorers and photographers, and connect with our global community. Join us today at nationalgeographic.org/joinus

For rights or permissions inquiries, please contact National Geographic Books Subsidiary Rights: bookrights@natgeo.com

ISBN: 978-1-4262-2223-8

Printed in South Korea

23/QPSK/1

The information in this book has been carefully checked and to the best of our knowledge is accurate. However, details are subject to change, and the publisher cannot be responsible for such changes, or for errors or omissions. Assessments of sites, hotels, and restaurants are based on the author's subjective opinions, which do not necessarily reflect the publisher's opinion.

We celebrated Dorothy's
third birthday on the
beach in Byron Bay.

The question we're always asking: Where to next?